SECRET LIVES

★★★★★
OF
THE
★★★★★
SUPREME COURT

**WHAT YOUR TEACHERS NEVER TOLD YOU
ABOUT AMERICA'S LEGENDARY JUSTICES**

BY ROBERT SCHNAKENBERG

ILLUSTRATED BY EUGENE SMITH

QUIRK BOOKS
PHILADELPHIA

"WE MUST REMEMBER THAT WE HAVE TO
MAKE JUDGES OUT OF MEN, AND THAT BY
BEING MADE JUDGES THEIR PREJUDICES ARE
NOT DIMINISHED AND THEIR INTELLIGENCE
IS NOT INCREASED"

—Robert Green Ingersoll

Private chambers. Voluminous robes. Closed conferences. The Supreme Court of the United States is forever cloaked in secrecy—its ways hidden and its deliberations largely obscured from public view. Luckily, such is not the case with the lives of the men and women who have populated the high court since it was first constituted in 1789. Their doings are matters of public record, at least up to the moment they first sat on the high bench. For most justices, gaining a seat on the Court wasn't their goal in life, and as a result they didn't bother to cover their tracks the way an ambitious politician might. So, with a little digging, we can easily discover which ones owned slaves, joined the Ku Klux Klan, or agitated to keep Jews, Catholics, or Chinese Americans mired in second-class citizenship. What's more, there's something about the life of a judge that seems to invite the cultivation of eccentric habits. Shielded from public scrutiny, Supreme Court justices are free to let their freak flags fly. They compose novelty songs, travel around the country in custom-built RVs, and do all their writing with a fountain pen—in an age when word-processing software has become ubiquitous. Some, it should also be noted, have preferred less idiosyncratic pursuits, like chasing skirts and guzzling liquor by the quart. A few were downright ornery, hated by colleagues and clerks alike.

In short, Supreme Court justices are just like the rest of us—subject to the same foibles and character flaws that beset every other upright ape walking through this vale of woe. This book will attempt to lift the robes and peek underneath, to provide a fresh, unromanticized take on the solemn-looking men and women who scowl down at us from the portraits in the National

Gallery. We'll learn who burned with every fiber of his being to be chief justice, and who was in it only for the chance to play poker with the president. We'll find out who hated whom, and how petty disagreements and personal prejudices may have changed the course of American judicial history. Focusing on the personalities and personal lives of Supreme Court justices may end up being one of the best ways to truly *understand* history. That so many contentious, cantankerous, and—in some cases—deeply disturbed individuals managed to come together around a conference table and hammer out so many epochal decisions is a testament to the sound craftsmanship of America's constitutional framework.

And so . . . may it please the court . . . let the witnesses approach the bench! Secret Lives Court is now in session!

JOHN JAY

December 12, 1745–May 17, 1829

BIRTHPLACE:

New York, NY

ASTROLOGICAL SIGN:

Sagittarius

TERM:

October 19, 1789–
June 29, 1795

APPOINTED BY:

George Washington

WORDS OF WISDOM:

"Those who own the country
ought to govern it."

America's first chief justice had limited judicial experience and little desire to be a judge. He found the burdens of the job irksome and bolted from the bench at the earliest opportunity. Asked to return to the Court five years after he resigned, he flatly declined, calling the federal judicial system "defective." Instead of strengthening the authority of the Supreme Court, he spent his final decades puttering around his farm, writing letters, and spreading the Christian Gospel. A crabby, slave-owning, anti-Catholic bigot, John Jay nonetheless still holds a place in the top ranks of America's revered "Founding Fathers."

Talk about an inauspicious beginning: America's first chief justice, John Jay, was hanged in effigy by angry mobs throughout the United States.

Jay was born into a wealthy New York mercantile family in 1745. As befit his status, he received a top-flight education, graduating from King's College (today known as Columbia University) at age nineteen. After gaining admission to the New York bar in 1768, he built a thriving law practice. In 1774, he married Sarah Livingston, daughter of the future first governor of New Jersey. Everything seemed teed up for Jay to enjoy the long and prosperous life of a colonial aristocrat. Then came the little matter of the American Revolution.

"Independency," as the colonists called it, wasn't exactly a cause dear to the conservative Jay's heart. He would have been content not to sever ties with England. Nevertheless, he bobbed along with the general tide and eventually became an advocate of separation. He held a series of diplomatic posts in the early days of the republic and seemed bound for a career in foreign affairs rather than law. In fact, his only experience as a judge was a brief stint serving as chief justice of the New York State Supreme Court in 1777–78. Despite these limitations, President George Washington tapped him to be the U.S. Supreme Court's first chief in 1789.

In those days, the Court met in the Royal Exchange Building in New York City and had little to do. The first session adjourned after only nine days for lack of legal business (a typical session today stretches from early October to late June). The justices spent much of their time "riding circuit"—traveling around the country trying cases in circuit courts. Like most of his colleagues, Jay hated this aspect of the job. In a letter, he lamented being "placed in an office . . . which takes me from my family half the year, and obliges me to pass too considerable a part of my time on the road, in lodging houses and inns." The poor food served on the road was a particular irritant, accustomed as Jay was to the finest New York dining. He began to chafe under the yoke of his thankless office and longed for new challenges.

He found an outlet in freelance diplomacy. In 1794, Washington sent him to England to negotiate a settlement with the British to halt their continued interference in American affairs. The resulting treaty, which bore Jay's name, generated tremendous controversy and was considered by some to be a capitulation to the British crown. Jay was denounced as a traitor and hanged in effigy. Yet, he retained enough support to be elected governor of New York in 1795. That was his ticket off the Court, off the circuit, and out of the line of fire.

He served six years as the state's governor and successfully rebuffed an attempt to rook him back onto the Supreme Court. In 1800, after the retirement of Jay's successor, Chief Justice Oliver Ellsworth, President John Adams nominated Jay to replace him. Unfortunately, he forgot to ask Jay's permission first. The steamed former jurist refused to accept the appointment and wrote

Adams a stern letter decrying the inconveniences of circuit riding. The next year, Congress enacted legislation to eliminate that function, for which generations of aging, infirm justices too sick to travel would be eternally grateful.

Upon leaving the governor's office, Jay retired to his farm in Rye, New York. He became increasingly religious, especially after the death of his wife, in 1802. His closing years were marked by ill health, and he largely avoided the public eye. He died in his sleep on May 17, 1829.

FOUNDING BIGOT

A devout Episcopalian, Jay harbored a visceral distaste for Catholics, which he repeatedly tried to enact into law. He proposed several amendments to the New York state constitution designed to bar Catholics from holding office unless they renounced their allegiance to the pope. These efforts ran aground, in part due to the arguments of Jay's slightly less intolerant young friend Gouverneur Morris. But in 1788, the state legislature, at Jay's urging, did enact a law requiring office seekers to "take an oath of allegiance to this State, and abjure and renounce all allegiance and subjection to all and every foreign king, prince, potentate, and State in all matters, ecclesiastical as well as civil." It was clearly designed as a slap against Catholics, whom Jay suspected of disloyalty.

BIBLE THUMPER

Given the prejudices of his time, Jay's anti-Catholicism could almost be overlooked. But America's first chief justice was also something of a Christian supremacist. In an 1816 letter, Jay asserted that "Providence has given to our people the choice of their rulers, and it is the duty, as well as the privilege and interest, of our Christian nation to select and prefer Christians for their rulers." In that same year, he helped found the American Bible Society, serving as its president from 1821 to 1828. A Biblical literalist, he renounced belief in any doctrine that didn't have its foundation in the Good Book. Jay also seized every opportunity to proselytize—even on secular occasions. Asked by the city of New York to send a message commemorating the fiftieth anniversary of the

Declaration of Independence in 1826, Jay expressed his "earnest hope that the peace, happiness, and prosperity enjoyed by our beloved country may induce those who direct her national counsels to recommend a general and public return of praise to Him from whose goodness these blessings descend." As his life drew to a close, Jay became even more devout. He made sure to thank Jesus in his last will and testament. On his deathbed, when asked if he had any final words for his children, Jay said only: "They have the Book."

FREE AT LAST? NOT SO FAST

Like a lot of America's founding fathers, Jay had a, shall we say, "nuanced" record on the issue of slavery. An outspoken abolitionist before that cause was cool, Jay took a stand against the expansion of slavery into the territories and opposed the Missouri Compromise. He was one of the founders of the New York Manumission Society, an organization dedicated to boycotting businesses that profited from the slave trade. As governor of New York, Jay lobbied for, and eventually signed into law, a bill to abolish slavery in that state.

That all sounds good—so far. But many are surprised to learn that this passionate advocate of emancipation was himself a slave owner. In fact, in 1798, the year before the New York law was passed, Jay owned eight human beings. Even worse, he made a point of keeping them enslaved until he decided they had "earned back" what he paid for them. Jay's abolition law itself allowed for this practice. Slave owners could keep their younger slaves in servitude for years as a means of recouping their investment. Also buried in the fine print: a provision deeming all slaves born before July 4, 1799 (an ironic date choice) to be reclassified as "indentured servants" and held in bondage in perpetuity.

PUBLIC ENEMY

Enormously controversial at the time, Jay's Treaty is now credited with staving off war between America and Britain for 16 years. For Americans spoiling for another go-around with the Redcoats—and others who saw themselves as disadvantaged by the terms Jay had negotiated—the treaty was tantamount to treason. It tainted everyone associated with it, no matter their stature. A group of Virginians toasted "a speedy death to General Washington" for signing it. Alexander Hamilton was stoned at a public meeting for supporting it. And Jay, whose name it bore, found himself on the receiving end of the most vehement denunciations. Vulgar rhymes began appearing in the anti-Federalist press accusing Jay of selling out to the British king. One such masterpiece began:

> May it please your highness, I, John Jay
> Have traveled all this mighty way,
> To inquire if you, good Lord, will please,
> To suffer me while on my knees,
> To show all others I surpass,
> In love, by kissing of your [ass] . . .

A Kentucky versifier waxed along similar lines:
> I think Jay's treaty is truly a farce,
> Fit only to wipe the national [arse].

It got worse. Meetings were organized at which Jay and his treaty were vilified by torch-wielding mobs. Jay himself joked that he could travel from Boston to Philadelphia by the light of his own figure burned in effigy. Graffiti scribbled on the fence of one of Jay's New England friends summed up popular sentiment: "Damn John Jay! Damn everyone that won't damn John Jay! Damn everyone that won't put lights in his windows and sit up all night damning John Jay!"

JOHN
MARSHALL

September 24, 1755–July 6, 1835

BIRTHPLACE:
Germantown, VA

NICKNAME:
"Silver Heels"

ASTROLOGICAL SIGN:
Libra

TERM:
February 4, 1801–
July 6, 1835

APPOINTED BY:
John Adams

WORDS OF WISDOM:
"The power to tax is the power to destroy."

He attended school with James Monroe, was boyhood friends with George Washington, and was distantly related to Thomas Jefferson. With a pedigree like that, is it any wonder that John Marshall ended up on the U.S. Supreme Court? But being well connected is not necessarily a harbinger of high achievement. Marshall took the opportunities that were presented to him and became, by force of intellect and personality, the most influential chief justice in American history. "My gift of John Marshall to the people of the United States was the proudest act of my life," declared John Adams, who had appointed him. Or, as Oliver Wendell Holmes, one of his successors on the Court, once observed: "If American law were to be represented by a single figure, skeptic and worshipper alike would agree that the figure could be one alone, and that one, John Marshall."

How disheveled was John Marshall? A neighbor once mistook the chief justice for a servant and threw him some change.

Beyond his noble birthright, there was nothing much about Marshall's upbringing that screamed "father of American jurisprudence." He had only a

year of formal schooling and attended law lectures for less than three months. Like all good patriots of his day, he was a soldier in the Revolutionary army, serving under his childhood chum and future political patron, Gen. George Washington. As a lieutenant at Valley Forge, Marshall became known for his athleticism. According to biographers, he could jump up more than six feet from a standing position. He also took part in foot races, wearing distinctively colored socks that his mother had sent to him. The odd leggings earned him the nickname "Silver Heels."

Silver Heels aimed higher than a career in track and field, however. After the war, he was admitted to the Virginia bar and entered politics. A staunch Federalist, he won favor with President John Adams, who sent him on a diplomatic mission to France in 1797. The mission culminated in clumsy French attempts to extract a bribe from Adams's envoys—the so-called XYZ Affair, named after the three French agents involved—and the immediate recall of the delegation. America's distaste for the French was only in its infancy, but even then it was enough to stoke an opportunistic young man's political career. At the urging of George Washington, Marshall ran for Congress, using the notoriety earned in the affair as his springboard to fame and fortune. The next year, Adams named him Secretary of State.

Marshall's ascent continued in 1800, when Chief Justice Oliver Ellsworth stepped down from the Supreme Court and Adams nominated Marshall to succeed him. Others were more favored in Federalist circles, however, and the Senate wasn't exactly enthusiastic about Marshall's nomination. Federalist senator Jonathan Dayton voted in favor only after fretting that the rejection of Marshall "might induce the nomination of some other character more improper, and more disgusting." Despite serious senatorial misgivings, the final vote to confirm was unanimous.

Once installed, Marshall set about putting his stamp on the high court. He instituted the practice of issuing one majority opinion on behalf of the entire Court, rather than having each justice issue a separate opinion. In the case of *Marbury v. Madison*, he established the Court's right to undertake judicial review of the constitutionality of legislation passed by Congress. With

McCulloch v. Maryland, he put the Court's imprimatur to the creation of the Bank of the United States—an enormous expansion of federal power. In the words of James A. Garfield, "Marshall found the Constitution paper; and he made it power. He found a skeleton, and he clothed it with flesh and blood." The Court's power and prestige swelled under Marshall's leadership. (When he arrived, the Court met in a dank, half-finished committee room on the first floor of the Capitol and was widely considered to be a backwater branch of government.)

Unsurprisingly, those who favored devolution of states' power, like Thomas Jefferson, found a natural enemy in Marshall. That dislike was exacerbated by Marshall's affable and unpretentious personality. He dressed in a plain, occasionally disheveled, manner and did all his own grocery shopping. A Virginia neighbor once saw him lugging a turkey home from the market, mistook him for a servant, and threw him some spare change. Marshall humbly pocketed the money and went on his way with his bird. A truly genial man, he won many a legal argument through conciliation and persuasion rather than confrontation and coercion—a fact that infuriated his political opponents.

Marshall spent 34 years as chief justice. In later years, ill health and the Court's changing political composition sapped him of some of his influence, but he remained a force to be reckoned with until the end. When he died, three months shy of his eightieth birthday, he was widely regarded among the greatest Americans in the nation's brief history. Legend has it that the Liberty Bell cracked as it tolled to mark his passing, although, like most legends involving the Liberty Bell, this one is untrue.

★ ★

BLOOD FEUD

Marshall and Thomas Jefferson were distant cousins, but that didn't stop them from despising each other. The enmity was both political and personal. Marshall was a Federalist, committed to a strong central government and a powerful, independent judiciary. Of Jefferson's small government party, he once remarked: "The Democrats are divided into speculative theorists and absolute terrorists," though he was quick to exempt Jefferson from the latter grouping. Irritated by the Sage of Monticello's self-professed reputation as a visionary, he mocked Jefferson as "the great Lama of the Mountain." For his part, the dandified Jefferson derided the unpretentious Marshall for his "lax lounging manners" and accused him of scheming to steal the presidency from him. Elsewhere he vented: "The state has long suffered from the want of any counterpart to the rancorous hatred which Marshall bears to his country and from the cunning and sophistry within which he is able to surround himself." Despite their mutual antipathy, the two men briefly put aside their differences for Jefferson's inauguration as president. In the interest of bipartisanship, Jefferson allowed Marshall to swear him in to office, though even that didn't go off without a hitch. In the middle of the ceremony, the Chief Justice pointedly turned his back on the incoming chief executive.

Shoe Fetish

While away from the bench, Marshall spent much of his downtime enjoying a game of quoits, an ancient form of horseshoes played with a round disc. A longtime fixture at the Richmond Quoits Club, he often combined disc-tossing with another of his favorite pursuits—drinking. He would down copious quantities of Madeira and rum punch, then engage in a spirited quoits game that invariably ended with him down on his hands and knees measuring his tosses against those of his opponents.

ANIMAL HOUSE

Marshall was famous for fostering a convivial air among fellow justices. He even insisted that all the Court's members live together in a boarding house. The environment soon resembled that of a college dorm, with rumors of excessive drinking flying around Washington. To keep up appearances, Marshall and his fellow boozehounds resolved to refrain from tippling during conferences, provided it wasn't raining. During one particularly tedious consultation, Marshall asked his friend Justice Joseph Story to go check on the weather from the window. When Story reported back that not a cloud loomed in the sky, Marshall upbraided him. "Justice Story," he said, "I think that is the shallowest and most illogical opinion I have ever heard you deliver. You forget that our jurisdiction is as broad as the Republic, and by the laws of nature it must be raining some place in our jurisdiction. Waiter, bring on the rum!"

I'M SURROUNDED BY IDIOTS!

Drunken revelry aside, Marshall's Court is widely considered to have been one of the effective and important bodies in American legal history—unless you're a Jeffersonian Democrat. Describing the state of the Supreme Court as he found it, writing to his patron Thomas Jefferson, Justice William Johnson was cutting in his assessments of several colleagues. "[William] Cushing was incompetent," Johnson wrote. "[Samuel] Chase could not be got to think or write, [William] Patterson was a slow man . . . and the other two judges [Marshall and his fellow Federalist, Bushrod Washington] you know are commonly estimated as one judge." (By Congressional order, the Court at that time consisted of only six members, not the nine we know today.) It was one of the first—but certainly not the last—times that a member of the Court saw fit to slag fellow jurists with a poison pen.

AMBLER ALERT

Next to alcohol and horseshoes, Marshall loved his wife, Mary Willis Ambler Marshall, above all things. Known as "Polly," she was born into a prominent Virginia family. Marshall met her at a party in 1780 when she was thirteen years old. He was twenty-five, but that didn't stop him from courting Polly for the better part of three years; they were married in 1783. Marshall's college notebooks are filled with her name doodled in all its variations: "Polly," "Polly Ambler," "Miss M. Ambler," and so on. In fact, he seems to have been more interested in scribbling her moniker than in doing his legal work.

Once married, Marshall spent many hours writing letters home to Polly from wherever his job took him. But the correspondence might not have provided all that much consolation. Polly suffered from severe depression, caused in part by the deaths of four of the couple's ten children. She may also have caught wind of a weekend tryst Marshall once had with his Parisian landlady. Even when faithful, he would often report back to her about the ladies he flirted with in the nation's capital. Whatever the reason, Polly spent more and more of her waking hours in bed, lolling around in a melancholy stupor. When she died in 1831, Marshall was devastated.

Author, Author!

Today it is commonplace for Supreme Court justices to write memoirs, autobiographies, and books of homespun accumulated wisdom. As with so many things Court-related, Marshall was a pioneer in this regard. Yet, he wasn't one to toot his own horn too loudly. When in 1827 his friend Justice Joseph Story asked him to pen an autobiography, Marshall responded with a brief sketch that began with the lines "The events of my life are too unimportant . . . to render them worth communicating or preserving." The rest was similarly self-effacing.

Biography was more up Marshall's alley. Between 1804 and 1807, he penned a magisterial five-volume life of George Washington, which he continued to revise and abridge until his death in 1835. Sadly the book was not well received, being little more than a bombastic mash note to his childhood friend and political patron. In a characteristically catty move, Marshall's old rival Thomas Jefferson ensured that the book's sales would falter by directing federal postmasters to refuse orders for it.

RITE ON, BROTHER!

Roughly one out of every three Supreme Court justices has been a freemason, an ancient fraternal order known for its obscure rituals and secret handshakes. By most accounts, Marshall was the first mason to occupy the chief justice's chair. He was active in the organization for most of his adult life and even served as the Worshipful Master of the Grand Lodge of Virginia from 1793 to 1795.

The Judge Who Was Kicked Off the Bench—
and Other Noteworthy Eighteenth-Century
Justices

JAMES WILSON (1789–98)

One of the original six justices, Wilson was a crook and a tool of the rich. During the American Revolution, he defended wealthy British loyalists in their efforts to retain their colonial property. Local patriots held him in such low esteem that a group of them once used a cannon to open fire on his home. An inveterate scam artist, Wilson helped mastermind a scheme to bribe the Georgia legislature to secure land grants—the so-called Yazoo Land Fraud Scandal. Another scheme involved petitioning Congress for the reimbursement of moneys he claimed to have paid to Indians for land tracts on the Illinois and Wabash rivers. Wilson's various con games eventually caught up with him. He spent much of his time on the Supreme Court "riding circuit" in a frantic effort to stay one step ahead of creditors. After two stints in debtor's prison, he died in disgrace in 1798. In a break with custom, the Supreme Court issued no eulogy.

JOHN RUTLEDGE (1790–91, 1795)

Rutledge remains the only Supreme Court justice to be kicked out of office. Beset by health problems during his brief stint as an associate justice from 1790 to 1791, he was invariably too sick to show up at the Court. In 1792 his wife died, and Rutledge began a long, slow descent into madness. By 1795, when President George Washington named him chief justice, he was a raving lunatic. The Senate rejected his nomination that December, and Rutledge was forced to surrender his seat after barely five months on the job. Distraught and increasingly unhinged, he attempted suicide by jumping into Charleston Bay. Two passing slaves saved his life—ironic, since he was an ardent slaveholder—and he spent his last five years in seclusion.

John Blair (1790–95)

Another of the early, crazy justices, Blair suffered from severe headaches and constantly complained about a "rattling, distracting noise in my head" that made it impossible for him to perform his official duties. He periodically descended into a fugue state in which his face would go numb and he would lose the ability to think clearly. Sensing this state of mind was undesirable for a judge, he resigned from the Court in 1795, after almost six years on the bench.

William Cushing (1790–1810)

Cushing served as chief justice for all of two days in 1796. Selected by Washington to replace the insane John Rutledge, the aged and infirm Cushing feared he had cancer and would soon die. He may also have been peeved that Washington failed to notify him of his appointment as chief justice until after the Senate had confirmed him. In any case, he quickly dashed off a letter to the president refusing the commission on account of his "declining state of health." He continued serving as associate justice for another fourteen years.

ROGER BROOKE

TANEY

March 17, 1777–October 12, 1864

BIRTHPLACE:

Calvert County, MD

NICKNAME:

"King Coody"

ASTROLOGICAL SIGN:

Pisces

TERM:

March 28, 1836–
October 12, 1864

APPOINTED BY:

Andrew Jackson

WORDS OF WISDOM:

"The African race in the United States even when free are everywhere a degraded class, and exercise no political influence. . . . Where they are nominally admitted by law to the privileges of citizenship, they have no effectual power to defend them, and are permitted to be citizens by the sufferance of the white population and hold whatever rights they enjoy at their mercy."

You have to hand it to Roger Taney. Without his example to live by, America's long line of vicious, racist Supreme Court justices would have no historical standard-bearer. Taney was the founding father of judicial racism, the Darth Vader to Abraham Lincoln's Luke Skywalker, and a pivotal figure in the nation's descent into bloody civil war. His keynote decision as chief justice, *Dred Scott v. Sanford*, went down in judicial infamy and permanently stained an otherwise distinguished legal career.

Did it really have to be that way? Well, actually, yes. Taney came from a family of Maryland tobacco planters, and he grew up around slaves and owned them for much of his adult life. (The fact that he freed some and gave others "pensions" is really beside the point.) He rarely traveled outside his native Tidewater region and never developed a worldview wider than that of the planting aristocracy. As a child, he attended boarding school, but withdrew after his teacher went insane. (Apparently suffering the effects of some type of dementia, the man became convinced he could walk on water and tried to cross the Patuxent River by foot. He drowned. The Taneys sent Roger to a private tutor instead.) Denied the chance to inherit his father's estate through the ancient right of primogeniture, Taney set his sights on a legal career. He was admitted to the bar in 1799.

Tall, gaunt, and hollow-eyed, young Taney recalled a character out of a Nathaniel Hawthorne novel. One friend described him as "as lean as a Potomac herring, and as shrewd as the shrewdest." When he married a fetching farmer's daughter in 1806, their improbable union was likened to that of "a hawk with a skylark." Nevertheless, the happy couple got along famously, for Taney had his soft side. He adored flowers and the natural world and could often be observed puttering in his garden. His law practice flourished.

> When Roger Taney abandoned formal knee breeches in favor of plain old trousers, many of his fellow justices were outraged.

During the War of 1812, Taney caught the political bug. He joined the pro-war faction of the Federalist Party known as the Coodies, quickly rising to a prominent position and earning the sobriquet "King Coody." A few years later, he abandoned the Federalists and hitched his star to the Democrats, under Andrew Jackson. Old Hickory liked the cut of Taney's gib and invited him into his cabinet. Taney briefly served as attorney general and secretary of war, drawing both salaries. Today such double dipping would be considered unethical, if not illegal, but at the time the practice was common. He made out like a bandit. "I performed the duties of both offices, I received the salaries of both," he later crowed. "I thought then and still think that it was right."

Following a controversial stint as secretary of the Treasury, Taney returned to private practice in Baltimore. That all changed in 1835, however, with the death of Chief Justice John Marshall. Eager to fill the opening with a loyalist, Jackson tapped Taney for the job. The choice was met with derisive howls from Marshall partisans who wanted Joseph Story, Marshall's ideological soul mate, to fill the slot. ("The Supreme Court—may it be raised one Story

higher!" gushed Josiah Quincy, president of Harvard.) Others thought the nomination smacked of favoritism. "The pure ermine of the Supreme Court is sullied by the appointment of that political hack, Roger B. Taney," complained a New York newspaper. Nevertheless, Taney was confirmed by the Senate and took his seat in March of 1836. Daniel Webster spoke for many of those disappointed by Taney's ascension when he lamented: "Judge Story . . . thinks the Supreme Court is gone, and I think so too."

Taney made several important changes while on the Court. He was the first Roman Catholic to sit on the high bench—itself a significant departure. He discontinued Marshall's tradition of all the justices sharing the same living quarters. He instituted a new custom whereby associate justices (rather than the chief) were assigned to write opinions in important cases, which continues to this day. Yet, all Taney's good work in Court administration was wiped from the history books by his majority opinion in the 1857 case of *Dred Scott v. Sandford*.

The legal battle pitted Scott, an erstwhile slave asserting his freedom because he had lived in the free state of Illinois, against the family of his former owner. In writing his opinion, Taney ignored the facts in favor of offering a sweeping denunciation of the citizenship of African Americans. Black slaves, he wrote, "had for more than a century before been regarded as beings of an inferior order; and altogether unfit to associate with the white race, either in social or political relations; and so far inferior that they had no rights which the white man was bound to respect; and that the Negro might justly and lawfully be reduced to slavery for his benefit." Not only was Scott not a U.S. citizen, Taney asserted, he never could be, nor could slavery be outlawed by act of Congress.

The decision sparked outrage in the antislavery community. "The name of Taney," fumed abolitionist senator Charles Sumner of Massachusetts, "is to be hooted down the page of history." Undoubtedly, it helped lead to Abraham Lincoln's election as president in 1860 and the subsequent outbreak of the Civil War. During that conflict, Taney compounded his problems by acting as a constant thorn in Lincoln's side. He opposed most of the Great Emancipator's wartime security measures and openly mocked the president in conversation. For his part, Lincoln ignored most of Taney's judicial directives and encouraged his supporters to smear Taney as a traitor. Many of them were thrilled when Taney died in 1864, paving the way for Lincoln to name loyalist Salmon P. Chase as his replacement.

Even after his death, Taney was vilified in print. An anonymous pamphlet entitled "The Unjust Judge" compared him to Pontius Pilate and charged that he was "perhaps the worst that ever occupied the seat of judgment among men." Recent scholars have tried to rehabilitate his reputation, suggesting that apart from the Dred Scott decision he actually left a fairly admirable record. That's a bit like saying that apart from the Holocaust, Hitler was a swell guy. Certainly the millions of African Americans who spent decades climbing out from under the yoke of the unconscionable *Dred Scott* decision would prefer to see him remain where he has long been consigned—in history's toilet bowl of repudiated racists.

★ ★

ALL IN THE FAMILY

Oh, to be a fly on the wall at a Taney family reunion. The future chief justice's relatives were a mixed bag of rogues and American royalty. His father was a violent hothead who, in 1819, stabbed a dinner companion to death in an argument over a woman's honor. To escape prosecution for murder, dear old dad fled Maryland for Virginia, where he died in a horse-riding accident the next year. On the plus side, Taney's mother was a descendant of William the Conqueror; by all accounts she acted as a positive formative influence in his life. One of his best friends was the composer of "The Star Spangled Banner," Francis Scott Key—or "Frank Key," as Taney called him. In 1806, the two became brothers-in-law when Taney married Key's sister Anne.

MASSA ROGER

As slave owners go, Taney was one of the good ones. He doled out silver pieces to those people he enslaved and fashioned tiny wallets in which they could keep their allowance. Together with his pal Francis Scott Key, he served as an officer in a "colonization society" dedicated to returning enslaved Africans to their homeland.

Bank Fraud

As if being a racist and a slave driver wasn't enough, Taney was probably a crook as well. When President Andrew Jackson named him Secretary of the Treasury in 1833—without Senate approval—Taney still owned stock in the Union Bank of Maryland, where he had worked as an attorney. After Jackson vetoed the recharter of the Second Bank of the United States, Taney set up a network of state banks into which federal funds were deposited. One of these so-called pet banks was—surprise, surprise— the Union Bank of Maryland. It was clearly a conflict of interest, and the ensuing scandal cost Taney his job. After nine months in office, during which Jackson had scrupulously avoided sending his name to the Senate for confirmation, Taney was rejected for the post of Treasury Secretary. He was the first U.S. cabinet secretary to be rejected by the Senate.

FASHION FORWARD

Sure, he consigned millions of Americans to a life of involuntary servitude and helped spark the Civil War, but there's one innovation for which all future Supreme Court justices can thank Chief Justice Taney. He was the first justice to wear ordinary trousers, rather than formal knee breeches, underneath his robes. The new fashion statement caused a mild stir at the time, with some observers fearful that such democratic attire signaled that unwashed rabble would soon take over government.

STAYIN' ALIVE

Was Taney psychic . . . or just a hypochondriac? In the spring of 1862, the chief justice asked each colleague to place a call on him before they left Washington for the summer. He was certain his death was imminent and wanted one last chance to bid adieu to his brethren. There was just one problem—he lived. In fact, Taney hung on for another two years. However, his physical condition did deteriorate such that his doctor likened him to a disembodied spirit. Unable to sit up, Taney spent most of his waking hours in bed reading. His dogged refusal to shuffle off his mortal coil prompted

Republican senator Benjamin F. Wade to crack: "No man ever prayed as I did that Taney might outlive James Buchanan's term, and now I am afraid I have overdone it."

All's Well That Inks Well

Dred Scott may have marred his reputation, but Taney did make one positive contribution to the cause of African American civil rights. When Justice John Marshall Harlan I was struggling to compose his dissent in the *Civil Rights Cases* of 1883, his wife helped him overcome writer's block by digging out the inkwell Taney had used to write the *Dred Scott* decision. Harlan was so taken with the idea of writing with the ink used to frustrate the aspirations of black Americans to defend their rights that "his pen fairly flew," and the dissent came out "like magic."

SALMON P.
CHASE

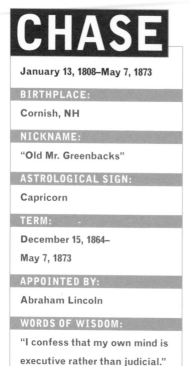

January 13, 1808–May 7, 1873

BIRTHPLACE:
Cornish, NH

NICKNAME:
"Old Mr. Greenbacks"

ASTROLOGICAL SIGN:
Capricorn

TERM:
December 15, 1864–
May 7, 1873

APPOINTED BY:
Abraham Lincoln

WORDS OF WISDOM:
"I confess that my own mind is executive rather than judicial."

Abraham Lincoln deserves much of the glory historians have accorded him. For freeing the slaves, winning the Civil War, and giving eloquent voice to some of America's highest ideals, he has earned a rightful place in the top ranks of U.S. presidents. So whatever possessed him to saddle the nation with one of the worst chief justices in Supreme Court history?

Salmon Portland Chase never wanted to sit on the Court, much less lead it, and when he got there he found himself dwarfed by his more intellectually endowed associates. He had a mediocre legal mind and precious few qualifications for the position. What's

As secretary of the Treasury, Salmon Chase ordered that his own face be put on the one dollar bill.

more, he was bedeviled by what Lincoln himself called "the Presidential maggot in his brain" and was constantly angling for a shot at the White House. Even Lincoln's own cabinet members were befuddled by the Chase appointment. "The President sometimes does some strange things," wrote Secretary of the Navy Gideon Welles, "but this would be a singular mistake." Tell us about it.

Oddly enough, if Chase had simply steered clear of the Supreme Court he

would have gone down in history as an accomplished—if unspectacular—public servant. The eighth of eleven children, he worked himself up from modest circumstances through Dartmouth College and into the Ohio bar. Thrice widowed and deeply religious, he found an outlet for his moral fervor in the abolitionist cause. He reportedly never refused to offer legal help to any person, black or white, and he used his antislavery activism as a springboard into politics. Finding neither the Whigs nor the Democrats to his liking, he joined the nascent Republican Party and was elected governor of Ohio in 1855.

His appetite whetted for bigger game, Chase set his sights on the presidency. But he failed to win the support of the Ohio delegation in 1860 and lost the Republican nomination to Illinois senator Abraham Lincoln, who went on to capture the White House. Eager to unite the party, and keenly aware of Chase's total ignorance of economic policy, Lincoln awarded him the plum job of secretary of the Treasury. It was the beginning of a long and rocky relationship.

Convinced that he should be running the country, Chase undermined Lincoln at every turn. He meddled in foreign policy, dragooned Treasury agents into his own personal political army, and even intrigued to replace Lincoln on the Republican ticket in 1864. Astonishingly, Lincoln took all this backstabbing in stride. He likened Chase's all-consuming ambition to a bothersome "chin fly" whose irritable behavior makes a horse run faster. "If Mr. Chase has a presidential chin fly biting him," Lincoln mused, "I am not going to knock it off; if it will only make his department go." Besides, Lincoln had a plan to get Chase out of his hair when the time was right: appoint him to the Supreme Court.

"There is not a man in the Union who would make as good a Chief Justice as Chase," declared Lincoln, though one wonders how he could have thought so. Despite his nonexistent judicial experience, Chase was highly esteemed within the party. The belief that he would provide a rubber stamp for Lincoln's emancipation policy likely influenced the decision, as did the imperative to move a nettlesome political rival into a lifetime appointment. "He wants to be president," Lincoln said shortly before naming Chase to the Court in December 1864, "and if he doesn't give that up, it will be a great injury to him and a great injury to me. He can never be president."

Almost upon assuming office, Chase knew he was in over his head. He found his new duties tedious and beneath him. He bemoaned "the painful monotony of hearing, reading, thinking, and writing on the same class of subjects and in the same way, all the time—morning, noon, evening, and night." Being a judge, he griped, consisted of "working from morning till midnight and no result, except that John Smith owned this parcel of land or other property instead of Jacob Robinson; I caring nothing, and nobody caring much more about the matter." Sensing Chase's apathy, his colleagues quickly tired of him. They found him imperious, complained about the way he doled out opinions, and wondered aloud how such a legal lightweight came to be their boss.

There were some bright spots. In a break from Roger Taney, his rabidly racist predecessor, Chase made it one of his initial acts as chief justice to appoint the first African American attorney to argue before the Court. In 1868, he became the first chief justice to preside over the impeachment of a president, when Andrew Johnson stood trial for high crimes and misdemeanors. But mostly Chase left no lasting footprint on constitutional law and provided little of the leadership that Lincoln had counted on. In fact, on several key issues—such as the printing of paper money and the suppression of civil liberties—he veered strangely from his political roots. In the words of John Usher, Lincoln's secretary of the Interior, Chase's "opinions as a jurist were the opposite of his views as a statesman."

History has not been kind to Chief Justice Chase. Noted his successor Morrison R. Waite: "In my judgment, my predecessor detracted from his fame by permitting himself to think he wanted the presidency. Whether true or not, it was said that he permitted his ambitions in that direction to influence his judicial opinions." Indeed, until the day he died of a paralytic stroke in 1873, Chase was still scheming—to the bitter end—to win entrance to the White House.

★ ★

HAVE A DRINK ON ME

As a young lawyer in Ohio in the 1830s and '40s, Chase defended so many fugitive slaves that proponents began to refer to him derisively as the "Attorney General for Runaway Negroes." In 1845 in Cincinnati, to show their gratitude, a group of poor African American churchgoers pooled their resources to present him with a sterling silver pitcher. Later, as governor of Ohio, Chase pointedly used the same pitcher to serve lemonade to the proslavery men who visited him in the governor's mansion.

BOSS FROM HELL

Chase's tenure at the Treasury Department was tumultuous, and he quickly became known for his volatile temper. Early in his tenure, he was accosted by the building's security guard after failing to show proper identification. The watchman horse-collared Chase and was about to punch his lights out when he realized whom he was manhandling. He was lucky to escape with his job—not to mention his life. Chase's underling, Assistant Secretary of the Treasury Maunsell B. Field, called his boss "a man of extremely nervous temperament" who could "sometimes be very violent, and occasionally even unjust, while swept by a gale of passion." Victims of Chase's rages included prominent Republican senators, such as William P. Fessenden of Maine, and Chase's own cabinet colleagues. Secretary of War Edwin Stanton, who meekly refused to fight back when subjected to Chase's verbal whippings, was a favorite punching bag.

ROOM WITH A VIEW

One thing is true about Salmon Chase—he never lost sight of his goal. When plans were drawn up to move his office from the south to the west side of the Treasury building, Chase asked why he was being relocated. So that you can always keep one eye on the White House, came the reply, and Chase cheerfully consented.

My Rival

No one was spared from Chase's ill will—not even the president. Chase considered Lincoln to be an uncouth boob who had somehow cheated him of his rightful place. A humorless martinet, he took a particularly dim view of Lincoln's penchant for telling homespun jokes and stories. "Personal relations between Mr. Lincoln and Mr. Chase were never cordial," observed one White House insider. "They were about as unlike in appearance, in education, manners, in taste, and temperament, as two eminent men could be."

For his part, Lincoln respected Chase's intellect and abilities. He once called his Treasury chief "about one and a half times bigger than any other man that I ever knew." Nevertheless, he saw his White House rival for what he was. "I will tell you how it is with Chase," Honest Abe once remarked. "Chase has fallen into two bad habits. He thinks he has become indispensable to the country. . . . He also thinks he ought to be president. He has no doubts whatever about that. It is inconceivable to him why people have not found it out, why they don't as one man rise up and say so."

HE'S SO MONEY

If money is the root of all evil, then what does that make Salmon P. Chase? He is the root of all money—U.S. paper money, that is. America's first federal currency was introduced in 1862, at the instigation of Treasury Secretary Chase, to fund the Civil War. Chase also took a hands-on role designing the banknotes. Eager to keep his image in the public's mind for a future presidential run, he ordered that his own face be put on the $1 bill. This naked act of self-promotion earned him the nickname "Old Mr. Greenbacks." Oddly enough, after the war Chief Justice Chase ruled that paper currency was unconstitutional.

Chase was also instrumental in putting the words "In God We Trust" on U.S. currency. A devout Episcopalian, he read the Bible daily and constantly sought to insert God into civic documents. (It was Chase who urged President Lincoln to include a mention in the last line of the Emancipation Proclamation.) When letters started pouring in demanding that the Almighty be recognized on the proposed currency, Chase seized on the idea. Declaring that "no nation can be strong except in the strength of God, or safe except in His defense," he instructed the director of the U.S. Mint to "cause a device to be prepared without unnecessary delay with a motto expressing in the fewest and tersest words possible this national recognition." Thus, "In God We Trust" was coined, in both senses of the word.

Salmon Chase's mug was eventually removed from the dollar bill, of course, but it graced the $10,000 bill from 1928 to 1946. Chase remains one of only three non-presidents to be commemorated on U.S. money. The other two are Alexander Hamilton ($10 bill) and Benjamin Franklin ($100 bill). In recognition of his monetary accomplishments—and despite his having nothing to do with its founding—Chase Manhattan Bank is named in his honor.

The 32-Year-Old Supreme Court Judge— and Other Noteworthy Nineteenth-Century Justices

JOSEPH STORY (1812–45)

The youngest person ever appointed to the Supreme Court, Story was only thirty-two when James Madison nominated him; he went on to serve more than thirty-three years. Before joining the judiciary, Story had made a name for himself as a poet. He published his first book of poetry at age twenty-six. Even after joining the Court in 1812, Story continued to multitask. He moonlighted as a bank president, taught law at Harvard, and wrote magazine articles. In an odd twist on the notion of art imitating life, twentieth-century Supreme Court justice Harry Blackmun played the role of Joseph Story in Stephen Spielberg's 1997 historical film *Amistad*.

STEPHEN JOHNSON FIELD (1863–97)

Field was the first Supreme Court justice to be the victim of an assassination attempt. It came at the hands of a fellow judge. David S. Terry, the former chief justice of the California State Supreme Court, vowed revenge against the associate justice after Field ruled against Terry's wife in a lawsuit involving her late, rich husband's estate. (The fact that Field was also old friends with a U.S. senator Terry had once killed in a duel may have entered into the drama as well.) By sheer happenstance, Terry, his wife, and Field all ended up on the same train to San Francisco in August 1889. When an enraged Terry attacked Field one morning at breakfast, Field's bodyguard shot him dead. Unfortunately, that incident was just the start of Field's troubles. His final years on the Court were marked by a slow descent into senility. According to legal historian David Garrow, the Lincoln appointee acted "like a madman" during some cases, and it became increasingly clear he could not understand the arguments made before him. Despite the urging of his colleagues, he refused to resign, determined to break John Marshall's record of 34 years of service. He did that—just barely—before finally relinquishing his seat in 1897. He died two years later.

John Marshall Harlan I (1877–1911)

Harlan earned a reputation as an early civil rights champion for his impassioned dissent in the 1896 case of *Plessy v. Ferguson*, which established the "separate but equal" segregation doctrine. The full truth, alas, is a little more complicated. Harlan was a former slaveholder who had once threatened to quit the Union army if President Lincoln signed the Emancipation Proclamation. Harlan turned against slavery only when he became a Republican and ran for office after the Civil War. Even in his *Plessy* dissent, he called the white race "the dominant race in this country . . . in prestige, in achievements, in education, in wealth, and in power" and vowed that it would continue to be so "for all time." And when it wasn't African Americans who were getting under his skin, it was the Chinese population. He once branded immigrants from China as a "distinct race and religion, remaining strangers in the land, residing apart by themselves, tenaciously adhering to the customs and usage of their own country, unfamiliar with our institutions and religion, and apparently incapable of assimilating with our people."

Oliver Wendell

HOLMES JR.

March 8, 1841–March 6, 1935

BIRTHPLACE:

Boston, MA

NICKNAME:

"Leany"

ASTROLOGICAL SIGN:

Pisces

TERM:

December 8, 1902–

January 12, 1932

APPOINTED BY:

Theodore Roosevelt

WORDS OF WISDOM:

"If my country wants to go to

Hell, I am here to help it."

The first question one must ask when discussing Justice Oliver Wendell Holmes Jr. is: What was *up* with that moustache? The possessor of one of the most formidable soup strainers of the Progressive Era, Holmes brought a decidedly martial severity to the high court—not surprisingly, considering he had served with distinction in the Union army during the Civil War. Like many ardent militarists, Holmes took a dim view of human nature. He was an avowed Social Darwinist who believed that humankind was fated to engage in a struggle of "all against all" for the world's limited resources, and he brought this cynical philosophy to bear on the cases he adjudicated. Only his quick wit and flair for the pithy turn of phrase saved him from being completely impossible to deal with. H. L. Mencken may have best summed up Holmes when he described him as "a soldier whose natural distaste and contempt for civilians, and corollary yearning to heave them all into Hell, was cooled and eased . . . by occasional doubts, hesitations, flashes of humor, bursts of affability, moments of sneaking pity."

He was born March 8, 1841, into the archetypal family of Boston Brahmins. (In fact, it was Holmes's father, Dr. Oliver Wendell Holmes Sr., the noted physician, poet, and intellectual gadabout, who first coined that term to denote the leading families of the New England Protestant establishment.) The eldest child of Oliver and Amelia Lee Jackson Holmes, a staunch abolitionist, young Oliver earned the nickname "Leany" for his lithe frame. He counted Henry Adams and William and Henry James among his childhood friends. As if a young man of his lineage had any other choice, he attended Harvard College, where, like his father before him, he was elected class poet. He graduated in 1861.

> According to his friends, Oliver Wendell Holmes Jr. was impotent and had a strictly platonic relationship with his wife, Fanny.

It is at this point that Holmes began to step out of his famous father's shadow. Rather than pursue a literary or medical career, he enlisted in the Union army, just in time for the Civil War. For the next three years, like a musket-toting Zelig, Holmes seemed to be on the scene for every major battle in the Eastern theater. He was thrice wounded—at Ball's Bluff in 1861; at Antietam the following year; and again at Fredericksburg in 1863. Only a shrapnel wound in that battle kept him out of the action at Gettysburg. Holmes's regiment was so decimated in the fighting that he was able to rise to the rank of brevet colonel. Combat experience—which Holmes increasingly blamed on the idealism of the abolitionist cause—considerably darkened his worldview.

After the war, Holmes returned to Boston and took up the study of law. He married, passed the bar, and established a practice with his asthmatic brother, Ned. He also taught, wrote, and lectured on the law and joined the Metaphysical Club, a floating philosophical bull session founded by pragmatist wisemen William James and Charles Peirce. In 1882, Holmes abandoned the life of academic windbaggery to accept an appointment as an associate justice to the Supreme Judicial Court of Massachusetts. There he wrote more than one thousand opinions and rose to the rank of chief justice in 1899.

In 1902, when President Theodore Roosevelt was casting about for a Supreme Court justice who would help him fight the "big railroad men and other members of large corporations," a speech Holmes had delivered to the

Harvard graduating class on Memorial Day years earlier caught his eye. The address extolled martial virtues and seemed to embody the full-throated jingoism that T. R. hoped to bring to the country. Assured by Republican senator Henry Cabot Lodge of Massachusetts that Holmes was "our kind right through," Roosevelt nominated him to the post of associate justice. It was to become one of the biggest regrets of his presidency. Just more than one year after taking his seat on the bench, Holmes voted against the trust buster in a major case involving the railroad monopoly. Roosevelt blew a gasket, announcing to anyone who would listen that he "could carve out of a banana a judge with more backbone" than Holmes.

He never got the chance. Holmes outlasted and outlived Roosevelt, serving on the Court for another twenty-eight years. Though he preached judicial restraint, he became something of a darling of Progressives and civil libertarians, most notably for his contention that the government should not abridge the right to free speech in the absence of a "clear and present danger." Holmes also became known for his lucid and artfully worded opinions, often given in dissent. He is one of the most quotable justices in history. The hiring of Supreme Court clerks, typically drawn from the ranks of recent law school graduates, was one of his innovations.

A believer in the virtues of strenuous exercise, Holmes walked to work two miles each morning until he was eighty-six years old. When he finally retired in 1932, at age ninety, he was a living legend and the oldest Supreme Court justice in American history. He died three years later after a brief bout with pneumonia. In the end, the man who had once declared that "taxes are the price we pay for civilization" put his money where his mouth was. He bequeathed his entire estate to the U.S. government.

★ ★

DEAR OLD DAD

Holmes had quite a legacy to live up to. His father, Oliver Wendell Holmes Sr., was one of the intellectual titans of the nineteenth century. A double threat as a doctor and a man of letters, he cofounded *The Atlantic* literary journal and coined the word *anesthesia*. He also huffed ether like a fiend and once claimed that the secret of life had been revealed to him while he was high. Unfortunately, when he sobered up and returned to his desk, where he had recorded the secret before passing out, he found only the following inscription: "A strong smell of turpentine prevails throughout." Not exactly the revelation the world was waiting for.

Of more lasting importance to mystery readers, the elder Holmes may have provided the inspiration for one of world literature's most popular and enduring characters. Sir Arthur Conan Doyle is said to have based his coke-sniffing consulting detective, Sherlock Holmes, in part on old Oliver Wendell.

SAY MY NAME

Not to be outdone by his old man, Holmes Jr. is also the namesake of several fictional characters. Oddly enough, two of them are black: Oliver Wendell "Spearchucker" Jones, the javelin-tossing surgeon in the book, movie, and TV series *M*A*S*H*; and Oliver Wendell Jones, the mischievous computer hacker in Berke Breathed's popular 1980s comic strip *Bloom County*. Oliver Wendell Douglas, the bumpkin protagonist of TV's *Green Acres*, may have a Supreme Court pedigree as well. His name is a mash-up of Holmes's and that of one of his successors on the bench, William O. Douglas.

Potent Quotables

Holmes was famous for his pithy observations, which invariably reflected his dour, pessimistic view of human nature. "I loathe the thick-fingered clowns we call the people" was one of his more representative pronouncements. Some of his other notable quotations address specific aspects of life, the law, and his conception of democracy.

Speaking about morality, Holmes (a lifelong atheist) once wrote that it was "more or less arbitrary. . . . Do you like sugar in your coffee or don't you? . . . So as to truth."

Although he helped clarify First Amendment rights and coined the term *clear and present danger*, Holmes disapproved of free speech. He once likened it to disease, declaring that, in the eyes of the law, it "stands no differently than freedom from vaccination." Writing to a friend, he proposed that "we should deal with the act of speech as we deal with any other overt act that we don't like."

Holmes also had no use for social reformers, an odd stance for the son of an abolitionist. "Doesn't this squashy sentimentality of a big minority of our people about human life make you puke?" he once lamented in a letter to a friend. When discussing those "who believe there is an onward and upward—who talk of uplift—who think that something in particular has happened and that the universe is no longer predatory," Holmes nearly gagged again. "Oh, bring in a basin!" he wailed.

To those "levelers" who promulgated the idea that all people are due a comparable slice of the economic pie, Holmes had this to say: "I have no respect for the passion for equality, which seems to me merely idealizing envy."

Holmes's misanthropy was largely borne of his Civil War experiences, where he witnessed unspeakable acts of carnage that prompted him to question the value of human life. "I see no reason for attributing to a man a significance different in kind from that which belongs to a baboon or to a grain of sand," he once remarked. On another occasion, he asserted that "the sacredness of human life is a purely municipal ideal of no validity outside the jurisdiction."

In place of human dignity, Holmes substituted a reverence for war and the survival of the fittest. "I believe that force, mitigated so far as may be by good manners, is the ultima ratio," he declared. "Every society rests on the death of men." To a friend who took a more humane view, he wrote: "You respect the rights of man—I don't, except those things a given crowd will fight for."

IDIOT'S DELIGHT

Nowhere was Holmes's ruthless Social Darwinism more on display than in the 1927 case *Buck v. Bell*. That case involved the forced sterilization of a retarded teenager by the state of Virginia in an effort to forestall the generation of what the state called "socially inadequate offspring." In a stunning 8–1 decision, the Supreme Court voted to uphold the sterilization on the grounds that the girl was a "deficient" mother. Writing for the majority,

> Holmes laid down the law in words that would warm the heart of the most committed Nazi eugenicist. "It is better for all the world," he argued, "if, instead of waiting to execute degenerate offspring for crime, or to let them starve for their imbecility, society can prevent those who are manifestly unfit from continuing their kind. . . . Three generations of imbeciles are enough."

SHORT AND SWEET

Holmes was famous for his concise opinions, which he often wrote standing up, saying: "Nothing conduces to brevity like a caving in of the knees."

SHOOTING BLANKS

The "Yankee from Olympus" was no love god. According to friends, Holmes was sexually impotent and had a strictly platonic relationship with his wife, Fanny Dixwell Holmes. (Insert your own salacious pun here.) Some biographers have speculated that the bullet that lodged in Holmes's neck at the Battle of Antietam damaged a nerve connected to his genitals. Holmes also complained of frequent lower back pain, which may have been related to his problems "down below." Whether his flag was flying or not, however, Holmes was known to be a bit of a flirt and corresponded by mail in a suggestive manner with several women. There is no evidence he consummated any of these relationships.

Duck, Abe!

Throughout his long judicial career, Holmes performed many great services for the nation, but none more important than that undertaken in July 1864 as a brevet colonel in the Army of the Potomac at the Battle of Fort Stevens. The story goes that young Colonel Holmes was assigned to escort President Lincoln on an inspection tour of the front lines. Apparently, Honest Abe neglected to remove his trademark stovepipe hat, making him an easy target for Confederate sharpshooters taking aim at the Union breastworks. Only a quick-thinking Holmes saved Lincoln from premature assassination. "Get down, you fool!" he barked, pulling the commander-in-chief behind the fortifications and out of the line of fire. Embarrassed by his breach of decorum, Holmes tried to apologize afterward, but Lincoln would have none of it. "I'm glad to see you know how to talk to a civilian," he told the future associate justice.

WAR WOUNDS

Holmes's Civil War service was the formative experience of his life, and he kept it with him till the day he died. Each year, he drank a toast on the anniversary of the Battle of Antietam, where he had been gravely wounded. Long after leaving the service, he was known to visit the gravesite of his unit commander at Arlington National Cemetery (where Holmes himself would later be buried). After his death, his executors found two musket balls in his safe deposit box, along with an explanatory note that read: "These were taken from my body in the Civil War." In his closet they found two gore-spattered Union army uniforms, with another note attached: "These uniforms were worn by me in the Civil War and the stains upon them are my blood."

CHARLES EVANS
HUGHES

April 11, 1862–August 27, 1948

BIRTHPLACE:
Glens Falls, NY

NICKNAME:
"Whiskers," "Chilly Charlie"

ASTROLOGICAL SIGN:
Aries

TERM:
October 10, 1910–June 10, 1916;
February 24, 1930–June 30, 1941

APPOINTED BY:
William Howard Taft

WORDS OF WISDOM:
"The Constitution is what the
judges say it is."

"Nobody ever slapped me on the back and called me Charley," Charles Evans Hughes once proclaimed. He may not have been your typical glad-handing Washington pol, but America's eleventh chief justice clearly knew how to play the game. Through sheer hard work and political tenacity, he managed, during a thirty-five-year period, to secure a succession of high-profile positions—governor, secretary of state, Supreme Court justice (twice)—and to come within a hair's breadth of the biggest prize of all, the U.S. presidency. Not a bad résumé for a poster child for home schooling.

Born in upstate New York in 1862, Hughes was a precocious student. He could read at age three and a half and displayed an uncanny knack for memorization. Weaned on the Bible by devout Baptist parents, by toddlerhood the future chief justice had committed to memory "a fairly large repertoire of biblical lore." At age six, he was sent briefly to a public school but grew so bored with the slow pace that he begged his parents to allow him to continue his studies at home. He even prepared a personal curriculum, entitled "Charles Evans Hughes' Plan of Study." The insanely detailed document lists every course he wished to pursue in one column, with an adjacent column indicating the time of day he planned to study it. Impressed, or perhaps mortified, his parents relented. By age eight, he had mastered Greek; at nine, he had read the complete works of William Shakespeare. The family moved to New York City, where Hughes attended elementary school and wrote learned essays with such titles as "The Evils of Light Literature" and "The Limitation of the Human Mind." He earned his high school diploma at age thirteen and enrolled in college the next year.

After graduating Phi Beta Kappa from Brown University in 1881, Hughes worked his way into Columbia Law School by teaching Greek, Latin, and algebra. He passed the bar with a near-perfect score and then joined a prominent New York law firm, married one of the senior partners' daughters, and became a partner in just under five years. A long and lucrative career in private practice awaited, but overwork and ill health began to take a toll. Burnt out, Hughes gave it all up for a teaching career, and later a chance at public service. In 1906, in a landslide victory, he defeated William Randolph Hearst to become governor of New York. In office, he shepherded progressive measures into law. He was reelected four years later on a promise to eliminate horseracing and gambling in the state.

Hughes was now a rising star in Republican politics. He declined William Howard Taft's offer of the vice-presidential nomination in 1908—his eye fixed, some speculated, on bigger game. Sensing that Hughes might challenge him for the Republican nomination in 1912, the wily Taft nominated him to fill an opening on the Supreme Court. Hughes was confirmed unanimously after

> Somehow Charles Evans Hughes rose to be chief justice without ever learning how to properly shave. He wore a thick, full beard for most of his adult life.

about five minutes of debate in the Senate. Two months later, when Chief Justice Melville Fuller died, Taft strongly considered selecting Hughes, but ultimately he chose Associate Justice Edward D. White. Was it possible that Taft, who coveted the chief justice role for himself, feared the consequences of installing the young and hardy Hughes in that position, where he could presumably serve another three to four decades? Taft admitted that the thought

had crossed his mind. In any event, Hughes would have to wait another twenty years for his chance to lead the Court. By that time, Taft had served and gone.

Once Taft was out of the way, Hughes set his sights on the White House. He resigned from the Court after six years and captured the Republican presidential nomination in 1916. His opponent was Woodrow Wilson, the pallid Princetonian who had ousted Taft in 1912. Despite running against an incumbent, Hughes mounted a stiff challenge and seemed on the verge of winning. On election night, some two hundred thousand supporters filled Times Square, chanting "Hughes, Hughes" in unison as the lights on the side of the *New York Times* building flashed the message: "Hughes Elected." Hughes went to bed convinced that he had captured the presidency. The next morning, he woke to the grim reality that Wilson had eked out a 23-vote Electoral College victory. An unflappable Hughes took it all in stride. "While of course I did not enjoy being beaten," he said, "the fact that I did not have to assume the tasks of the presidency in that critical time was an adequate consolation."

After a brief sojourn in private practice, Hughes returned to Washington in 1921, as secretary of state under President Warren G. Harding. The austere diplomat was noticeably out of place among the back-slapping poker players in Harding's cabinet. Indeed, he was such a cold fish that they called him "Chilly Charlie" behind his back. Nevertheless, Hughes bided his time, and in 1930, when Taft's declining health once more put the chief justiceship within his grasp, he was ideally positioned to seize the opportunity. From his deathbed, Taft whispered to President Herbert Hoover that he should name Hughes as his successor. Hoover agreed and submitted Hughes's name to the Senate.

This time, his nomination met with fierce opposition—a stark contrast to his first confirmation, in 1910. Senator George Norris, an outspoken progressive from Nebraska, led the opposition. "No man in public life so exemplifies the influence of powerful combinations in the political and financial world as does Mr. Hughes," he railed, convincing twenty-five colleagues to join him. When Hughes was finally confirmed as chief justice in February 1930, the 52 to 26 tally represented the largest vote against a confirmed chief justice nominee.

At age sixty-eight, Hughes was also the oldest chief justice. Nevertheless, he proved himself an astute jurist and an especially able administrator. Felix Frankfurter, who joined the Court in 1939, compared Hughes's work in conference to a great conductor striking the pitch for a group of musicians. "To see him preside was like witnessing Toscanini lead an orchestra," he gushed. Hughes's judiciary magnum opus may have been his opposition to President Franklin D. Roosevelt's obnoxious "court packing" scheme. In a naked power grab, FDR wanted to name one additional justice for every current justice over age seventy who refused to retire, thus "packing" the judiciary branch with hand-picked cronies. Hughes had the stature to lead a high-profile campaign against the plan—which was clearly unconstitutional—but he chose instead to defuse FDR's anger by upholding several key New Deal measures dear to the president's heart. This "tough love" approach showed true political dexterity as well as an awareness of the Court's need to change with the times.

Hughes himself changed little during his eleven years as chief justice. He remained a pragmatic jurist not easily pigeonholed as a conservative or liberal. His lodestar was the integrity of the Court as an institution. Toward the end of his life, he became so obsessed with not overstaying his welcome that he asked family members to vote by secret ballot if they felt he was becoming too senile to serve. Ultimately, it was not his mind but his digestive system that betrayed him. Weakened by a duodenal ulcer, Hughes sent his resignation to President Roosevelt in June 1941. He died seven years later while summering with his family on Cape Cod.

A BEAUTIFUL MIND

Hughes had a photographic memory, which he developed in early childhood. He could recite entire verses from the New Testament by the time he was six years old. As a grown man, he was known to deliver long speeches verbatim, without notes, after having read them only once or twice. It was said he could read "a paragraph at a glance, a treatise in an evening, a roomful of papers in a week"—a talent that gave him no small advantage when squaring off against other, less-prepared lawyers. Nevertheless, he was initially reluctant to pursue a legal career. "I know that I could do well in law, but the profession is repugnant to me," he told college classmates. His first choice was a life in the ministry. "God's glory is my only aim," he once declared. His aim was off. By his senior year in college, he had decided to go to law school.

No Brother!

For a politician, Hughes wasn't exactly the most gregarious person. Herbert Hoover once remarked that he had "no instinct for personal friendship that I could ever discover." From an early age, Hughes preferred to be alone. One time, when he overheard his parents discussing the possibility of adopting another child, he marched into the room and argued the case against. The family had limited resources, he charged, and providing him with an adequate education was much more important than providing him with a playmate. Young Charles remained an only child.

SAVE YOUR PRAYERS

Though known to be a deeply religious Christian, Hughes disdained prayer. Faith, he once wrote to his mother, was "too wonderful and mysterious and sacred to be cheapened by formalism and vain repetitions." Saying grace was particularly irksome to Hughes, who once called "prayers before meals and the so-called family prayers . . . a wretched business."

THE WEIGHT

By his own admission, Hughes suffered from "nervous depression" as a young man, chiefly due to the stress of his job as a partner in the firm of Carter, Hughes & Cravath. He was also profoundly disturbed at being turned down for a life insurance policy despite a clean medical record. The reason? Weighing about 125 pounds soaking wet, Hughes was considered danger-ously underweight by the insurance carrier. For the rest of his life, he period-ically vacationed in the Alps to recharge his mental batteries. When President Taft implored him to run for reelection as governor of New York in

1910, Hughes initially demurred, saying, "I do not dare to run the chance of breaking down mentally."

SMOKE BREAK

Hughes's overall health and well-being improved considerably after he gave up smoking in 1914. An excessive cigar smoker from early adulthood, he blamed the habit for his hypertension and, despite his doctor's qualms that quitting cold turkey might do more harm than good, resolved to abstain from stogies entirely—and immediately. "I think I won't smoke anymore for a little while," he announced to some fellow puffers at a dinner party. He never smoked again.

"WHISKERS"

Hughes's distinctive physical appearance always attracted attention. In 1890, having never learned how to shave himself and tired of going to the barber, he grew a thick, full, red beard, which he maintained for the rest of his life. William Randolph Hearst, his opponent in the 1906 New York gubernatorial election, called him an "animated feather duster." Albany wags dubbed him "Whiskers" behind his back. In 1909, during President William Howard Taft's inaugural parade, a heavy snowstorm descended on Washington. Those in attendance commented afterward on the sight of Hughes, mounted on a large white horse, his coat tails flapping and red whiskers billowing in the cold wind. After Hughes became chief justice, his trademark bush became even more famous. He once received a piece of fan mail at the Court with no name or address printed on the outside— just a crude drawing of his facial hair.

THE SHIRT OFF HIS BACK

That wasn't the only piece of fan mail Hughes received—or the most unusual. (It was said that only President Roosevelt and Huey Long got more mail than Hughes.) An editor at the *Des Moines News* once wrote to him asking if he would mail her one of his shirts. She planned to cut it up and sell it at a public auction of "kitchen aprons made from the shirttails of famous men." The letter asked Hughes to attach an identifying mark to the shirt, as well as "a short biography of the garment, as to what important events it has shared in your life." Amused, Hughes had the letter framed and periodically brought it out to show guests at his parties. There's no indication he ever acceded to the request.

EXTREME MAKEOVER, SUPREME COURT EDITION

In his early days in Washington, Hughes was known for his lack of fashion sense. He wore tacky department store clothes and did little to control the growing forest on his face. In later years, he made more of an effort to ingratiate himself with Washington society. He started trimming his beard, bought his suits from the finest tailors in town, and hired a valet to dress him in the morning. Before long, the one-time fashion nightmare was one of the capital's foremost style icons. During Hughes's time as secretary of state, *Time* magazine remarked that he "resembled nothing so much as a Russian grand duke under the empire."

You Again?!

Because their time in public office coincided almost perfectly, Hughes and Franklin D. Roosevelt will forever be linked in the public mind. Although often at odds, the two men managed to make the most of the situation. When Hughes administered the oath of office to Roosevelt for the third time, he admitted that "I had an impish desire to break the solemnity of that occasion by remarking: 'Franklin, don't you think this is getting to be a trifle monotonous?'"

BUNT AND CENTER

Hughes's brother-in-law was Walter F. "Dutch" Carter, a one-time Yale baseball star turned lawyer who, with his teammate George Case, co-invented the squeeze play in a game against Princeton on June 16, 1894.

MOUNTAIN MAN

How many Supreme Court justices can boast that they have a mountain range named after them? The next time business or pleasure takes you to

Antarctica, visit the Hughes Range, located in the Queen Maud Mountains on the Polar Plateau. The massive mountain range was named in Hughes's honor by its discoverer, longtime Hughes crony Rear-Admiral Richard Evelyn Byrd. For a less awe-inspiring tribute, drop by Cornell Law School, where Hughes once taught. A dormitory there is also named in the chief justice's honor.

A "Surprising" Connection to a "Popular and Useful" Guidebook

In 1888, Hughes signed on as a partner in what would become one of America's most prominent and distinguished law firms. Known today as Hughes Hubbard & Reed, the firm boasts a stellar roster of high-profile legal alumni, including one who made his mark in the culinary arena. Tim Zagat, cofounder of the popular Zagat's restaurant guide, was once an associate in the firm.

HUMAN GUINEA PIG

Not content to leave a mark in the fields of law, geography, and restaurant criticism, the Hughes clan blazed a trail in the medical realm. In 1919, Hughes's eleven-year-old daughter Elizabeth contracted severe diabetes. Within three years, the disease had weakened her near death. Admitted to private care under the supervision of Canadian physician F. G. Banting, she became one of the first diabetes patients to be injected with insulin, which was then considered an experimental treatment. Elizabeth went on to live another fifty-eight years and helped found the Supreme Court Historical Society in 1972.

James Clark
McREYNOLDS

February 3, 1862–August 24, 1946

BIRTHPLACE:
Germantown, VA

NICKNAME:
"Scrooge"

ASTROLOGICAL SIGN:
Aquarius

TERM:
October 12, 1914–
January 31, 1941

APPOINTED BY:
Woodrow Wilson

WORDS OF WISDOM:
"My God, another Jew on the court!"

The Archie Bunker of the Supreme Court, James Clark McReynolds left a legacy of racial and religious bigotry unrivalled by any other justice. An abrasive boor and virulent anti-Semite without an ounce of common decency or professional courtesy, he came to the high court after a decidedly undistinguished legal career. In fact, rumor has it that President Woodrow Wilson nominated him to the bench for one reason only: to get him out of his cabinet, where he was serving unspectacularly as attorney general.

A native Kentuckian, McReynolds affected the courtly air of a Southern gentleman, a posture utterly belied by his belligerent personality. After receiving his law degree from the University of Virginia in 1884, he practiced law in

> **How disliked was James Clark McReynolds? When he died of pneumonia in 1941, not a single one of his fellow justices attended his funeral.**

Nashville for the better part of two decades before embarking on a political career. But his arrogance alienated voters, and he lost his only bid for Congress, in 1896. Instead, McReynolds pursued a career in the Justice Department, first as an assistant U.S. attorney and later as Wilson's attorney

general beginning in 1913. He made so many enemies both inside and outside the administration, however, that Wilson saw fit to elevate him to the Supreme Court after barely a year into the job.

Once thought to be a progressive, McReynolds surprised most observers by becoming one of the court's conservative stalwarts. In the 1930s, he was one of four justices—dubbed the "Four Horsemen"—to openly oppose President Franklin D. Roosevelt's New Deal. He was notorious for his hysterical, over-the-top dissenting opinions, at one point declaring the workmen's compensation law "a measure to stifle enterprise, produce discontent, strife, idleness, and pauperism." Roosevelt's program, he warned, represented "Nero at his worst. The Constitution is gone!"

McReynolds may have been entitled to his reactionary legal opinions, but his lack of social graces was another kettle of fish. Dubbed "Scrooge" by journalist Drew Pearson, he was a vicious misanthrope widely loathed by his colleagues, irrespective of their political stripe. Chief Justice William Howard Taft, who served with McReynolds for nearly nine years, declared him "selfish to the last degree" and "fuller of prejudice than any man I have known." Taft added, "He has a continual grouch and is always offended because the court is doing something that he regards as undignified." Echoing those sentiments was McReynolds's fellow justice and personal bête noire, John Hessin Clarke, who claimed he was "too much of a grouch to have a good opinion even of himself." Clarke in particular grew so weary of McReynolds's unremittingly unpleasant manner that he quit after barely six years on the bench, just to get away from him. Characteristically, McReynolds refused to sign a letter congratulating Clarke on his retirement. "This is a fair sample of McReynolds's personal character and the difficulty of getting along with him," a beleaguered Taft commented afterward. Oliver Wendell Holmes was even more cutting, calling McReynolds "a savage, with all the irrational impulses of a savage." Nor did McReynolds's bilious personality go unnoticed outside the court's hallowed halls. The British socialist theorist Harold Laski is said to have remarked that "McReynolds and the theory of a beneficent deity are quite incompatible."

McReynolds died of pneumonia in 1941, five years after leaving the bench. His colleagues were surprised to learn that he bequeathed the bulk of his estate to charity—but not surprised enough to change their opinion of him. Not one of his fellow justices showed up at his funeral.

★ ★

Jew Foe

McReynolds wasn't the first anti-Semite to serve on the court, but he was easily the most devoted to the cause. An unapologetic Jew-hater of the old-school variety, the crabby Kentuckian refused to eat, shake hands with, or talk to "Hebrews," as he usually called Jewish people. "For four thousand years the Lord tried to make something out of Hebrews," he once wrote, "then gave it up as impossible and turned them out to prey on mankind in general—like fleas on the dog for example."

Amazingly, McReynolds's "No Jews Allowed" policy extended even to his judicial colleagues. When Louis Brandeis was appointed to the Supreme Court in 1916, becoming America's first Jewish justice, McReynolds refused to speak to him for three years. Even worse, he would get up and leave the chamber whenever Brandeis began to speak, returning only after his oration was finished. As a consequence, the court delegation was invariably one man short at ceremonial gatherings. "I do not expect to attend," McReynolds informed Chief Justice Taft when declining a dinner invitation with his fellow justices and the U.S. attorney general, "as I find it hard to dine with the *Orient*." On another occasion, McReynolds begged off a court-sponsored visit to Philadelphia, telling Taft: "As you know, I am not always to be found when there is a Hebrew abroad. Therefore, my 'inability' to attend must not surprise you." In 1924, the court's group photograph became a sticking point. McReynolds adamantly refused to sit next to Brandeis, whom he immediately preceded in seniority. A flummoxed Taft implored McReynolds to swallow his distaste long enough to allow the picture to be taken, but to no avail. McReynolds held firm, and the photograph session was cancelled.

In 1932, a second Jewish justice was appointed, prompting another round of the vapors. The news of Benjamin Cardozo's pending appointment inspired

McReynolds to implore President Herbert Hoover not to "afflict the court with another Jew." Unmoved, Hoover nominated Cardozo anyway, prompting McReynolds to declare that "the only way you can get on the Supreme Court these days is to be either the son of a criminal or a Jew, or both." Apparently pleased with the freeze-out tactics he had used on Brandeis, McReynolds rolled out some new variations for Cardozo. He ostentatiously read a newspaper throughout Cardozo's swearing-in ceremony, declined to speak to him after taking his seat on the court, and made a point of covering his face whenever Cardozo delivered his opinions. When Cardozo died in 1938, McReynolds refused to attend the memorial service. The next year saw the appointment of yet another Jewish justice, Felix Frankfurter, giving McReynolds an opportunity to issue one final blast of anti-Semitic vitriol: "My God, another Jew on the court!" This time he skipped the swearing-in ceremony altogether.

To be fair, McReynolds was an equal opportunity bigot. He observed that blacks were "ignorant, superstitious, immoral and with but small capacity for radical improvement." He had no love for Germans either. He once cheered on a judge who made prejudicial remarks about German Americans, calling them descendants of a country "engaged in hunnish warfare" whose natives "unhappily had obtained citizenship here." McReynolds even offered a legal argument for the use of ethnic hatred in the administration of justice. "Intense dislike of a class does not render the judge incapable of administering complete justice to one of its members," he opined.

Can't Live with 'Em, Can't Even Listen to 'Em

When Jews, blacks, and Germans weren't grinding McReynolds's gears, he found time to detest women as well. "I see the female is here again," he once complained when a woman attorney appeared before the court. Female lawyers were often denied a hearing. McReynolds simply vacated the bench in disgust as soon as they started to speak.

SMOKE SCREEN

Declaring that "tobacco smoke is personally objectionable to me," McReynolds forbade people to smoke in his presence. He had "No Smoking" signs put up throughout the Supreme Court building and refused to hire smokers to serve as his law clerks. Among his other pet peeves: wrist watches for men (he considered them effeminate) and red fingernail polish on women (he found it vulgar). An avowed fussbudget, McReynolds was also notorious for bolting early from dinner parties if he disliked the seating arrangements.

Permanent Vacation

Besides being a hateful anti-Semite, misogynist, and all-around curmudgeon, McReynolds was a chronic shirker who often skipped out on judicial responsibilities to go duck hunting with his cronies. "An imperious voice has called me out of town," he once mischievously informed Chief Justice William Howard Taft before leaving on one such excursion. "I don't think my sudden illness will prove fatal, but strange things some time happen around Thanksgiving." On another occasion, he left for vacation without notifying Taft at all.

TAKE THAT, HARLAN

McReynolds was openly contemptuous of his colleagues on the court, often cutting them down with caustic remarks. Little pretext was required to draw his verbal venom. When Justice Harlan Fiske Stone commented that one attorney's long-winded brief was "the dullest argument I ever heard in my life," McReynolds replied: "The only duller thing I can think of is to hear you read one of your opinions."

LOUIS
BRANDEIS

November 13, 1856–
October 5, 1941

BIRTHPLACE:
Louisville, KY

NICKNAME:
"The People's Attorney"

ASTROLOGICAL SIGN:
Scorpio

TERM:
June 5, 1916–February 13, 1939

APPOINTED BY:
Woodrow Wilson

WORDS OF WISDOM:
"We can have democracy in
this country, or we can have
great wealth concentrated in
the hands of a few. But we can't
have both."

On June 5, 1916, James McReynolds's worst nightmare took his seat on the Supreme Court. America's first Jewish justice arrived with impeccable credentials. He'd earned the highest grade point average ever in the history of Harvard Law School and built a thriving private law practice. But the so-called People's Attorney was considered a dangerous radical by many in the Protestant legal establishment, for whom anti-Semitism was an inbred state of mind. During twenty-three years on the Court, Brandeis would earn the respect—if not the affection—of many of his detractors, with the notable exception of the irredeemably spiteful McReynolds.

The appointment of Louis Brandeis—the first Jewish justice on the Supreme Court—generated plenty of controversy.

Though revered by a generation of northeastern Jewish liberals (many of whom sent their children to his namesake university), Brandeis was born, of all places, in Louisville, Kentucky. The son of a wholesale grain and produce dealer who saw his fortunes dashed in the "Long Depression" of the 1870s,

Brandeis spent part of his formative years living abroad in Germany, where he mastered several languages as well as physics, chemistry, and mathematics. He returned to the United States in 1875 and enrolled at Harvard Law School at age eighteen—without a college diploma. (The things you could do in those days!) One of his early brushes with fame came when he attended a lecture on education delivered by an aged Ralph Waldo Emerson.

After two years of law school, Brandeis deemed himself fit to enter private practice. He went into business with one of his Harvard classmates and quickly built a client list in Boston's well-to-do German Jewish community. He also married his second cousin, Alice Goldmark, in 1891 and started living the abstemious lifestyle for which he became famous. "Some men buy diamonds and rare works of art," Brandeis said. "Others delight in automobiles and yachts. My luxury is to invest my surplus effort, beyond that required for the proper support of my family, to the pleasure of taking up a problem and solving, or helping to solve, it for the people without receiving any compensation." Though a noble sentiment, it was also something of an exaggeration. *Someone* must have been compensating Brandeis, because by 1900 he was a millionaire.

During these years, Brandeis developed his "radical" reputation. He mediated a strike in a shoe factory, opened his home to the wife of anarchist Nicola Sacco during the latter's murder trial, and advocated against the concentration of corporate power. In 1907 he appeared before the Supreme Court to defend an Oregon law establishing a ten-hour workday for women—buttressing his case with only two pages of legal precedent and more than one hundred pages of sociological data. This so-called Brandeis Brief revolutionized the way lawyers argued before the Court.

Although hardly a devout Jew (he never went to synagogue and was not bar mitzvahed), Brandeis took up the cause of Zionism, beginning in his mid-1950s. The dream of establishing an egalitarian, agrarian Jewish homeland in Palestine became the abiding crusade of his later life. He donated millions of dollars and delivered countless speeches in support of the effort.

In January 1916, President Woodrow Wilson rewarded Brandeis for his agitation against monopoly power by nominating him to the Supreme Court.

"I am not exactly sure that I am to be congratulated," Brandeis wrote to his brother, "but I am glad the president wanted to make the appointment and I am convinced, all things considered, that I ought to accept." Perhaps he was envisioning the bruising four-month-long confirmation battle that lay ahead.

Once that hurdle was cleared, Brandeis enjoyed a remarkably successful twenty-three-year run on the high bench. A staunch defender of free speech, the dignity of the individual, and a Constitutional right to privacy, Brandeis voted consistently with the Court's liberal bloc in favor of progressive reforms and, later, Franklin D. Roosevelt's New Deal policies. With his erudite dissents and carefully reasoned majority opinions—always supported by the latest sociological and economic data—he won over many of his erstwhile foes and blazed a trail to be followed by his fellow Jewish jurists Benjamin Cardozo and Felix Frankfurter.

THE "STOP BRANDEIS" CAMPAIGN

Decades before the word *bork* entered the popular lexicon, Brandeis was the target of an organized—and highly personal—campaign to deny him a seat on the Supreme Court. Leading the charge was ex-president and future chief justice William Howard Taft, who groused that "it is one of the deepest wounds I have had as an American and a lover of the Constitution and a believer in progressive conservatism, that such a man as Brandeis could be put on the Court." Harvard University president A. Lawrence Lowell echoed Taft's criticism. "Are we to put on our supreme bench a man whose reputation for integrity is not unimpeachable?" he railed. "It is difficult—perhaps impossible—to get direct evidence of any act of Brandeis that is, strictly speaking, dishonest; and yet a man who is believed by all the better part of the bar to be unscrupulous ought not to be a member of the highest court of the nation."

Determined to smother this baby in its crib, Taft, Lowell, and fifty-four other "concerned citizens"—including six former presidents of the American Bar Association—submitted a petition to the Senate protesting Brandeis's nomination. "An appointment to this court should only be conferred upon a member of the legal profession whose general reputation is as good as his legal attainments are great," they kvetched. "We do not believe that Mr. Brandeis has the judicial temperament and capacity which should be required in a Judge of the Supreme Court. His reputation as a lawyer is such that he has not the confidence of the people." A whispering campaign was started to spread rumors about unspecified improprieties in Brandeis's past.

Why such vehement opposition? Anti-Semitism may have played a part; Brandeis himself thought as much. Writing in the third person about the confirmation imbroglio, he said, "The dominant reasons for the opposition to the confirmation of Mr. Brandeis are that he is considered a radical and is a Jew." The New York *Sun* added fuel to this fire when it complained in an editorial that President Wilson had only nominated Brandeis to win the city's Jewish vote in the 1916 election. But there was personal animosity as well. Brusque and standoffish, Brandeis was not well liked in the legal community. Even one of his friends admitted that "if Mr. Brandeis had been a different sort of man, not so aloof, not so isolated, with more of the camaraderie of the bar," he would have had no trouble getting confirmed.

When push came to shove, the campaign against Brandeis was doomed to fail. Unlike subsequent confirmation battles (see "Clarence Thomas"), there was no "smoking Coke can," no specific allegation on which Brandeis's detractors could pin their hopes of derailing his nomination. The nominee himself mounted a spirited counterattack, charging that the establishment was out to get him. One of Brandeis's law partners even drew up a chart showing that everyone who signed Taft's petition was intimately interconnected through private clubs, corporate directorships, and intermarriage. In the end, Brandeis was confirmed by the Senate, 47–22, on a largely party-line vote.

No Hard Feelings

William Howard Taft may not have wanted Brandeis on the Court, but the subject of his petition drive apparently didn't hold a grudge. Brandeis became one of Taft's staunchest supporters when Taft was named chief justice in 1921. Given their political differences, that was a development neither man

could foresee. "Impossible!" Brandeis had harrumphed when word first began circulating that Taft would be tapped to lead the Court. He later described the rotund ex-president as resembling a "good-natured" liquor salesman. Taft, he complained, possessed "a first-rate second-rate mind," as well as "all the defects but also the advantages of the aristocratic order that has done well by him." Over time, however, "Big Bill" won him over, not so much by his legal acumen as his deft administration of the Court. "It's very difficult for me to understand why a man who is so good a chief justice . . . could have been so bad as president," Brandeis once mused. For his part, Taft came to regret his public opposition to Brandeis's nomination. One night, when they ran into each other on the streets of Washington D.C., Taft formally apologized: "Mr. Brandeis, I once did you a grave injustice. I am sorry." "Thank you, Mr. Taft," Brandeis replied. The two men shook hands and went their separate ways.

PROPHET STATEMENT

Although best known to the general public as "The People's Lawyer," Brandeis possessed a prophetic mien (and Jewish heritage) that earned him another nickname—"Isaiah"—used only by his law clerks and President Franklin Roosevelt.

GONE FISHIN'

Brandeis spent as little time as necessary in his Supreme Court offices, preferring to do most of his work from his home in Dedham, Massachusetts. He also loved vacations—at one point mocking a Court colleague who had returned to private practice for having to work during the summer. On the eve of one important case, Brandeis was criticized for taking time off. "I need the rest," he countered. "I can do a year's work in eleven months, but I can't do it in twelve!"

HORSEPLAY

The American Zionist movement wasn't the only cause to which Brandeis devoted his energy. He was also a member in good standing of the Society in Dedham for Apprehending Horse Thieves. The whimsical affinity group—still in existence—describes itself as "the oldest continually existing horse thief apprehending organization in the United States" and accepts applications from anyone willing to pay the $10 membership fee. Past members include George Armstrong Custer, Jane Fonda, Mikhail Gorbachev, several U.S. presidents, and former Massachusetts governor Michael Dukakis.

I Scream, You Scream

How do the rich stay rich? They live frugally, as Brandeis did. A notorious cheapskate, the millionaire justice didn't bother to provide food for his house-guests. One fellow judge confessed that he made a point of eating before and after going to Brandeis's home for dinner. An avowed teetotaler, the People's Lawyer refrained from all personal indulgences. His only weakness? Ice cream, which he consumed like it was going out of style.

TECHNOPHOBE

Brandeis never used the telephone and didn't own an automobile until late in life.

CLOSET FRANKIST?

Did Brandeis worship a false messiah? A court officer cleaning out his chambers after he left the bench discovered a large bust of Jacob Frank, the eighteenth-century Jewish heretic who claimed to be the reincarnation of King David. On his desk in the Supreme Court, Brandeis also kept a portrait of Frank's daughter Eva, a family heirloom passed down from his mother's relatives, whose forebears were followers of Frank.

WILLIAM HOWARD

TAFT

September 15, 1857–March 8, 1930

BIRTHPLACE:

Cincinnati, OH

NICKNAME:

"Big Bill"

ASTROLOGICAL SIGN:

Libra

TERM:

July 11, 1921–February 3, 1930

APPOINTED BY:

Warren G. Harding

WORDS OF WISDOM:

"Presidents come and go,
but the Supreme Court goes
on forever."

On March 3, 1913, his last night as president, William Howard Taft sat at his desk until midnight signing autographs for his most devoted supporters. When the muscles in his bear-sized hands grew tired, he went to bed, only to rise again at 2:30 a.m. and sign for another half hour. To the fifty-five-year-old chief executive unceremoniously voted out of office the previous fall, it must have seemed like an appropriately tedious end to a decidedly undistinguished political career. All his life, Taft had craved one post above all others: Chief Justice of the Supreme Court. Instead he ended up as president—a job he hated. Now, with a Democrat in the White House, it looked like he would never get a chance to fulfill his fondest ambition.

"I love judges, and I love courts," Taft once declared. "They are my ideals that typify on earth what we shall meet hereafter in heaven under a just God." He seemed destined for a judicial career from birth. His grandfather Peter Rawson Taft was a county court judge in Vermont, and his father, Alphonso Taft, served on the Ohio Superior Court. Young William Howard, after graduating from Cincinnati Law School, followed him there in 1887. He was only twenty-nine years old.

In 1890, after Republican Benjamin Harrison became president, Taft made his first play for a Supreme Court seat. But he was too young, and "Little Ben" had other plans for him. "My chances of going to the moon and donning

a silk gown at the hands of President Harrison are about equal," Taft cracked. Instead, he accepted the consolation prize of an appointment as solicitor general, hoping to use that as a stepping stone to an eventual Court nomination. Two years later, he secured a gig as a U.S. District Court judge in his native Ohio, serving for the next eight years.

Taft loved being a judge, but his ambitious wife, Nellie, had bigger plans. She had set her sights on the White House and encouraged him to accept a series of administrative and cabinet posts in the administrations of William McKinley and Theodore Roosevelt. In 1908, the retiring T. R. hand-picked Taft—then secretary of war—to succeed him in the White House. Hoping to cement his progressive legacy, Roosevelt campaigned vigorously on his protégé's behalf and helped carry him to victory.

> **Did William Howard Taft suffer from early Alzheimer's disease? While administering the oath of office to Herbert Hoover, Taft forgot the words and made them up on the spot.**

Taft now had a job he'd never wanted, having run on a platform he didn't really believe in. Is it any wonder that his presidency was an unmitigated disaster? Taft loathed politics, and his conservative, pro-big-business policies were out of step with the times. History remembers him merely as an oddity, a morbidly obese mountain of a man who had to be lifted in and out of an enormous custom-fitted bathtub. By the time he lost reelection in 1912, even Roosevelt had turned against him, mounting a third-party candidacy in a futile effort to reclaim the legacy he believed Taft had spoiled.

Routed from office, Taft seemed destined for the elephant's graveyard of American history. Only the election of Republican Warren G. Harding in 1920 held any hope of salvaging his career, though Taft still considered a Supreme Court appointment to be a long shot. While president, he had vowed not to appoint anyone over age sixty to the Court—and now Taft himself was sixty-three. When Harding invited him for breakfast to discuss a role in his administration, Taft wasn't expecting the Supreme Court to be on the agenda. Perhaps he was just intoxicated by the prospect of a free meal, given his report home to Nellie: "They were very cordial. They had waffles and creamed chipped beef . . . coffee and toast. They offered me eggs, but as I saw this was extra, I declined." When Taft was through stuffing his face, Harding took him into his private study and asked if he would be interested in a Supreme Court appointment. Taft replied that it was the great ambition of his life. Over the next months, he made it clear that he would accept nothing less than the chief justiceship. In June 1921, Harding finally granted his wish, nominating Taft to succeed the recently deceased Edward Douglass White.

Taft took to his new post like a whale to water. He loved working on cases late into the night and reveled in the status of a robed judicial mandarin. "In my present life, I don't remember that I ever was president," he crowed. He also proved quite effective in the job. He was well liked by colleagues and put his executive experience to work pushing through many administrative and procedural reforms that made the Court run more smoothly. In 1929, Taft successfully won approval for the construction of the Supreme Court Building, freeing future justices from working in the old Senate Chamber of the Capitol and holding their conferences in a dank basement where, in his words, "the shelves are so high it takes an aeroplane to reach them."

The only bad thing about Taft's time as chief justice was that it didn't last longer. Plagued by declining health, he retired in February 1930. When he stepped down, his colleagues told him: "We call you Chief Justice still—for we cannot give up the title by which we have known you all these later years and which you have made dear to us. We cannot let you leave us without trying to tell you how dear you have made it. You came to us from achievement in other fields and with the prestige of the illustrious place that you lately had held, and you showed us in new form your voluminous capacity for getting work done, your humor that smoothed the tough places, your golden heart that brought you love from every side and most of all from your brethren whose tasks you have made happy and light. We grieve at your illness, but your spirit has given life an impulse that will abide whether you are with us or away." A month later, he died.

Have a Cow

In an otherwise undistinguished administration, Taft did have one enduring distinction: He was the last president to keep a pet cow in the White House. Pauline Wayne, also known as Miss Wayne, was a Holstein who called the White House lawn her pasture from 1910 to 1913. She produced 7½ gallons of milk a day—more than enough to feed the gargantuan Taft and the rest of the First Family.

AFTER YOU. NO, AFTER YOU

As president, Taft appointed both his predecessor (Edward Douglass White) and his successor (Charles Evans Hughes) as chief justice.

I Oath You

Taft is the only former president to have sworn a new president into office. He swore in Calvin Coolidge in 1925 and Herbert Hoover in 1929. (He would have sworn in Coolidge twice, but in 1923 the oath was administered by Coolidge's father, a notary public and justice of the peace.)

Scales of Justice

Taft's mountainous body is his principal claim to fame, but by the time he became chief justice he was positively buff by his own standards. Within a year of leaving the White House, Taft had shed nearly seventy pounds of lard off his 340-pound frame, largely by cutting pork, bread, and potatoes out of his diet. (He joked that it was because the weight of the presidency was finally off his shoulders.) His systolic blood pressure plummeted from a scary high of 210 in 1910 to a more manageable 160 in 1926.

His days of being helped out of the bathtub may have been behind him, but Taft remained an extra-large man, with the attendant jolly disposition. While serving as chief justice, he had an electric elevator installed in his home to carry him to and from his office on the third floor. He took great pleasure in playing elevator operator for his wife, Nellie, bowing grandly as she got on and pushing the buttons like a conductor.

Dead Man Walking

Ironically, as his weight declined, so did Taft's health, probably as a consequence of age and decades of overindulgence. He endured a battle with gout, brought on by years of eating fatty foods, and in December 1922 admitted to having "gravel," or kidney stones, removed from his bladder. He also suffered from sleep apnea and often dozed off during public appearances. By 1925, Taft's mental state was deteriorating noticeably. While administering the oath of office to Herbert Hoover in 1929, he forgot the words and made them up on the spot. Some have even suggested that he was in the early stages of Alzheimer's disease.

"I am older and slower and less acute and more confused," Taft wrote to his brother in November 1929. But he was determined to cling to his position on the high court. "As long as things continue as they are," he went on, "and I am able to answer in my place, I must stay on the court in order to prevent the Bolsheviki from getting control." The next month, his health took a turn for the worse. By the end of January 1930 he was hallucinating, and by late February he was shifting in an out of a coma. On his father's behalf, his son Robert traveled to Washington to announce his retirement from the Court. Taft died on March 8.

TRICKY BLOODLINES

Through his mother, Taft was a seventh cousin twice removed of President Richard M. Nixon.

OUT OF SIGHT, OUT OF MIND

In an illustration of how fleeting the fame that goes with being president can be, a young boy crossed paths with Chief Justice Taft one day on the streets of Washington D.C.

"I know who you are!" cried the boy. "You used to be President Coolidge."

BENJAMIN N.
CARDOZO

May 24, 1870–July 9, 1938

BIRTHPLACE:
New York, NY

ASTROLOGICAL SIGN:
Gemini

TERM:
March 14, 1932–July 9, 1938

APPOINTED BY:
Herbert Hoover

WORDS OF WISDOM:
"Justice is not to be taken by storm. She is to be wooed by slow advances."

H istory hasn't been kind to Herbert Hoover. Widely blamed for his inaction in the face of the Great Depression, America's thirty-first president did manage to distinguish himself in the arena of judicial nominations. In 1930, he appointed Charles Evans Hughes, one of the Supreme Court's most respected chief justices, and two years later he plucked Benjamin Nathan Cardozo off the New York State Court of Appeals to replace retiring justice Oliver Wendell Holmes. It was a decidedly bold move. Cardozo was three things most experts said Holmes's successor could *not* be: a New Yorker (there were already two on the Court at the time), a Democrat (Hoover was a rock-ribbed Republican), and, most important, a Jew. Louis Brandeis already occupied what was thought of as "the Jewish seat," and the prevailing anti-Semitism argued for a Gentile fanny to fill Holmes's vacated chair. The fact that Hoover bucked this anti-Jewish sentiment (present even among some of the Court's own members) and nominated the man widely considered to be the country's preeminent jurist says a lot about "The Grand Old Man's" fair-mindedness and integrity.

For Cardozo, the appointment was the culmination of a stellar legal career, one he seemed destined for from birth. A Sephardic Jew of Portuguese descent, he was born into one of America's oldest and most distinguished families. His ancestors, who had immigrated to the New World in the mid-eighteenth century, were among the founders of one of the oldest Jewish congregations in

North America. For centuries, the Cardozos served as pillars of New York's Sephardic community. One of the future justice's ancestors helped found the New York Stock Exchange in 1792. Poet Emma Lazarus, who wrote the inscription on the base of the Statue of Liberty, was his first cousin.

Along with a gold-plated family name, Cardozo benefited from a top-shelf education. His childhood tutor was Horatio Alger, the celebrated author of "rags-to-riches" children's stories emphasizing the values of hard work and perseverance. (Alger was also, as it happens, a pedophile who preyed upon his male students, although there is no evidence that he made any untoward advances on Cardozo.) A precocious youth, Cardozo enrolled at Columbia College at age fifteen, graduating with top honors at nineteen. He opted to forego his third year of law school (obviously, school was boring him) and

> A voracious reader, Benjamin Cardozo lived a hermit's life. He never married or even dated and in all likelihood died a virgin.

passed the bar in 1891 without ever earning a law degree. After a period of private practice, he was elected to the New York Supreme Court and then to the Court of Appeals, where his perspicacity and analytical rigor won him wide acclaim in the legal community.

He seemed like a rocket ship bound for the Supreme Court, but his religion and political ideology delayed his ascent throughout the 1920s. Chief Justice William Howard Taft, in particular, fretted about the prospect of another progressive on the Court. Taft was dead by 1932, however, and whatever "religious or sectarian repercussions" Hoover foresaw were swallowed up in a groundswell of support for Cardozo's nomination. Backed by leading Republican senators (and despite objections of the Court's resident anti-Semite, James McReynolds), Cardozo was unanimously confirmed.

He served only six years and was plagued by health problems, culminating in his death from a stroke in 1938. Nevertheless, Cardozo left his mark. He crafted more than one hundred opinions and was known for his eloquent and highly literate writing style. With Brandeis and Stone, he was one of the "Three Musketeers" devoted to upholding the constitutionality of Franklin Roosevelt's New Deal legislation. Like Brandeis, and later Felix Frankfurter, Cardozo became a household god in the American Jewish community—a role model for a generation of aspiring Jewish lawyers and judges. Though famous for his steely reserve, Cardozo seemed to revel in his rock star status. He once confessed to a friend: "I find that I am rapidly developing into a myth. If I were not a Jew, I should expect to be transformed pretty soon into a Greek god." To another acquaintance, he wrote: "Of course I like the applause, but it has been so dreadfully overdone that I can hardly look the knowing ones in the face. . . . Such a fuss and bother, and see the ordinary creature who stirred it all up!"

ONE TOUGH JEW

Although he considered himself an agnostic, Cardozo maintained his Jewish cultural identity throughout his life. He refused to allow pork or shellfish into his home, served on the board of the American Jewish Committee, and lent his name to various Zionist causes. He was always on guard for signs of anti-Semitism as well. A lifelong Democrat, Cardozo had a visceral revulsion for the Republican Party. In the GOP ranks, he once wrote to one of his relatives, "will be found all the narrow-minded bigots, all the Jew haters, all those who would make of the United States an exclusively Protestant government." Not surprisingly, Cardozo supported Catholic Al Smith for president in 1928 and Franklin Delano Roosevelt against the man who nominated him to the high bench, Herbert Hoover, in 1932 (although FDR, he confessed, "leaves me cold"). One wonders if Hoover would have been so eager to appoint him had he known Cardozo's true feelings about his party.

(ARCHIE) BUNKER MENTALITY

He may have been a liberal and a member of a persecuted minority group, but Cardozo was hardly immune to spewing racial and ethnic prejudices. He called Italians "dagos" and frowned upon interracial relationships as "repellent" and "revolting," likening them to "sex perversions." Of the Japanese, Cardozo once groused: "I find myself casting furtive glances here and there, wondering when and where the Japs will be upon us." The legendary jurist's bigotry may have been the product of his cloistered lifestyle. Reportedly, the only black people Cardozo ever met were domestic servants: chauffeurs, valets, and messengers.

THE BACHELOR

Monkish is the term usually used to describe Cardozo's personal habits. "The bachelor judge has led an almost hermitlike existence," remarked one profile. Indeed, he was famous for working from the break of dawn until late at night and had few close friends. He rarely left his home except to take the occasional stroll and spent most of his downtime reading Greek and Latin for pleasure. As for women, Cardozo had little use for them and in all probability died a virgin. His closest female confidant was his sister Ellen, who lived with him until his death and likewise never married. Some have speculated that Cardozo may have been gay, or at least a closet case, but it seems just as likely that he was devoutly celibate. Sex, Cardozo's close friend and fellow judge Learned Hand once observed, "was as nearly absent from his [life] as it is from anybody I ever knew that wasn't gaited the other way."

Heave Ho

Cardozo may not have been a ladies' man, but he did have his lighter side. He was known to have a self-deprecating wit and a flair for legal humor. Once, while sailing with some fellow justices, he got seasick and was in clear and present danger of throwing up all over the deck. Another robed eminence approached and asked if he could do something to help. "Yes," Cardozo replied. "Overrule the motion."

NOTHING TO SEE HERE

"There is not anything very interesting about me," Cardozo once noted. Elsewhere he described himself as "nothing but a plodding mediocrity." Most legal scholars would disagree, ranking him among the near-great jurists of the twentieth century. His reputation might have been higher still had he not worked so assiduously to deflect attention from himself. Where other justices courted would-be biographers, Cardozo reflexively threw them off the scent. He complained about even the most complimentary newspaper and magazine profiles and tried to have collections of his own writings barred from publication. He dubbed one compilation of his legal opinions "a crime against good taste."

This policy of nondisclosure persisted even after Cardozo's death. For years, his close friend and literary executor, Irving Lehman, rebuffed all attempts by scholars to gain access to Cardozo's papers. He even went so far as to set fire to Cardozo's personal correspondence, which one of the late justice's pen pals described as "very intimate and personal." Whatever secrets they held—about the buttoned-down jurist's private life or otherwise—have unfortunately been lost to history.

AND HERE'S TO YOU, MR. CARDOZO!

Stern and unsmiling, Cardozo was well known for his morose disposition. Yet that grim visage allowed him to make at least a tiny mark on rock 'n' roll history. As a child growing up in Queens, future Rock and Roll Hall of Famer Paul Simon was so preternaturally solemn that his parents nicknamed him "Cardozo," in the justice's honor. Eventually, Rhymin' Simon cheered up and ditched the moniker. Otherwise, Cardozo & Garfunkel might have blazed a trail up the pop charts in the mid-sixties.

HUGO BLACK

February 27, 1886–
September 25, 1971

BIRTHPLACE:
Harlan, Alabama

NICKNAME:
"Ego"

ASTROLOGICAL SIGN:
Pisces

TERM:
August 19, 1937–
September 17, 1971

APPOINTED BY:
Franklin Delano Roosevelt

WORDS OF WISDOM:
"Uncontrolled and uncontrollable liberty is an enemy to domestic peace."

How does a frothing white supremacist with a fifty-year track record of trampling on the rights of racial and ethnic minorities achieve the status of a liberal judicial icon? Only in America, baby. Proving that it pays to have friends in high places wearing white sheets, small-time Alabama lawyer Hugo LaFayette Black parlayed his Ku Klux Klan connections into a seat in the U.S. Senate and then onto the highest court in the land. Once there, he forged an admirably progressive record that served to expand the pie of Constitutional liberty for all Americans. Unless you were Japanese or black, that is. Then he wanted to throw you in a concentration camp and strip away your voting rights.

Black was the youngest of eight children, born into a family of merchants in the hill country of central Alabama. "I'm just a Clay County hillbilly," he liked to say, and he enjoyed a conventional hillbilly upbringing. His father was a drunk. His mother was emotionally unstable. "I was the family pet," he noted. He found refuge in reading and spent the rest of his free time hanging around the town courthouse, playing checkers and dominos with the alter kockers who gathered there.

Hoping to follow his older brother into the medical profession, Black attended two years of medical school but soon realized that law was his true

calling. He enrolled at the University of Alabama law school, graduating with honors in 1906. He practiced law in Ashland and then Birmingham, where he honed his political skills by joining every lodge, club, and fraternal organization that would take his application. That list included the Ku Klux Klan, which fitted him for a sheet in 1923. He spent only two years in the sinister racist fraternity, but the association paid off handsomely. When Black ran for the U.S. Senate in 1926, he barnstormed the state, addressing nearly all 148 Klan klaverns, or chapters, in Alabama. He is said to have told one such assembly: "I desire to impress upon you as representatives of the real Anglo-Saxon sentiment that must and will control the destinies of the stars and stripes, that I want your counsel." The Klan responded to his appeal by handing Black an upset victory.

In the Senate, Black earned a reputation as a pugnacious champion of the "little guy." An ardent foe of lobbyists, he introduced legislation requiring that all of them register with the government. In speeches, he railed against the "high-powered, deceptive, telegram-fixing, letter-framing, Washington-visiting" practices of the Alabama utilities lobby. During one committee hearing, Black accused an Alabama newspaper editor of being on the power companies' payroll. The witness responded by calling Black a "contemptible cur," at which point Black challenged him to take it outside. Black's aggressive style caught

Hugo Black spent two years in the Ku Klux Klan, where his duties included administering the oath of white supremacy to new members.

the attention of President Franklin D. Roosevelt, who needed someone to defend his New Deal policies on the Supreme Court. In 1937, FDR nominated Black to fill the vacant seat of retiring justice Willis Van Devanter. Black was confirmed by the Senate despite a swirling controversy over his Klan membership. The New York Times decried Black's ascension, and protestors picketed outside as he was sworn into office.

Once ensconced on the bench, Black did much to assuage the fears of political progressives. He became one of the staunchest advocates of free speech, which he considered virtually absolute. Black also became known for the doctrine of "incorporation," the contention that the Bill of Rights applied to the individual states as well as the federal government. This concept formed the basis for sweeping Court decisions in the areas of privacy, criminal process, and abortion rights, to name just a few. An increasingly cautious Black dissented in several of these cases. Indeed, although generally thought of as quite liberal, he could also be something of an old foof. He dissented in *Griswold v. Connecticut*, for example, which forbade states from banning the use of contraceptives by married couples. "The right of a husband and wife to assemble in bed is a new right of assembly to me," he harrumphed. Even more troubling was Black's assertion: "I like my privacy as well as the next one, but I am nevertheless compelled to admit the government has a right to invade it unless prohibited by some specific constitutional provision." Such statements earned him a reputation as the conservative movement's favorite liberal justice.

Cantankerous to the end. Black died of a stroke on September 25, 1971. He left behind a decidedly mixed judicial legacy and a whole mess of white-hooded skeletons in his closet. In fact, we may never knew exactly how many. Shortly before his death, he ordered his son to destroy all his papers, in a move he impishly dubbed "Operation Frustrate the Historians."

★ ★

The Man from the Klan

If Black had merely joined the Klan briefly to advance his political career, that would have been bad enough. But historical evidence suggests he was quite the active member of America's preeminent homegrown terrorist organization. Soon after joining his local branch, Black became "Kladd of his Klavern"—Klanspeak for the officer who initiates new members by administering the oath of white supremacy. (How interesting it would have been had Black ever ascended to the post of Supreme Court chief justice, and had to administer the oath of office to the incoming president; would he have gotten the two oaths mixed up?)

Once Black even lent his considerable legal acumen to the Klan cause.

In 1921, he represented a Klansman charged with the murder of a Catholic priest in Birmingham. After ensuring that the jury box was well seeded with Klan members, Black reportedly used secret Klan gestures to signal his sympathies to the jury. He repeatedly asked prosecution witnesses if they were Catholic in a blatant attempt to play off the biases of the panel. Not surprisingly, the accused Klansman was acquitted, and Black had earned a few more brownie points with the local Grand Dragon.

None of this sordidness seemed to bother President Franklin D. Roosevelt when he was considering Black for a seat on the Supreme Court. "I've felt from the beginning of all this Klan talk that perhaps he did belong to the Klan," FDR said at the time, "but that did not necessarily mean that he might not make a very great judge on the Supreme Court." The public, however, felt differently, and when Black's Klan activities were revealed after his confirmation, he was forced to explain himself in a nationally broadcast radio address.

He may have renounced his youthful membership in the Ku Klux Klan, but Black remained a lifelong cracker. In the U.S. Senate, he led the filibuster against a bill to outlaw lynching. In 1965, as a member of the Court, he voted to uphold the constitutionality of poll taxes, designed to make it impossible for African Americans to vote. "Unfortunately there are some who think that Negroes should have special privileges under the law," he groused to a friend.

SWEET HOME ALABAMA

Life wasn't all necktie parties and poll taxes where Black's views on race relations were concerned. To his credit, the Alabama-born justice voted in favor of the *Brown v. Board of Education* desegregation decision—a courageous stand that won him the everlasting enmity of his fellow peckerwoods. "I hope he dies and burns in hell," fumed Alabama secretary of state Betty Fink. For years, Black couldn't travel to his home state without donning a bulletproof vest. The Alabama state legislature even passed a resolution denying him the right to be buried there. (Black's ambivalent record on racial justice, his colleague Earl Warren joked, merely reflected his desire to win back his eternal resting place.)

WELCOME TO THE CAMP

Black didn't just hate and fear black people; he had no use for Japanese Americans either. In 1944, he authored one of the most morally heinous opinions in Supreme Court history: the *Korematsu v. United States* decision that validated the government's forced internment of Japanese Americans during World War II. Black explicitly disavowed race as a component in his decision, but even fellow justices found it hard to swallow. In his dissent, Justice Frank Murphy called *Korematsu* the "legalization of racism," which he deemed "utterly revolting among a free people."

Gaydar Love

Not surprisingly, Black was no fan of gays. Once, during a brief stint as a police court judge in Alabama, he heard the case of a man charged with assault who claimed his male accuser had made a pass at him. Disgusted, Black threw out the assault charge and had the accuser jailed for disorderly conduct. "That kind of thing will destroy a society, son," he remarked afterward to his namesake, Hugo Black Jr.

SUIT YOURSELF

The one part of his job that Black really hated was the dress code. He chafed at wearing judicial robes, preferring to work in a business suit. This preference was partly due to the cost, for Black was a notorious cheapskate. "I shall be compelled in the very near future to purchase a new garment at an outlay of about $100," he complained to a friend in 1945, "a sum which could buy many other things I would prefer to have."

Where's the Beef?

Convinced by his doctor that eating copious amounts of red meat was the key to maintaining good health, Black adhered to a somewhat severe form of what would later be known as the Atkins Diet. He ate a steak every day for most of his adult life.

THE 'ROID WARRIOR

Years before Barry Bonds and Roger Clemens, Black was the original juiced-up gangsta. After the death of his first wife, Josephine Foster Black, in 1951, Black married his secretary, Elizabeth DeMeritte. She was vivacious, fun-loving—and twenty-two years his junior. To keep up with her, Black began giving himself testosterone shots. His sex drive quickly exploded. "I feel almost as much a man as I've ever been," he crowed to his son Hugo Jr.

BLACKSTABBER

Though not as bumptious as, say, Felix Frankfurter, Black could rub some of his colleagues the wrong way. "You just can't disagree with him," complained his principal nemesis, Justice Robert H. Jackson. "You must go to war with him if you disagree." Black and Jackson had a running feud dating to the mid-1940s, when the Court took up a case from which Jackson believed Black should have recused himself on conflict-of-interest grounds. Jackson made the mistake of expressing his objections publicly, which made Black an enemy for life. In 1946, when Chief Justice Harlan Stone died, Jackson was primping himself for what he assumed would be his elevation to the chief justice's chair. Black saw his chance to exact a little revenge. Along with his ideological ally William O. Douglas, he let it be known that he would resign from the Court if Jackson were nominated to replace Stone. President Truman relented and selected Fred Vinson instead. Black's relationship with Jackson was poisoned forever. For the record, Black also ground the gears of Frankfurter, who called him "a self-righteous, self-deluded part fanatic, part demagogue, who really disbelieves in Law."

KILLER ON THE ROAD

Black was a notoriously wreckless driver. He rarely obeyed the speed limit and often disregarded road signs. A police officer once stopped him for going the wrong way down a one-way street. "Don't you know the law?" the cop asked. "You can get an argument on that," the justice replied.

"BLONDIE" IS THE ROOT OF ALL EVIL

As a father, Black was quite the taskmaster. He refused to give his children any positive feedback and upbraided them for the slightest fall from grace. He also found novel explanations for poor academic performance. Once when his son Hugo Jr. came home with a less-than-perfect report card, Black became convinced that newspaper comic strips were to blame. He forbade the boy from reading them.

RACQUET MAN

An avid tennis player, Black tried to work in several sets a day on his private tennis court at his home in Alexandria, Virginia. When his doctor informed him it was inadvisable for a man in his forties to play so much, Black quipped that he could hardly wait until he turned fifty so he could start playing again. He continued to serve and volley until the age of eighty-three.

Mourning Constitutional

A strict constructionist, Black was famous for carrying around a ten-cent copy of the Constitution in his front pocket. When he died, a copy was buried with him.

> ## Near Misses, Rejects, and Also-Rans: Four Men (and One Woman) Who Could Have Been Supreme Court Justices

LEARNED HAND (1872–1961)

If ever there were a person whose very name screamed "Supreme Court justice," it was Billings Learned Hand. Hand tops most experts' lists of greatest American judges never to sit on the Supreme Court. He came close to being nominated on a couple occasions, but the highest he ever got was the U.S. Court of Appeals. "The greatest living American jurist is not *on* the Supreme Court," Justice Benjamin Cardozo once declared when asked to name his most erudite colleague. Learned he may have been, but if truth be known Hand hated his famous name, thinking it made him seem unmanly. An insecure bookworm who had trouble fitting in with other boys, he instead channeled his energies into his studies. Hand spent more than a half century on the bench and became one of the nation's preeminent legal scholars. He was also a prolific folk singer who left behind a substantial catalog of recorded songs and was known to break into hymns, sea shanties, and Gilbert & Sullivan numbers in his chambers.

G. HARROLD CARSWELL (1919–1992)

"There are a lot of mediocre judges and people and lawyers," said Nebraska senator Roman Hruska about G. Harrold Carswell. "They are entitled to a little representation, aren't they? We can't have all Brandeises, Frankfurters, and Cardozos." With endorsements like that, Carswell must have known it would be tough sledding getting confirmed to the high court. President Richard Nixon's last-second substitute for his first rejected Supreme Court nominee, Clement Haynsworth, Carswell was widely regarded as a nonentity, even by the Republican legal community. A Georgia native, he had served barely a year on the Court of Appeals and was selected principally out of Nixon's desire to get a Southerner on the Court. As it played out, Southern lawmakers provided the bulwark of his support in the Senate. "Does it not seem that we have had enough of those upside-down, corkscrew thinkers?" asked Louisiana's Russell Long in his speech endorsing Carswell. "Would it not appear that it might be well to take a B student or a C student who was able to think straight, compared to one of those A students who are capable of the kind of thinking that winds up getting a 100 percent increase in crime in this country?" Unfortunately for Carswell, not enough of Long's colleagues agreed with this bizarro assessment. His nomination was rejected on a vote of 51 to 45.

ROBERT BORK (1927–)

Robert Bork came achingly close to becoming a Supreme Court justice, but he'll have to settle for being a little-used eponym. Since 2002, the verb "to bork" has appeared in the Oxford English Dictionary. Meaning "to attack unfairly," the word reflects the lingering animosity of Bork's contentious 1987 confirmation fight, which prefigured the Clarence Thomas hearings by three years and set the stage for two decades of senatorial wrangling over judicial nominations. Bork was eminently qualified to sit on the Supreme Court—if a trifle scary-looking, in a fire-and-brimstone sort of way. He resembled the man on the Quaker Oats Box, who most likely shared the same crabby, "get off my lawn you damn kids" worldview. A five-year veteran of the Court of Appeals by the time President Ronald Reagan nominated him, Bork had also served as solicitor general and acting attorney general during the Nixon administration. (It was Bork who fired Watergate special prosecutor Archibald Cox on Nixon's orders in the so-called Saturday Night Massacre.) But it was his right-wing judicial philosophy, not his résumé, that scared the bejesus out of liberals. A proponent of constitutional "originalism," Bork made Antonin Scalia look like George McGovern. Senator Ted Kennedy denounced him in a nationally televised speech, declaring that "Robert Bork's America is a land in which women would be forced into back-alley abortions, blacks would sit at segregated lunch counters . . . and the doors of the federal courts would be shut on the fingers of millions of citizens." The ensuing confirmation hearings resembled a political campaign, complete with negative TV ads and opposition research. A Washington D.C. alternative newspaper even snooped into Bork's video rental records, presumably looking for porn. Sadly, Bork's tastes ran more to harmless fluff like *Ruthless People*, *The Man Who Knew Too Much*, and the Marx Brothers comedy *A Day at the Races*. Still, by the time Democrats were through demonizing Bork in the media, the corpse of Zeppo himself would have stood a better chance of getting confirmed. The Senate rejected his nomination, 58–42. A distinguished legal career had effectively come to an end—even as a new verb was born.

DOUGLAS H. GINSBURG (1946–)

Try, try again. After the debacle of the Bork nomination, Ronald Reagan returned to the conservative judicial trough for another nominee to carry his banner on the high court. This time he found what may have been the nation's only pot-smoking Republican law professor. Ginsburg, a judge on the same D.C. appeals court whence Bork had been plucked, lasted only a few weeks as a high court nominee before withdrawing his name in disgrace. His crime? Toking up a few times while teaching law at Harvard in the early 1970s. At first, Reagan tried to explain away Ginsburg's marijuana use as a "youthful fancy," but, having previously equated drug-taking to terrorism, he was ultimately compelled to ask his nominee to stand down. With the third bite of the apple, Reagan nominated the squeaky clean Anthony Kennedy to replace the retiring Lewis Powell—and the republic was spared the indignity of always wondering whether one of its highest judges was hiding a bong under his robes.

HARRIET MIERS (1945–)

"The Old Maid." "Bush's Cleaning Lady." "Harriet the Hack." These are just a few of the epithets lobbed at White House counsel Harriet Miers, George W. Bush's first choice to replace retiring justice Sandra Day O'Connor. Miers's most vehement opposition came from her fellow Republicans—conservatives in particular—who objected to her perceived lack of ideological bona fides, as well as her complete lack of judicial experience. A longtime retainer of Bush from his days as Texas governor, Miers was in fact a former Democrat who had once given money to Al Gore's 1988 presidential campaign. Her unmarried status raised eyebrows on the anti-gay right, some of whose members intimated she might be a lesbian. Her fanatical devotion to Bush should have dispelled that suspicion. Who has time for relationships when so much of your time is spent composing mash notes to your boss? In one of them, Miers wrote to Bush: "You are the best governor ever—deserving of great respect!" In another, she pined for the day when Bush's daughters realized that their parents were "cool." A 1995 Miers note gushed about a recent visit from Bush, declaring the airplane ride they had shared as "Cool!" The leaking of this odd correspondence alone probably wouldn't have torpedoed Miers's candidacy, but her meetings with Republican senators did not go well, and she gave vague and insufficient answers on questionnaires designed to smoke out her judicial philosophy. The truth was, she had none. Exposed as an empty suit, Miers withdrew her name from consideration less than a month after Bush had nominated her.

FELIX
FRANKFURTER

November 15, 1882–
February 22, 1965

BIRTHPLACE:
Vienna, Austria

ASTROLOGICAL SIGN:
Scorpio

TERM:
January 30, 1939–August 28, 1962

APPOINTED BY:
Franklin D. Roosevelt

WORDS OF WISDOM:
"Does a man become any different when he puts on a gown? I say, 'If he is any good, he does.'"

"Whatever you see in Felix," remarked Felix Frankfurter's wife, Marion, "the opposite is true as well." Indeed, he is one of the most maddening justices ever to sit on the Supreme Court. A left-wing radical in his youth, he matured into one of the most eloquent and effective advocates of liberal causes, helping to found the American Civil Liberties Union and agitating for more progressive labor laws. On the Supreme Court, however, Frankfurter reversed course, voting the conservative line in cases involving civil liberties and criminal procedure. What's more, he alienated most of his colleagues with his haughty personality and penchant for catty put-downs. Once thought to be a judicial legend in the making, Frankfurter is remembered today almost as much for his overbearing crabbiness as for his contributions to American law.

The Court's third Jewish justice was born in 1882 in Vienna, Austria, and arrived in the United States at age twelve. He grew up on New York's Lower East Side, on the same streets as another legendary Jewish American, Arnold Rothstein, the mobbed-up gambler who fixed the 1919 World Series. In those early days, Frankfurter was a degenerate gambler who loved to play dice with fellow tenement dwellers. "There was a very intense crapshooting period," he recalled. "I also played chess. But crapshooting on the street was the thing."

When he wasn't busy "rolling the bones," Frankfurter had a job delivering chemicals for $4 a week. He worked his way through New York's City College and on to Harvard Law School, where he graduated with highest honors in 1906. He worked in Washington as an aide to Secretary of War Henry L. Stimson before accepting a teaching position at Harvard in 1914. It was during this period that he became active in the Zionist movement and helped found the *New Republic*, the nation's preeminent liberal opinion journal.

Left-wing causes consumed Frankfurter throughout most of the teens and twenties. He helped defend suspected Communists rounded up during the "Palmer Raids" of the early 1920s, and he spoke out in the case of Sacco and Vanzetti, Italian immigrant anarchists executed for murder in 1927 after a controversial trial marred by civil liberties violations. Progressives thus eagerly anticipated Frankfurter's nomination to the Supreme Court in 1939. President Franklin D. Roosevelt, whose administration was staffed largely with lawyers trained by Frankfurter, expected his new justice to be a liberal bastion in defense of New Deal policies.

> Thanks to Felix Frankfurter, millions of American schoolchildren were forced to recite the Pledge of Allegiance every morning—whether they lived "under God" or not.

To an extent, FDR got what he wanted: Frankfurter did vote to uphold the New Deal. However, in most other legal areas, his tack was decidedly conservative. In the case of *Minersville School District v. Gobitis*, Frankfurter wrote the majority decision upholding a Pennsylvania school board's requirement that all students recite the Pledge of Allegiance, even if doing so violated their religious beliefs. "National unity is the basis of national security," Frankfurter thundered in his opinion, dismaying many of his ACLU cohorts. "To deny the legislature the right to select appropriate means for its attainment presents a totally different order of problem from that of the propriety of subordinating the possible ugliness of littered streets to the free expression opinion through handbills." After the *Gobitis* decision, Frankfurter received a torrent of angry letters from former supporters who saw his decision as a betrayal of the civil liberties cause he had once championed. Many referenced Frankfurter's own heritage as a Jewish immigrant, suggesting he should have been more sensitive to the dilemma faced by religious minorities. Undaunted, he stuck to his guns. When the Court overturned *Gobitis* three years later, Frankfurter penned the lone written dissent.

He bucked the liberal line on many other issues as well, becoming a leading advocate for the school of thought known as "judicial restraint." His cavalier treatment of fellow justices undoubtedly handicapped him in cases in which he could have persuaded some to come over to his side. Simply put, Frankfurter was an arrogant man who held his colleagues' intellectual capacities in low regard. That flaw, more than anything, likely cost him the chance to take his place in the first rank of Supreme Court justices. When he died of a stroke in 1962, he was thought of instead as a brilliant, but vexing, judicial misfire.

★ ★

CLASS CLOWN

Today Frankfurter is remembered almost as much for his work as a law professor as for his tenure on the Supreme Court. Some say teaching was his true calling, but you'd never know that from the response of some of his students. Several accused him of allowing his left-wing political biases to seep into his work in the classroom. Others charged that he played favorites, reserving his praise only for the most brilliant and those from wealthy families. "There were no neutrals about Felix," recalled one former student. "You either thought the sun rose and set down his neck; or you despised him." Chief among the professor's detractors was that student's father, who had warned his son upon learning of his enrollment at Harvard Law: "When you get there, you will find a professor with the ridiculous name of Felix Frankfurter. He is said to have a great influence with his students. You just watch out. He is a Communist, an anarchist, or worse."

PAY IT FORWARD

A born networker, Frankfurter cultivated numerous high-powered acquaintances. "Felix has two hundred intimate friends," his wife once observed. He liked to give back for his good fortune by serving as mentor for the next generation of lawyers and activists. He recommended dozens of young reformers for jobs in the Roosevelt administration, stocking the New Deal apparatus with eager foot soldiers who called themselves "Happy Hot Dogs" in his honor.

MR. CONGENIALITY

A supercilious snob, Frankfurter routinely rubbed his Court colleagues the wrong way. He wasn't shy about expressing his distaste for *them*, either. Not even Chief Justice Fred Vinson escaped his scorn; Frankfurter accused him of being an intellectual lightweight and openly questioned his fitness to sit on the bench. Their relationship grew so toxic that Vinson once leapt from his chair during a private conference and nearly punched Frankfurter in the nose. When Vinson died of a heart attack in 1953, a gleeful Frankfurter couldn't resist one final dig. Riding home from the funeral by train, he cracked, "This is the first indication I have ever had that there is a God."

Flak Attack

Someone as brusque as Frankfurter could have used a good P.R. rep. Yet the dyspeptic jurist was dismissive of public relations people, calling them "professional poisoners of the public mind, exploiters of foolishness, fanaticism, and self-interest."

COMIC RELIEF

For all the interpersonal inadequacies, Frankfurter did have a playful side. He was known to wave hello to friends from the bench while the Court was in session. When a law professor from Australia was visiting, Frankfurter allowed the man's young daughter to sit on each of the justice's chairs. On another occasion, while the solicitor general was delivering his oral argument, Frankfurter passed a note to the man's wife: "Anyhow—I'm for your hat." He could often be heard whistling "The Stars and Stripes Forever" as he sauntered through the Court building's hallowed marble halls.

Gift of Gab

In a long line of long-winded justices, Frankfurter was the undisputed king of the gasbags. He was a nonstop talker who literally did not know when to shut up. When Dean Acheson was serving as Secretary of State in the Truman administration, each morning he and Frankfurter would walk the two-mile route from their Georgetown homes to work. Frankfurter would drone on and on the whole way, to the point where Acheson secretly contemplated shoving him into oncoming traffic. Desperate to escape and get on to the work of diplomacy, Acheson demanded that Frankfurter agree to shut his pie hole at a specified point in their walk. Efforts were futile. They reached the agreed-upon point, but Frankfurter kept on blabbing.

TAPPED OUT

In the 1952 decision in *Lee v. United States*, Frankfurter came out against government wiretapping of criminal suspects, calling it a "dirty business" that "makes for lazy, and not alert, law enforcement." He knew whereof he spoke. In the 1920s, he had been among the first Americans subjected to telephonic surveillance. Future FBI director J. Edgar Hoover tapped Frankfurter's phone to monitor the young lawyer's links to the radical labor group Amalgamated Clothing Workers and what Hoover called Frankfurter's "communistic propaganda activities."

A FRANK RESPONSE

Asked by a friend to preside over his wedding ceremony, Frankfurter declined, citing lack of jurisdiction. When the friend pressed him to explain how a Supreme Court justice could lack the authority to marry people, Frankfurter replied: "Because marriage is not considered a federal offense."

WILLIAM O.
DOUGLAS

October 16, 1898–January 19, 1980

BIRTHPLACE:
Maine Township, MN

NICKNAME:
"Wild Bill"

ASTROLOGICAL SIGN:
Libra

TERM:
April 17, 1939–November 12, 1975

APPOINTED BY:
Franklin D. Roosevelt

WORDS OF WISDOM:
"I don't follow precedents,
I make 'em."

America's longest-serving justice was also "the oddest duck to ever serve on the United States Supreme Court" according to eminent legal scholar Raoul Berger. In his thirty-six years on the high court, William Orville Douglas set new records for most opinions written, most dissents issued, and most speeches delivered. Court watchers nicknamed him "Wild Bill" for his cowboy wardrobe and decidedly libertine lifestyle. He was a high-living, hard-drinking limousine liberal who occasionally dashed off opinions on the back of cocktail napkins and cycled through a seemingly endless succession of sex partners that would have made Bob Crane blush. His chaotic personal life made him a constant target of impeachment threats, but it only marginally affected his judicial work. He forged a solidly progressive record, especially in the areas of civil rights, free speech, and environmental protection. One of the Court's most steadfast defenders of wildlife, Douglas was also a bit of a kook who thought trees and rivers should be granted standing to sue if they felt threatened by overdevelopment. His dream of one day becoming president remained unfulfilled—a fortunate thing for the republic, for he might have nominated a shrub to take his place on the bench.

Douglas was born in Minnesota but spent most of his formative years in Yakima, Washington. His father, a Presbyterian minister, died when he was five years old. His domineering mother raised him to believe he would never be as good as his father unless he ascended to the U.S. presidency, an unreasonable burden that in fact explains a lot of Douglas's subsequent pathological behavior. As a young man, he took a series of odd jobs, including pin boy at the local bowling alley and assembly-line worker at an ice cream factory. At one point, he was hired by the town to deliver legal papers to the hard-working residents of area bordellos. Sadly, "whorehouse errand boy" was not an official header on his Supreme Court résumé.

Speaking of résumés, Douglas became notorious for inflating his own. He claimed he graduated second in his class at Columbia Law School (he actually finished fifth) and to have served in the U.S. Army during World War I (he hadn't). There was really no reason for such embellishments, aside from Douglas's own need to self-aggrandize. He was in fact an able law student who was snatched up by Yale Law School soon after he graduated and became one of the preeminent law professors in the country. He befriended Joseph Kennedy, the Camelot paterfamilias who was then head of the Securities and Exchange Commission. In 1937, Douglas ascended to that position, where he won praise as a vigilant corporate watchdog whose personal motto was "Piss on 'em." His skills as a poker player won him the favor of President Franklin D. Roosevelt, who nominated him to succeed the retiring Louis Brandeis on the Supreme Court in 1939.

> In one of the loopiest dissenting opinions in Supreme Court history, William Douglas argued that trees and rivers should have the right to file suit in cases involving environmental protection.

On the bench, Douglas railed against elites, corporations, and other manifestations of "The Establishment." He also chafed at the monastic life of an associate justice, occasionally pining for the political career his mother had once planned for him. Restless, and repeatedly frustrated in his ambitions, Douglas sought release through drink, sex, and the cultivation of his own outlaw persona. He wore a Stetson cowboy hat everywhere and occasionally canoodled with his secretaries. He picked fights with political rivals and went on self-pitying alcohol

binges. He loathed his own law clerks, whom he derided as "the lowest form of human life." (They, in turn, called him "shithead" behind his back.) He was also extremely vain, seizing every opportunity to have his picture taken.

All this weird behavior won Douglas a lot of enemies in high places. Richard Nixon couldn't stand him, both for his unabashed liberalism and his erratic personal morality. Through his proxy Gerald Ford, Nixon spearheaded an attempt to impeach Douglas in 1969—one of many such attempts that ultimately failed for lack of just cause. The ultimate survivor, Douglas clung to his seat even after a stroke in late 1974 robbed him of most of his faculties. He outlasted Nixon, but eventually the debilitating aftereffects of his stroke caught up with him, and he reluctantly resigned from the Court in November 1975. He died a little more than four years later, at age eighty-one.

BENCH PLAYA

The terms *Supreme Court justice* and *man slut* rarely appear in the same sentence, but in Douglas's case the juxtaposition is apt. To call "Wild Bill" a ladies' man would be to devalue that label. He was, quite simply, the horniest man ever to sit on the high court. Famous for hitting on everyone from secretaries to stewardesses, Douglas may have had hundreds—perhaps thousands—of lovers, in addition to his four official (and long-suffering) wives. One prominent Washington journalist labeled him "a tomcat" who would "go after anything that would wear a skirt—or wasn't wearing a skirt." A female friend of Douglas's called him "the biggest whorer around." "He would lay anyone anywhere," quipped one male pal. Another family friend even had a special "love shack" built for him at her ranch in the mountains of Washington state. There the randy justice could kick back on periodic booty calls with his mistress du jour. To become one of Wild Bill's *comare*, candidates typically had to meet one or more of the following qualifications: be blonde, younger than he was, or inferior in social status. Douglas had a particular affection for flight attendants and college co-eds—one of whom, twenty-three-year-old Cathleen Heffernan, became the fourth Mrs. Douglas in 1965. He was sixty-seven.

For all his dalliances, Douglas seemed to like being married, though each of his wives grew weary of his horndogging, especially as it became increasingly brazen. During one trip to the Soviet Union with wife number two, Mercedes Davidson, Douglas bragged in a letter to an associate back home that he was still able to procure Russian ladies capable of "satisfying his most precious drives." A classic sex addict, Douglas did little to conceal his affairs or the lavish amounts of money and gifts with which he showered his mistresses. When one of his wives got fed up with his behavior, he simply divorced her and moved on to the next. Yet he always went into a marriage believing his latest bride to be his soul mate. Douglas, one of his friends observed, "was always happy just before a marriage and one week afterward."

What's in a Name?

While "Wild Bill" remains the most colorful (and appropriate) of Douglas's nicknames, he is more widely known in legal circles as "The Great Dissenter," in honor of his predilection for writing dissenting opinions. Douglas penned more than three hundred in his long career. In many cases, he was the sole dissenter, a fact that earned him yet another distinctive moniker: "The Lone Ranger."

SING A SONG OF CONSTIPATION

With fellow law school professor Thurman Arnold, Douglas is the author of "Humoresque for Passengers," a popular bawdy ditty about wise use of bathroom facilities on trains. It includes such lines as

> Passengers will please refrain
> From flushing toilets while the train
> Is in the station . . .
> We encourage constipation
> While the train is in the station
> Moonlight always makes me think of you.

The two were inspired to write the song, whose melody they pinched from a fanciful composition by Anton Dvorák, while on a train on the New Haven Line bound for Yale University—presumably after eating some high-fiber cereal.

ALWAYS A BRIDESMAID

When he was a child, Douglas's mother drummed into his head that his life would be a failure if he never became president. As a result, Douglas repeatedly flirted with the idea of running for the White House and connived for a place on every Democratic ticket from 1944 to 1960. When John F. Kennedy passed him over in favor of Douglas's old poker buddy Lyndon B. Johnson, the hard-drinking justice reportedly went on a week-long bender.

NOT WILD ABOUT HARRY

Douglas was President Franklin D. Roosevelt's second choice for a running mate in 1944. If he had been chosen, then he, and not Harry Truman, would have succeeded FDR as president in 1945. It was the beginning of a long-standing rivalry between the two men. Douglas briefly considered running against Truman for the Democratic nomination in 1948. A "Draft Douglas" movement even bubbled up, but Douglas soon realized the folly of running against an incumbent president—even one as unpopular as Truman—and withdrew his candidacy. Truman later sought out Douglas for the vice-presidential nomination that eventually went to Alben Barkley, but the Justice demurred, declaring: "I have no wish to be the number two man to a number two man." What exactly he meant by "number two," given his feelings about Truman, is open to interpretation.

JERRY'S JIHAD

It took a lot to rile Gerald Ford. But America's genial thirty-eighth president sure got his knickers in a twist when he first crossed paths with William O. Douglas. In 1969, then Congressman Ford introduced a resolution calling for Justice Douglas's impeachment. (It was the fourth time in his Supreme Court career that Douglas had faced a serious impeachment threat; formal charges had also been filed in 1953, after he temporarily stayed the execution of atomic spies Julius and Ethel Rosenberg.) What was Jerry's beef? He claimed that Douglas had taken what amounted to $12,000 in kickbacks from a shady hotelier, along with the usual litany of complaints against the high-living jurist. Douglas, Ford claimed, "defied the conventions and convictions of decent Americans" and behaved like a "dirty old man" by consorting with younger women, several of whom he later married. For good measure, America's soon-to-be unelected president accused Douglas of fomenting "hippie-yippie-style revolution" and excoriated him for writing a magazine article that allegedly praised "the lusty, lurid, and risqué along with the social protest of left-wing folk singers." He also added one of the more ludicrous bon mots to the lexicon of American constitutional law. "An impeachable offense," Ford said, "is whatever a majority of the House of Representatives considers it to be at a given moment in history."

At the conclusion of a seven-month investigation, a House Judiciary subcommittee determined there was no basis for Ford's charges and no grounds for Douglas's impeachment. Ford did get the last laugh, however. As president in 1975, he accepted Douglas's resignation and named his successor on the Court, John Paul Stevens. At Stevens's swearing-in ceremony, the two old foes met for the final time. "Good to see you, Mr. Justice," Ford told a stroke-addled, wheelchair-bound Douglas. "Yeah. It's really nice seeing you," Douglas caustically replied. "We've got to get together more often." And with that, he had his attendant roll him out of the room.

LET'S BE FRANK

Another name on Douglas's personal enemies list was that of Felix Frankfurter, the famously disagreeable justice who regularly slagged his colleagues in his letters and diaries. Douglas, Frankfurter once wrote, was one of the "two most completely evil men I have ever met" and "the most cynical, shamelessly amoral character" he had ever known.

I'm Walkin' Here!

An avid outdoorsman, Douglas believed that vigorous walking was the best exercise. He recommended that everyone "get in at least twenty miles on foot every weekend—rain, shine, or snow." Elsewhere he observed that "it is only by foot that one can really come to know the nation." And he practiced what he preached. From age eleven to age twenty-one, Douglas made annual week-long treks through the Cascade Mountains of Washington state. By the time he was finished, he had hiked most of the trails in Yakima, Mount Rainier, and Mount Adams. He later hiked the Long Trail in Vermont, through the Berkshires of western Massachusetts and the White Mountains of New Hampshire. In his most ambitious excursion, he hiked the length of the Appalachian Trail, from Maine to Georgia—a distance of more than two thousand miles. Canoeing and mountain climbing were also regular elements of his outdoor regimen.

DUMB AS A STUMP

With his love of the outdoors and the natural landscape, Douglas developed a reputation as an ardent environmentalist. In honor of that legacy, a wilderness area in Washington state and a waterfall in the Appalachian Mountains of North Carolina are named in his honor. But it's a subalpine valley in the Sequoia National Park in California that owes him the real debt of gratitude. In 1972, in one of the loopiest dissenting opinions in Supreme Court history, Douglas argued in *Sierra Club v. Morton* that inanimate objects should have the right to file suit in cases involving environmental protection. Specifically, Douglas named "valleys, alpine meadows, rivers, lakes, estuaries, beaches, ridges, groves of trees, swampland, or even air" as potential litigants before the Supreme Court. "The voice of the inanimate object . . . should not be stilled," Douglas thundered from the bench. "Perhaps they will not win," he concluded, in language that would make Lisa Simpson blush. "Perhaps the bulldozers of 'progress' will plow under all the aesthetic wonders of this beautiful land. That is not the present question. The sole question is, who has standing to be heard?" Amazingly enough, America's trees and estuaries have thus far not seen fit to heed Douglas's call to seek redress before the nation's highest judicial body.

LIAR, LIAR

In our age of celebrity, no one would blink twice at a Supreme Court Justice writing a score-settling tell-all memoir. But the Establishment was aghast when Douglas's two-part memoir, *Go East Young Man* and *The Court Years*, was published in 1974 and 1980. Filled with self-serving boasts about his intellectual acumen and catty comments about colleagues, the book won praise in liberal circles. The *New York Times* even said the first volume "reads like the kind of novel one wishes would not end." How right they were. After Douglas's death, it was revealed that many of the autobiographical details were completely fictitious. He didn't grow up poor, never had polio as a child, wasn't a private in the army, and didn't work his way through law school, as he had claimed. (In fact, his first wife had supported him.) He also contended to have once heard Enrico Caruso sing at the Metropolitan Opera, though that was impossible. The legendary tenor had died the year before Douglas arrived in New York.

Bitter End

Douglas's final days on the Court were dark and depressing. After suffering a severe stroke in late 1974, he insisted on returning to the bench. The *New York Times* observed sadly that he "appeared for the first time as a frail and fragile old man, his voice thin and uncertain, his left arm hanging useless at his side, most of the once remarkable vigor of the outdoorsman drained away." Wracked with constant pain, Douglas grew increasingly demented and paranoid. He called people by the wrong names and nodded off during oral arguments. At one point, he called for a 12:30 lunch break—at 1 p.m. In his delirium, he believed plots were afoot to murder him or remove him from the bench. He also became convinced that he was chief justice and attempted to commandeer Warren Burger's chambers for his own.

FRANK
MURPHY

April 13, 1890–July 19, 1949

BIRTHPLACE:
Sand Beach, MI

NICKNAME:
"Wild Mustard," "Fragile Frank"

ASTROLOGICAL SIGN:
Aries

TERM:
February 5, 1940–July 19, 1949

APPOINTED BY:
Franklin D. Roosevelt

WORDS OF WISDOM:
"Speak softly and hit hard."

I seldom read novels," Frank Murphy once said, "because no novel could be so exciting as my life." Those seem like bold words coming from a Supreme Court justice, especially one who abstained from most material pleasures and may have died a virgin. But Murphy did have his moments. He fought in the First World War and served as viceroy of the Philippines in the Second. He was mayor of Detroit during one of the most tumultuous periods in the city's history, although his record in that office qualifies him as one of the most inept city managers in American municipal history. And he capped his career with nine years on the high bench during the heyday of the kind of paternalistic, big government liberalism he spent his life championing. Murphy's days may not have been exciting, but they certainly were eventful.

Was Frank Murphy America's first gay justice? He certainly had a long and close friendship with trusted aide Edward G. Kemp.

A short, slender, red-haired Irish Catholic, Murphy was the archetypal first-generation immigrant made good. His father—who had immigrated to the United States from Canada—was an Irish radical who had served jail time for his ties to the secret anti-British Fenian society. His mother was a devout

Roman Catholic who instilled in Frank the idea that he should devote his life to public service as a kind of "lay priest." Determined to use the courtroom as the forum for his evangelism, Murphy enrolled at the University of Michigan, where he earned his Bachelor of Laws in 1914. He also earned a lifelong nickname, "Wild Mustard," although its origins are obscure. It may have reflected the fury he brought to the game of football, which he played passionately until the day a 220-pound lineman fell on his 135-pound frame and cracked three of his ribs.

Taking time off for a tour of duty in World War I, Murphy began the practice of law, first in private practice and later as an assistant U.S. attorney. His professional motto was "All clients are bastards." In 1923, he became a judge for the Recorder's Court of Detroit, where he spent six years, adjudicating criminal cases. It was his only judicial experience before assuming his seat on the U.S. Supreme Court.

To be honest, judging bored Murphy. Politics was more up his alley, so in 1930 he ran for mayor of Detroit. His platform was progressive—and ambitious. "We'll have the dew and the dawn and the sunshine of a new era," he promised voters. "No man or woman will ever go hungry in this town." Newspapers derided him as the "dew and sunshine" candidate, but he won anyway. His term coincided with the worst years of the Great Depression: "dew and sunshine" were in short supply, but government handouts were not. Murphy reopened closed auto plants as dormitories for the homeless and greatly expanded the city's unemployment relief program. Such liberal largesse caught the attention of incoming president Franklin Roosevelt, who needed a man with Murphy's moxie to run things in the Philippines. FDR named Murphy governor-general of the islands in 1933.

The Philippines, Murphy soon learned, was a lot different from Detroit. ("Oh boy, it's some palace!" he gushed upon seeing his new headquarters in Manila—and in fact it *was* a palace.) During his three-year stay, he lived like an Eastern potentate. He had the army build him a steeplechase course for his riding pleasure and insisted that his hotel bills and bar tabs be paid for by the government. It was the time of Murphy's life, and he never forgot it. The national headquarters of the Philippine armed forces in Quezon City was named after him. For the rest of his life, he kept a Philippine flag in his office to remember the experience.

Still, all good things must come to an end. For Murphy, that meant returning to his native Michigan in 1936 to run for governor, at FDR's bidding. Once again Murphy ran on an aggressive New Deal platform and won. And once again he did not distinguish himself in office. As governor, he successfully mediated an end to the famous Flint Sit-Down Strike of 1937 but racked up precious few other accomplishments. He was defeated in his reelection bid in 1938, leaving him ripe for appointment to FDR's cabinet as attorney general and then, in 1939, as a Supreme Court justice.

Murphy was more or less a rubber stamp for Roosevelt's New Deal agenda. Unburdened by a fine legal mind, he ruled on cases almost exclusively on his gut feeling about what was fair or unfair. His best moments came in dissent, as in the 1944 case of *Korematsu v. United States*, in which he charged the Court with racism for upholding the forced relocation of Japanese Americans during World War II. He was a stalwart opponent of capital punishment ("Only the hapless hang," he once declared) and a defender of free speech. Murphy sided with Jehovah's Witnesses in a case affirming their right not to salute the American flag in school. It was quite a bold vote for a devout Catholic, prompting one onlooker to assert: "If Frank Murphy is ever sainted, it will be by the Jehovah's Witnesses."

Murphy may not have been a saint—nor the most distinguished justice in history—but he remains something of a minor deity in the Irish Catholic community, which is all his mother could have asked for. Stricken by coronary thrombosis, he died in his sleep on July 19, 1949, at age fifty-nine. More than ten thousand people attended his funeral in Detroit.

★ ★

MAYOR McSLEAZE

Murphy ran for mayor of Detroit promising "dew and sunshine," but the happy times proved to be short-lived. The depression cast a pall over the city's economic fortunes, while Mayor Murphy's response—which was basically to hand out money—hardly qualified as sensible financial management. In just three years, Murphy brought the city to the brink of bankruptcy. He ran up a $14 million deficit; $11 million in taxes went unpaid. Ten percent of the city's population was out of work, with jobless benefits totaling $1 million a month. Fraud and embezzlement were rampant. Henry Ford himself had to loan the city $5 million just to meet its payrolls. Even City Controller Gracie Hall Roosevelt, brother-in-law of the soon-to-be president, admitted: "If we had all this to do over, it would be done far more efficiently." In short, Frank Murphy's Detroit was a cesspool of graft and negligence.

SAINT FRANCIS

Murphy may have been the most devout Catholic ever to sit on the Supreme Court. Everywhere he went, he carried a Catholic Bible his mother had given to him as child. He made a point of reading a chapter from it every day. By the time he died, the Bible was so worn out from re-reading that he kept it wrapped in a towel to prevent it from falling apart.

Murphy cut a distinctly priestly figure to those who knew and worked with him. One observer likened his courtroom style to "a bishop hearing confession." Washington lobbyist Tommy "the Cork" Corcoran called him the "modern counterpart of the fighting abbots of the Middle Ages." George Cardinal Mundelein, the Archbishop of Chicago, once dubbed him a "lay bishop" and said: "Mr. Attorney General, you are one Catholic politician I don't have to worry about."

The Church was the lodestar of Murphy's existence, more important to him than even the prospect of becoming president. Asked if he would like to run for the White House someday, Murphy replied: "If I had to give up the Catholic Church for the most exalted position on earth, I'd gladly give up the glory and power. I don't think I'd have any trouble making the decision. I love my church."

COLD SHOWERS

Benjamin Cardozo may not have been the Supreme Court's only lifelong virgin. Columnist Drew Pearson, the ultimate Washington insider, was one of many convinced that Murphy went to his grave without ever having experienced carnal pleasure. Upon hearing that a woman claimed to have spent the night with Murphy, FDR's trusted advisor Harry Hopkins quipped: "Well, there's no place where you could be safer." When Murphy died, his *Washington Post* obituary snidely observed that he had been "romantically linked with names of a number of pretty girls, and one kissed him in public."

By all indications, Murphy lived a celibate life and dated only within the context of his busy party schedule. "He can and does charm women, though his courtships do not go beyond dancing and horseback riding," reported *Time* magazine in a 1939 profile of the then attorney general. A New Deal historian noted that Murphy blew off steam via "a steady routine of cold showers, calisthenics, horseback riding, and fruit-and-vegetable dinners." Apparently all those jumping jacks and broccoli spears weren't doing the trick, however. At the time of his death, Murphy was engaged to be married to Joan Cuddihy, a woman twenty-nine years his junior and the granddaughter of the publisher of *Literary Digest*.

BEEFEATER

Sex wasn't the only thing from which Murphy abstained. Tobacco, alcohol, tea, and coffee were also *verboten*, although the justice did occasionally indulge his love for three-pound steaks.

Trapped in the Closet

Murphy was no Casanova when it came to the ladies, but was he actually playing for the other team? The authors of the book *Courting Justice*, a history of gays and lesbians at the Supreme Court, make a convincing case that Murphy may have been America's first gay justice. "Fragile Frank," as he was known in society circles, fit the stereotypical profile of a closeted gay man: He was fastidious, physically fit, and impeccably dressed. One columnist called him "the answer to ladies' prayers," that is, the perfect nonthreatening date. President Roosevelt's son-in-law had another term for it: He called Murphy a "pansy."

For decades, rumors abounded about Murphy's purported homosexual affairs. Sidney Fine, the justice's biographer, uncovered what may be the closest thing we'll ever get to documentary evidence of Murphy's sexual preference. A letter from an American soldier in the Philippines congratulating Murphy on his appointment to the Supreme Court appears to refer to an affair they had while Murphy was governor general. Eyebrows were also raised by Murphy's long "friendship" with Edward G. Kemp, a trusted aide with whom he lived, worked, and socialized for more than forty years. "We have a gay society," Murphy once remarked of their unusual living arrangement. (They shared a suite in the same hotel in Washington D.C.) Near the end of his life, when Murphy was planning his wedding to Joan Cuddihy, he even instructed Kemp to find a house where all three of them could live together. "We would have great fun," the aging justice enthused. Sadly, whatever ménage à trois he was planning was not to be. Murphy dropped dead of a heart attack before his wedding day. In his will, he left all his possessions to Kemp and his personal secretary.

DIM BULB

Murphy wasn't the sharpest crayon in the box. "I write the law as my con-science bids me," he declared. Critics charged that he had no abiding judicial philosophy, just a priggish sense of what was "right" or "wrong." "The Supreme Court tempers justice with Murphy," became the standard joke among Court watchers baffled by the former attorney general's jurisprudence. Murphy, wrote one observer, "looked upon hallowed juridical traditions as a drunk views a lamppost—as a means of support rather than a source of light."

Even his fellow justices were somewhat bewildered by Murphy's approach to the law. The ever dyspeptic justice Felix Frankfurter derisively dubbed Murphy "the Saint" and "the Stooge" for his overly moralistic and insufficiently erudite opinions. He once wrote to Justice Stanley Reed: "The short of the matter is that today you would no more heed Murphy's tripe than you would be seen naked at Dupont Circle at high noon tomorrow." The animosity Frankfurter felt for his junior colleague grew increasingly personal. "Us girls call him Murph," Frankfurter once scoffed, in a reference to Murphy's supposed fondness for showgirls. Frankfurter's hostility may also have originated in a sense that Murphy's paternalistic liberalism was just a little phony. Although he championed the cause of civil rights and fair play for minorities, Murphy had his limits. He once admitted that he "really did not care much for Jews—until somebody jumps on them."

BARENAKED LADDIE

Murphy may have been a bit of a prude, but he is perhaps the only Supreme Court justice to have a nude male statue dedicated in his honor. "The Hand of God" by Swedish sculptor Carl Milles depicts a ten-foot-tall naked man standing on the thumb and forefinger of the Almighty. Today it sits outside the Frank Murphy Hall of Justice in Detroit, although for more than a decade after its completion in 1953 it was kept in storage, out of concern for "public decency." The United Auto Workers Union—one of Murphy's biggest supporters—footed the bill for the unusual tribute.

ROBERT H.
JACKSON

February 13, 1892–October 9, 1954

BIRTHPLACE:

Spring Creek Township, PA

ASTROLOGICAL SIGN:

Aquarius

TERM:

July 11, 1941–October 9, 1954

APPOINTED BY:

Franklin D. Roosevelt

WORDS OF WISDOM:

"The price of freedom of religion, or of speech, or of the press is that we must put up with a good deal of rubbish."

W hen the [Supreme] Court moved to Washington in 1800," Robert H. Jackson observed, "it was provided with no books, which probably accounts for the high quality of early opinions."

As the last Supreme Court justice not to have graduated from law school, Jackson was living proof that you don't have to be a man of letters to be a man of the law. In fact, the unassuming "country lawyer" from western Pennsylvania had almost no formal schooling beyond high school. He never attended college and took only one year's worth of classes at Albany Law School. Almost all his legal

Robert Jackson's greatest contribution to the law may have come in 1945, when he took a sabbatical from the Court to serve as America's chief counsel in the Nuremberg war crimes trials.

training came via the old-school method of "reading the law" with his attorney cousin, Frank H. Mott, a form of apprenticeship that vanished with the nineteenth century. Yet with only a humble educational background, Jackson became one of America's most accomplished attorneys and one of the wittiest, most graceful opinion writers in Supreme Court history. So much for that fancy "book learnin'."

Robert Houghwout Jackson was born into modest means—his father ran

a stable in upstate New York—but cultivated some powerful friends. Chief among these was Franklin Delano Roosevelt, whom he first encountered in his early twenties, while he was practicing law in Buffalo and FDR was assistant secretary of the Navy. Roosevelt later became New York governor, taking Jackson with him as a personal advisor/poker buddy. The two men would remain close friends for more than three decades, often taking fishing trips together to the Bahamas and the Florida Keys. In 1930, when Jackson applied for membership in the prestigious American Law Institute, one of the officials on the membership committee asked future Supreme Court justice Benjamin Cardozo, "Who is Jackson? I never heard of him." "You will," Cardozo replied, "in time." The story may be apocryphal, or it may reflect the high expectations already forming for the unlettered, but well-connected, young lawyer.

Once elected president, Roosevelt persuaded Jackson to give up his lucrative law practice and join him in Washington—first at the Bureau of Internal Revenue, then in the Justice Department, and finally as U.S. solicitor general. This last position, which entailed arguing the government's case before the Supreme Court, suited Jackson the best. He proved to be a passionate, effective constitutional advocate—so effective, in fact, that Justice Louis Brandeis suggested he should be named solicitor general for life. But FDR had bigger plans for his poker pal. In 1940, he named Jackson attorney general and, the next year, nominated him to be the next associate justice of the Supreme Court. With a nod and a wink, he also indicated that he would one day elevate his old buddy right into the chief justice's chair.

Few could argue that Jackson was qualified for his new post. The only objection came from Maryland senator Millard Tydings, who had a personal beef with Jackson from his time as attorney general. Jackson, Tydings raged, "has not the character, integrity, nor judicial temperament . . . to sit on the Supreme Court of the United States." Unfortunately for Tydings, none of his Senate colleagues would agree with that dubious opinion. On July 7, 1941, Jackson was confirmed by voice vote.

He spent thirteen years on the Court, and although his dream of becoming chief justice was never realized (FDR's death in 1945 put the kibosh on that), Jackson was an eloquent and effective backer of the New Deal and the liberal cause. His greatest contribution to the law may have come in 1945, when he took a sabbatical from the Court to serve as America's chief counsel in the Nuremberg war crimes trials. In this high-profile posting, Jackson squared off across a courtroom with Hermann Göring and other high-ranking Nazi officials. While his lawyering skills were a little rusty, Jackson's opening and closing statements went down in history as among the most powerful examples of advocacy in the arena of international law.

After returning to Washington after the Nuremberg trials, Jackson spent eight more years on the Court. He continued to perform his job but was increasingly consumed by his bitter feuds with other justices, specifically Hugo Black and William O. Douglas. The public spats created controversy for the Court and tarnished Jackson's otherwise stellar legacy. The country lawyer's last important vote came in the case of *Brown v. Board of Education*, in which he joined the majority in declaring school segregation unconstitutional. He died of a heart attack five months later.

★ ★

FEAR OF A BLACK PLANET

Jackson had a long-running feud with fellow justice Hugo Black (see page 89 for more). Essentially, Jackson viewed Black as an unprincipled hack who used his position on the Court to do his cronies' bidding. "With few exceptions, we all knew which side of a case Black would vote on when he read the names of the parties," Jackson once harrumphed.

The simmering personality conflict came to a head in 1945, when the Court took up the case of *Jewell Ridge Coal Corp. v. Mine Workers.* The workers' attorney, Crampton P. Harris, was Black's former law partner and had recently sponsored an award banquet in Black's honor. Jackson saw this as a clear conflict of interest and expressed his disgust by disassociating himself from Black's ruling in the case, which, not surprisingly, favored the mine workers. He also declined to attend the banquet.

From that moment, the two justices were mortal enemies. Black's chance for revenge came in 1946, when he spearheaded a campaign to deny Jackson the chief justiceship. Chief Justice Harlan Stone had died, and Jackson believed he had been promised the chair by President Roosevelt. There was just one small problem. Roosevelt was dead too, and his successor, Harry Truman, wasn't inclined to honor every one of his predecessor's political commitments. Sensing an opening, Black passed word that he would quit rather than serve under Jackson as chief justice. To keep the peace, Truman instead appointed one of his own cronies, Fred Vinson. An aggrieved Jackson cabled Truman, congratulating him on the Vinson nomination but adding the acid caveat: "I would be loathe to believe that you would concede to any man a veto over court appointments." Truman denied that Black had exerted any such influence, but Jackson was not mollified. He then sent a message to Congress, threatening to open a can of whup-ass on Black if anything like the Jewell Ridge fiasco took place again on his watch. "I will make my Jewell Ridge opinion look like a letter of recommendation by comparison," Jackson warned.

THE ENEMY OF MY ENEMY

Jackson's loathing for Black extended to Black's BFF William O. Douglas as well. After the Jewell Ridge imbroglio, Douglas noted that "it was very evident in almost all our conferences that Bob Jackson thoroughly disliked Hugo Black and was out to destroy him. I mean destroy him in the sense of discrediting him. And his words were very acid, very derogatory. A lot of that carried over to me also."

As he had with Jewell Ridge, Jackson looked for a suitable test case to make his point that Douglas was nothing more than an unscrupulous opportunist. He found one in the case of *Zorach v. Clauson*, in which the Court ruled 6–3 in favor of allowing public school students to leave school at midday to attend religious instruction. Douglas had voted in previous cases that such arrangements violated the constitutional ban on the establishment of religion, but now—with an eye on the presidency and the need to curry favor with Catholic voters—he switched his position. Jackson pounced. In a caustic dissent, he all but called Douglas a hypocrite, writing that Douglas's majority opinion in the case "will be more interesting to students of psychology and of the judicial processes than to students of constitutional law."

Wordsmith

Despite his lack of formal education, Jackson carved out a reputation as one of history's wittiest and most erudite justices. His opinions are often laced with literary allusions and impish humor. Writing about one case, he quipped that the parties involved "changed positions as nimbly as if dancing a quadrille." On another occasion, opining on Hugo Black's majority opinion in a case involving separation of church and state, he compared his nemesis to the character of Julia in Lord Byron's *Rape of the Lock*, who, "whispering 'I will ne'er consent,' consented."

GREAT JACKSON'S GHOST!

One of Jackson's law clerks during the 1952–53 term was future chief justice William Rehnquist. Their association would prove to be a source of great controversy decades after Jackson's death. During Rehnquist's Supreme Court confirmation hearings, a memo emerged that he had written while clerking for Jackson concerning the deliberations over *Brown v. Board of Education*. Entitled "A Random Thought on the Segregation Case," the memo argued against Supreme Court action in favor of desegregating U.S. public schools. "I think *Plessy v. Ferguson* was right and should be reaffirmed," Rehnquist wrote, signing the memo with his own initials. The embarrassing document could easily have killed Rehnquist's nomination— in 1972 and again in 1986, when he was promoted to chief justice—had he not invented a novel explanation. It was Jackson's opposition to desegregation he was espousing in the memo, he claimed, rather than his own personal opinion. Since at the time Jackson was already on the record in favor of integrating U.S. schools, this statement was a bit of a reach. But, as they say, dead men tell no tales, and Rehnquist was able to skate by, using his deceased boss as a convenient scapegoat.

EARL
WARREN

March 29, 1891–July 9, 1974

BIRTHPLACE:

Los Angeles, CA

NICKNAME:

"Super Chief"

ASTROLOGICAL SIGN:

Aries

TERM:

October 5, 1953–June 23, 1969

APPOINTED BY:

Dwight D. Eisenhower

WORDS OF WISDOM:

"Everything I did in my life that was worthwhile I caught hell for."

Earl Warren," observed the influential American journalist John Gunther, "will never set the world on fire or even make it smoke; he has the limitations of all Americans of his type, with little intellectual background, little genuine depth or coherent political philosophy; a man who has probably never bothered with an abstract thought twice in this life.... [He is] no more a statesman in the European sense than Typhoid Mary is Einstein."

Those words, written for the 1947 edition of Gunther's sociopolitical travelogue *Inside USA*, adequately capture the then California governor who went on to become one of the most consequential chief justices in Supreme Court history. The man dubbed "Super

> Like John Jay, John Marshall, and roughly one-third of all Supreme Court justices, Earl Warren was a member of the Freemasons.

Chief" by Justice William J. Brennan was no legal scholar, but he used his considerable political and interpersonal skills to mold the Court in his image more effectively than any high court headman since John Marshall.

Born in Los Angeles in 1891, Earl Warren grew up in the rough-and-tumble central California city of Bakersfield. His Norwegian immigrant parents "were

too poor to afford the luxury of a middle name," he later quipped. His father worked as a repairman for the Southern Pacific Railroad and later became a local slumlord. Bakersfield at that time had a violent, rowdy reputation. A turn-of-the-century oil boom attracted an influx of unsavory characters, but young Earl kept his nose clean. As a child, he spent much of his time tending to a sizable menagerie of dogs, a sheep, an eagle, several chickens, rabbits, and, his personal favorite, a burro named Jack. He worked a variety of odd jobs to pay his way, including newsboy, freight hustler, and farm hand. When he graduated from high school in 1908, he was one of the only students in his class to go on to college.

At the University of California at Berkeley, Warren was a somewhat indifferent student. He joined the Gun Club and flunked second-year Greek but managed to scrape by academically and earn his law degree in 1914. He served briefly and without distinction as an infantry private during World War I. During the 1920s, he worked as a deputy district attorney in and around the Bay Area in northern California. His days as a young lawyer were marked by severe panic attacks before court appearances. "I'd get on a street-car, and I'd be so tense I would hope the car would be wrecked on the way to the courthouse," he later admitted. Nevertheless, Warren worked his way up the ladder to become district attorney and was elected California attorney general in 1938. That same year, Warren's father was found bludgeoned to death in his home in Bakersfield. The grisly crime was never solved, although old Methias Warren's shady real estate machinations may have had something to do with it.

As attorney general, Warren earned a reputation as a vicious red baiter and racist. He fought against the nomination of Berkeley law professor Max Radin to the state supreme court because the left-leaning Radin, he railed, "constantly gives aid and comfort to Communists and other radicals." He also took the lead in expediting the forced internment of Japanese Americans after the attack on Pearl Harbor. "We don't propose to have the Japs back in California during this war if there is any lawful means of preventing it," Warren frothed. "If the Japs are released, no one will be able to tell a saboteur from any other Jap." In his testimony before Congress on the issue, Warren went even further: "The only reason that there has been no sabotage or espionage on the part of Japanese Americans," he said, "is that they are waiting for the right moment to strike." To his credit, Warren later recanted, stating: "I have since deeply regretted the removal order and my own testimony advocating it, because it was not in keeping with our American concept of freedom and the rights of citizens. Whenever I thought of the innocent little children who were torn from home, school friends, and congenial surroundings, I was conscience-stricken."

Whatever his subsequent misgivings, Warren's law-and-order reputation surely didn't hurt him when he ran successfully for governor of California in 1942. He was a popular chief executive, twice winning reelection and forging a generally progressive record. His large and attractive family—he and his wife Nina had five well-scrubbed children—won him a great deal of favorable press. In 1948, Warren ran unsuccessfully for vice president on the Republican ticket. In 1951, he announced his own run for president, but his ill-starred candidacy was dogged by dirty tricks and illness. (He was briefly hospitalized with an intestinal malignancy.) The forces of Senator Robert Taft, one of the other Republican contenders, spread rumors that Warren was dying of cancer and had taken a golf bag full of bribe money. Dwight Eisenhower eventually vanquished both Warren and Taft for the GOP nomination, but not before Warren extracted the promise of a Supreme Court appointment in exchange for his endorsement. Duly elected, Eisenhower made good on his promise, and the rest is judicial history.

As chief justice, Warren is best known for bringing together his fractious colleagues in unanimous support of the epochal *Brown v. Board of Education* desegregation decision. But his legacy also includes landmark cases in the areas of criminal process, prayer in schools, voting rights, and privacy. Warren's pronounced leftward drift once ensconced on the high court earned him the everlasting enmity of American conservatives, and many campaigned vigorously for his removal. Conspiracy theorists also bless the day he donned his robes for the first time. Warren headed up the Warren Commission, the body charged by President Lyndon Johnson with finding out the truth about John F. Kennedy's assassination. After nearly a year of study, the commission concluded that Lee Harvey Oswald acted alone, a finding that did little to quell widespread suspicions about Soviet, Cuban, and mafia-inspired plots.

After more than fifteen tumultuous years as chief justice, Warren resigned in June 1969. He was replaced by a man he did not respect—Warren Burger—who was appointed by a president he had come to detest, Richard M. Nixon. After barely five years in retirement, mortified by the state of the Court and the country in the Nixon era, Warren died of congestive heart failure at age eighty-three.

★ ★

Left Turn

For decades, the conservative press denounced Warren as a left-winger. Who knew how right they were? Born a southpaw, Warren was forced to write right-handed by his grade school teacher, who tied his left hand behind his back to facilitate "learning." For the rest of his life, Warren wrote with his right hand, but did everything else with his left.

THE CISCO KID WAS A FRIEND OF MINE

. . . or at least a friend of my friend. One of Warren's closest chums was Leo Carrillo, a Mexican American actor best known for playing "Pancho," the English-mangling, sombrero-wearing sidekick of the Western movie hero known as the Cisco Kid. The two met during army service in World War I. As governor, Warren appointed Carrillo to the California state parks commission.

I LIKE IKE, BUT HE DOESN'T LIKE ME

Warren's reward for endorsing Dwight Eisenhower in the 1952 presidential campaign was supposed to be the first vacant seat on the Supreme Court. Yet, as many historians have noted, Ike nearly balked when that opening turned out to be the chief justice's chair. After the sitting chief, Fred M. Vinson, died in September 1953, Warren demanded that Eisenhower honor their agreement and name him to the position. The president demurred, sending his attorney general, Herbert Brownell, to California to try to renege on the deal. "The first vacancy means the first vacancy," Warren insisted. He even threatened to resign as governor and stump the nation, branding the president as a liar, if he didn't get his way. Brownell returned to Washington, telling Eisenhower, "We're stuck with him, I guess." Ike named Warren to the bench the next month, later admitting that it was "the biggest damn fool thing I ever did."

RED SCARE

Eisenhower wasn't the only person dismayed by Warren's leftward turn on the high court. Robert Welch, the head of the right-wing John Birch Society, led a nationwide campaign to "Impeach Earl Warren," denouncing him as a Communist and a traitor. Bumper stickers bearing the sentiment soon began appearing on cars from coast to coast. One speaker at an anti-Warren rally even called for the chief justice to be hanged. Elected officials chimed in as well. Governor George Wallace of Alabama announced that Warren "doesn't have enough brains to try a chicken thief in my home county," while Senator James O. Eastland of Mississippi assailed Warren and his Court colleagues for "up[holding] the position advocated by the Communist Party."

AT EASE

When not caught up in the ideological crossfire, Warren was known to be one of the most affable, unassuming chief justices in Supreme Court history. A week into the job, while he was walking the halls of the Court, a court officer snapped to attention in his presence. Warren immediately approached the man and held out his hand, saying: "My name is Earl Warren. What's yours?"

Fighting Felix

One of the only justices who didn't get along with Warren was Felix Frankfurter. The intellectual jurist was exasperated by Warren's nonanalytical approach. During one conference early in Warren's tenure as chief justice,

Frankfurter erupted: "God damn it, you're a judge! You can't decide cases by your sense of justice or your personal predilections." Replied Warren: "Thank heaven I haven't lost my sense of justice."

TRICKY SITUATION

Warren and Richard Nixon felt a longstanding antipathy, dating to their days as up-and-coming California politicians. In fact, Warren tried to engineer the timing of his own resignation from the Court so that Lyndon Johnson, and not Nixon, could name his replacement. (The scheme fell apart when Johnson's choice for successor, Abe Fortas, became involved in an ethical scandal.) Nixon never forgot the slight. In May 1974, when the elderly Warren fell gravely ill in Washington, he asked President Nixon's permission to be treated at Bethesda Naval Hospital in Maryland. Nixon refused, and Warren was admitted to Georgetown University Hospital instead. He died two months later.

Warren may have had the last laugh, however. In an interview conducted shortly before his death, he unloaded on the man known as "Tricky Dick" over his Watergate indiscretions. "Nixon's not important," Warren railed. "The country, the country is important. But it's going to rot under Tricky." He went on to call Nixon the worst president in American history and lamented his decision to step down five years earlier, saying: "If I had ever known what was going to happen to this country—and this Court—I never would have resigned. They would have had to carry me out of here on a plank!"

Brother Earl

Like Fred Vinson, his predecessor as chief justice, and his colleague Thurgood Marshall, Warren was an active and dedicated freemason. He was a longtime member of an Oakland Masonic lodge and served as Grand Master of California from 1935 to 1936.

GAME ON!

Warren was an ardent sports fan. He often attended Washington Senators baseball games, accompanied by his limo driver, and traveled out of town each October (while the Court was in session) to watch World Series games. Each December, he organized a junket to Philadelphia so that he and fellow justices could attend the annual Army-Navy football game. Of his newspaper reading habits, Warren once observed: "I always turn to the sports section first. The sports section records people's accomplishments; the front page nothing but man's failures."

WHO'S YOUR DADDY?

Politics make strange bedfellows. Warren's son-in-law was *What's My Line?* game-show host (and ardent conservative) John Charles Daly.

John Marshall
HARLAN II

May 20, 1899–December 29, 1971

BIRTHPLACE:

Chicago, IL

ASTROLOGICAL SIGN:

Taurus

TERM:

March 28, 1955–
September 23, 1971

APPOINTED BY:

Dwight D. Eisenhower

WORDS OF WISDOM:

"One man's vulgarity is another's lyric."

I f you look the part, you'll get the job," goes an old saw, and no one looked the part of a Supreme Court justice more than John Marshall Harlan II. The last justice born in the nineteenth century, and the first descendant of a justice ever to serve on the Court, the grandson of John Marshall Harlan I was six feet tall, white haired, and dignified. Underneath his robes, he wore bespoke three-piece suits crafted by a London tailor. Across his vest he carried his grandfather's gold watch chain, a symbol of judicial rectitude passed down through the generations. "Harlan both on the bench and in the conference is to the manner born," wrote Justice Felix Frankfurter. Justice Tom Clark addressed Harlan as "'milord" and once sent him a get-well note that read: "Your Lordship should be more careful of your

> For years, John Marshall Harlan arranged private screenings of adult films in the basement of the Supreme Court building. The (ostensible) purpose? To help justices define what constituted obscenity.

whiskey and your habits." His aristocratic bearing and sober legal mind won him a legion of admirers. Several of the current justices have cited Harlan as a model, with the liberal Ruth Bader Ginsburg and the conservative chief justice John Roberts both declaring him as their judicial hero.

Harlan's establishment pedigree extended beyond his grandfather. George Harlan, one of his ancestors, served as governor of Delaware during the colonial period. His father was a prominent city alderman who twice ran for mayor of Chicago. Harlan himself breezed through exclusive private schools and into Princeton, where he was elected class president three years running. A natural leader, he became a Rhodes Scholar and earned his law degree in just one year.

After passing the bar, Harlan worked as an assistant to the U.S. Attorney in New York City. Tasked with heading up the office's Prohibition Division, he foreswore alcohol voluntarily. After two years of busting up bootlegging rings, he went into private practice in 1927. Taking on a diverse array of clients, Harlan made a name for himself as a tenacious litigator. He represented the New York City Board of Education in litigation arising out of its attempt to employ free-thinking philosopher Bertrand Russell. He handled the will of an eccentric old dowager, Miss Ella Wendel, whose $75 million estate was under siege from a host of greedy relatives. And he took on the case of heavyweight boxer Gene Tunney in a breach-of-contract suit. Over the course of two decades, he became one of America's most famous lawyers.

Harlan's renown made him a natural fit for a judicial appointment, and when Republicans recaptured the White House in 1952, the cake was baked. President Dwight Eisenhower appointed him to the federal Court of Appeals in January 1954. Less than one year later, when Supreme Court Justice Robert H. Jackson died suddenly, Harlan answered the call to take his place. He served for more than sixteen years and developed a reputation as one of the liberal Court's most prolific and impassioned dissenters. During one four-year stretch, he wrote an average of forty-three opinions per term, many of them in longhand.

In contrast to some of Eisenhower's other high-court appointments, Harlan remained remarkably consistent in his conservative judicial philosophy. His closest ideological ally was Felix Frankfurter, with whom he voted almost 80 percent of the time. Although the two men shared a contrarian worldview, Harlan had none of the older justice's acerbic temperament and thus became known around the Court as "Frankfurter without the mustard."

His staunch federalism was out of step with most other members of the Warren Court, but Harlan got along well with his more liberal colleagues. He became fast friends with both the libertine William O. Douglas and the cantankerous Hugo Black, who became his frequent dining companion at the Court cafeteria. "John Harlan is one of the few people who convince me that there is such a thing as a good Republican," Black once declared.

Cautious and restrained in both his personal manner and his judicial philosophy, Harlan impressed Court watchers with his keen legal mind and steel-trap memory. He could recite past decisions with uncanny accuracy and often delivered his own opinions extemporaneously. As time wore on, however, old age and disease caught up with him, and for his last six years on the Court, Harlan was functionally blind. His eyesight worsened such that he couldn't see the ash of his own cigarette. Once, a clerk visited him in his sickbed to ask him to sign some papers, and the fumbling justice leaned forward and signed his own bed sheet. Black, who was then dying of stroke disease, confessed to a relative: "I can't see. I've got to quit. . . . And I'll tell you something else: John Harlan can't see a thing. He ought to get off the Court, too." In September 1971, shortly after being diagnosed with cancer, Harlan did just that. He submitted his resignation letter to President Richard Nixon. Two months later, he was dead.

RUB-A-DUB-DUB

As the grandson of a legendary jurist, Harlan could easily have coasted on his family reputation. Yet, he was determined to make a name for himself in the legal community, and he did so by taking on high-profile cases. In 1926, as the top lawyer for the Prohibition Division of the U.S. Attorney's office in New York, he won national headlines for his successful prosecution of Earl Carroll, the flamboyant stage producer of the ribald musical "Vanities." The previous year, Carroll had thrown a raucous Washington's Birthday party in his theater, attended by some five hundred leading lights of New York's theatrical community. During the party, Carroll wheeled out a bathtub filled with champagne and

occupied by a naked showgirl named Chorine Joyce Hawley. Revelers proceeded to fill their glasses and ogle the nubile woman (in that order). The pruri-
ence of the case attracted all the attention, but Harlan's prosecution hinged on
Carroll's denial that any alcohol had been served at the event. A jury found
Carroll guilty of perjury—and Harlan's legal legend was born.

BOMBS AWAY!

**Not since Oliver Wendell Holmes had there been a Supreme Court justice
with a military record to match Harlan's. During World War II, he served
as an advisor to the Eighth Army's Strategic Bombing Group, counseling
them on ways to improve the accuracy of their bombing runs. He even
took a spin as a waist gunner during a daylight raid over Germany. His
efforts earned him the Legion of Merit for distinguished conduct, as well
as the Croix de Guerre from the governments of France and Belgium.**

**Bombing obviously got into Harlan's blood. During his years on the
Supreme Court, he adorned the walls of his office with photographs of
American planes dropping their payloads on defenseless European cities.**

RACE MAN

What is it with Supreme Court justices and their love of eugenics? Even the
generally sober-minded Harlan wasn't immune. In 1937, he was one of the founding directors of the Pioneer Fund, a creepy foundation whose stated purpose
was to promote the propagation of America by people "descended predomi-
nantly from white persons who settled in the original thirteen states prior to the
adoption of the Constitution of the United States and/or from related stocks, or
to classes of children, the majority of whom are deemed to be so descended."
The brainchild of two Nazi sympathizers (one of whom was dubbed "a pioneer
in the science of race cleansing" by the Hitler-loving University of Heidelberg),
the organization began by devising an incentive plan to encourage army avia-
tors, a group of purportedly "eugenically superior" white men, to have additional
children. Astoundingly, Harlan remained on the board of this blatantly racist
organization for seventeen years.

Nobody's Flunky

Harlan took the independence of the judiciary *very* seriously. He was so obsessed with not giving even the appearance of political favoritism that he refused to vote in presidential elections. He declined to stand up or applaud during the president's annual State of the Union address, and he lobbied to discontinue a tradition in which the justices paid a visit to the White House in top hats and tails at the commencement of the Supreme Court term in October.

THE LUST PICTURE SHOW

The straitlaced Harlan seems like an unlikely candidate for the position of Supreme Court Porn Commissioner, but it's a role he took to with surprising relish. For years, he was the justice in charge of setting up private screenings of adult films in the basement of the Supreme Court building. There the robed eminences would gather and feast their peepers on such cinematic masterpieces as *A Woman's Urge*, *Sexual Freedom in Denmark*, and *I Am Curious (Yellow)*. The ostensible reason was to determine what constituted obscenity, but more often than not the screenings provided an excuse for the justices to kick back and enjoy a little soft-core entertainment. "And so our nymphomaniac subject was never cured," intoned the narrator at the end of one purportedly "educational" offering. "Yeah, but I am!" quipped a satisfied Thurgood Marshall.

Harlan took great delight in his job, sending around memos to announce the week's screening schedule, with the mischievous notation "No tickets are required." Of all the justices, Harlan was the most avid porn watcher. On the rare occasions when he missed a showing, he sent some of his clerks in his stead, instructing them to take detailed notes of the on-screen sexcapades and report back. Later in life, when troubled by faltering eyesight, he relied on Justice Potter Stewart to narrate the events. "You don't say!" "By George!" "Extraordinary!" Harlan exclaimed as various acts of sexual gymnastics were recounted in detail.

THE FOUR-LETTER JUSTICE

From the Earl Carroll case to the porno film festival and beyond, obscenity seemed to be a running theme in Harlan's legal career. In 1971, he lobbied the Court to take on the case of *Radich v. New York*, in which a New York City art-gallery owner was charged with desecration of the flag for displaying a sculpture depicting an erect penis wrapped in Old Glory. (Harlan ruled that the artwork was protected under the First Amendment.) That same year, he wrote the majority opinion in the case of *Cohen v. California*, arguing that a teenager arrested for wearing a jacket bearing the legend "Fuck the Draft" inside a Los Angeles courthouse could not be charged with disturbing the peace. "Absent a more particularized and compelling reason for its actions," Harlan wrote, "the State may not, consistently with the First and Fourteenth Amendments, make the simple public display of this single four-letter expletive a criminal offense."

**Harry Truman's "Biggest Mistake"—
and Other Noteworthy Twentieth-
Century Justices**

TOM CLARK (1949–67)

Tom Clark was one of the least intelligent and most corrupt justices ever to sit on the Supreme Court. A fixture of bribery and racketeering scandals throughout his stint as U.S. attorney general in the 1940s, Clark was well known as a tool of organized crime. He once arranged to have four Chicago mob bosses released from prison before their terms were up, then sabotaged attempts by Congress to investigate. Amazingly, he somehow managed to convince President Harry Truman to nominate him to the high court in 1947. Even Truman came to regret the choice, calling the appointment "my biggest mistake." "It isn't so much that he's a *bad* man," Truman conceded. "It's just that he's such a *dumb* son of a bitch." As if his own dubious contributions to American law weren't enough, Clark also afflicted the nation with his son, Ramsey Clark, the former U.S. attorney general turned crackpot left-wing conspiracy theorist. Among his many questionable utterances, Ramsey Clark once likened Saddam Hussein to a freedom fighter and attended the funeral of Serbian dictator Slobodan Miloseviç, declaring, "History will prove [he] was right."

SHERMAN MINTON (1949–56)

Former U.S. senator Sherman Minton of Indiana was the last of Truman's four disastrous Supreme Court appointments. After the nondescript Harold Burton, the ineffectual Fred Vinson, and the dim, venal Tom Clark, Truman doubled down on stupidity with his selection of Minton, whose only distinguishing qualification was that he had once sat next to Truman at his Senate desk. A genial backslapper with the body of a linebacker, Minton was known primarily for his potty mouth and for being the last Supreme Court justice to use a spittoon while sitting on the bench. His judicial acumen, alas, left something to be desired, prompting Felix Frankfurter to remark that Minton "will not go down in history as a great jurist, but he was a delightful colleague."

POTTER STEWART (1958–81)

Potter Stewart is best known for providing the Supreme Court with an enduring definition of what constitutes pornography. "I know it when I see it," he famously said—and it turns out he had seen plenty of it. During World War II, Stewart served as a Navy lieutenant in Casablanca, where his shipmates often ventured ashore to troll for locally produced porn. Through hours of—*ahem*—hard experience, Stewart learned to tell the difference between the hardest of hardcore and harmless adult entertainment. He called it his "Casablanca Test," and through him it became the standard constitutional test for the entire country. Later in his Supreme Court career, Porno Potter earned the distrust of his colleagues for serving as the anonymous source for many of the unflattering portrayals of the Burger Court that were contained in the 1979 best seller *The Brethren*, by Bob Woodward and Scott Armstrong. It wasn't too hard to figure out Stewart was the mole; he is one of the only justices in the book not to be depicted as a complete buffoon. Fallout over the mini-scandal led to Stewart's resignation from the Court in 1981, at the relatively young age of seventy.

WILLIAM J.
BRENNAN JR.

April 25, 1906–July 24, 1997

BIRTHPLACE:

Newark, NJ

NICKNAME:

"Deputy Chief"

ASTROLOGICAL SIGN:

Taurus

TERM:

October 16, 1956–July 20, 1990

APPOINTED BY:

Dwight Eisenhower

WORDS OF WISDOM:

"Death is an unusually severe
and degrading punishment."

hat's the most important rule of the Supreme Court?" William Brennan was fond of asking his law clerks. "The rule of five!" he would answer, fanning out the fingers of his tiny hand. "With five votes, you can do anything around here. Five, count 'em, five!" As the Court's most gregarious member, and its most outspoken liberal, Brennan lived—and, less occasionally, died—by the rule of five during his more than thirty years on the high bench. He used his nose for votes and his considerable schmoozing skills to wrangle the necessary majorities for some of the Court's most progressive decisions.

William Joseph Brennan Jr. was born on April 25, 1906, in Newark, New Jersey. His mother kept house while his father stoked the coals at the local Ballantine Brewery. Growing up, Brennan worked a series of odd jobs—milking cows, selling suits, inspecting street repairs, pumping gas, making change for the trolley service—and also helped his father launch a burgeoning political career, first as a union leader and later as a municipal commissioner. Turned off by backroom politics, he sought a career in law, hoping to secure a job on Wall Street; he graduated from Harvard Law School in 1931.

During two decades in private practice, Brennan earned a reputation as one of New Jersey's top corporate lawyers. He married, started a family, and grew quite wealthy, but his pro-labor views made him ill-suited to serve as a

mouthpiece for big business. If his job boasted one perk, it was the ability to make powerful friends in both political parties. In 1949, when the Republican governor of New Jersey offered him a judgeship, he gave up his high salary for a chance at a more meaningful career. He ascended to the state supreme court three years later.

Brennan's nomination to the U.S. Supreme Court came as a result of blind luck. In 1956, while filling in for ailing chief justice Arthur Vanderbilt at

> William Brennan may be the only Supreme Court justice with a hardcore following. Indie rock band Fugazi lamented Brennan's retirement in their 1991 song "Dear Justice Letter."

a legal conference in Washington D.C., he delivered an address on the subject of overburdened courts. In the audience sat Herbert Brownell Jr., President Dwight Eisenhower's attorney general, who was so impressed by the speech that he filed Brennan away as a potential future Supreme Court nominee. The fact that Brennan was a Catholic and a Democrat, and that Ike was looking to curry favor with both those groups for his reelection campaign, was only the icing on the cake. When associate justice Sherman Minton resigned later that year, Brownell recommended Brennan. Eisenhower agreed, and Brennan was summoned to the White House the next day, completely unaware of what lay in store. He even stopped off for a hot dog on the way. He ended up getting dinner—as well as an offer to serve on the highest court in the land. As the nomination progressed, no one in the Eisenhower administration bothered to ask Brennan about his politics or judicial philosophy. If they had, they might have discovered they were nominating the most liberal justice in Supreme Court history.

There's something to be said for making the right kind of enemies. When Brennan came before the Senate for confirmation, only one senator voted against him: Joseph McCarthy, the muculent Red-baiter from Grand Chute, Wisconsin. McCarthy charged that Brennan was "hostile" to congressional investigations of Communism because of a speech Brennan had delivered two years before in which he said, "There are some practices in the contemporary American scene which are reminiscent of Salem witch hunts." But Tailgunner Joe was unable to convince even a single Republican colleague to join him in opposition. Brennan's elevation to the high bench marked the third time he had been appointed to a court by a GOP official. That such a dedicated progressive won the support of all but his most extreme ideological foes is a testament to Brennan's consensus-building skills and affable personality.

Brennan wasted no time showing off that genial nature. "I'm the mule in the Kentucky Derby," he declared upon taking his seat on the Court. "I don't expect to distinguish myself, but I do expect to benefit by the associations." Like a legal version of Seabiscuit, he quickly set about winning over his new colleagues. Slight of stature, Brennan had an impish quality that reminded some of a leprechaun. He greeted fellow justices with a hearty "Hiya pal!" and made a point of calling the buttoned-down conservative John Marshall Harlan "Johnny." Most people found his shtick charming. A few found it irritating. Even one of Brennan's closest friends admitted that "he had a bit of the blarney in him."

He had quite a bit of blarney in him, if his output is any indication. Brennan wrote 1,360 opinions throughout his thirty-three years on the Court, more than any other justice except William O. Douglas. A dyed-in-the-wool judicial activist, he helped effect a fundamental revolution in constitutional law. No justice was more eager to use the Court's power to produce social change, undertaken in areas as wide-ranging as free speech, voting rights, and the administration of criminal justice. One of the Court's most outspoken opponents of capital punishment, Brennan once declared electrocution to be "nothing less than the contemporary technological equivalent of burning people at the stake." The Court's job, he said, was to determine "whether a punishment comports with human dignity. Death, quite simply, does not."

Brennan's unapologetic liberal activism won him the enmity of conservatives. Along with Harry Blackmun, author of the *Roe v. Wade* opinion, he was number one on many a right-winger's enemies list. On the other hand, some progressives considered him too much of a compromiser, too willing to cut deals with ideological foes to reach his vaunted magic number five. Even until the end of his tenure on the Court, when a stroke forced him to retire at age eighty-four, he was still cobbling together majorities to overturn a ban on flag desecration. He died seven years later.

HIS NAME IS EARL

Brennan's best friend on the Court was Chief Justice Earl Warren. The two shared a passion for baseball. In fact, Brennan's first day was spent watching the 1956 World Series between the Yankees and the Dodgers, joining Warren and the other justices in the third-floor conference room. "Sit down so we can see the game!" one robed eminence bellowed as Brennan entered the room, making the new arrival feel right at home. Over the years, Brennan developed something of a father/son bond with Warren, who was fifteen years his senior. They often attended Washington Senators games together. But the relationship never got too chummy. Out of respect for Warren's position, Brennan refused to call him by his first name, insisting on referring to him only as "Chief."

Just Call Me When the Cake's Done

If Warren was Brennan's father figure, the other two chief justices under whom he served were more like distant uncles. He had little in common with the pompous Warren Burger, and the chilly, conservative William Rehnquist left him cold. Rehnquist, for his part, found Brennan to be a bit of a sanctimonious windbag. Remarking on the latter's opinion-writing skills, Rehnquist once observed: "Bill is usually thorough, but as often as not he sounds like someone reading aloud a rather long and uninteresting recipe."

FELIX THE PEST

If Brennan had a bête noire on the Court, it was Felix Frankfurter. One of the Warren Court's few unabashed conservatives, Frankfurter had also taught Brennan at Harvard, making him loath to concede to the younger man in an argument. Mix in Frankfurter's notoriously imperious personality, and the result is a recipe for conflict. "I always encourage my students to think for themselves, but Brennan goes too far!" Frankfurter reportedly complained, in characteristically patronizing fashion. He also went out of his way to demean Earl Warren behind his back, which made Brennan's blood boil. "Any encouragement in a chief justice that he is the boss, that he differs from the other members of the Court in matters other than administrative, must be rigorously resisted," Frankfurter once said, lecturing Brennan on his deference to "The Chief." Frankfurter, who considered himself the intellectual fulcrum of the Court, saw "keeping the chief justice in his place" as part of his job description. Brennan begged to differ. He constantly complained to his clerks about Frankfurter's "condescending nature." "He makes me so mad sometimes!" Brennan confessed—about the closest thing to an insult ever to exit the convivial justice's mouth. After a particularly obnoxious Frankfurter browbeating, Brennan finally lost it. He turned as red as a beet and demanded that Frankfurter stop treating him like a law student. A mortified Frankfurter was forced to write Brennan a letter of apology.

TIGAR TRAP

In 1966, Brennan courted controversy when he hired Michael Tigar, a recent graduate of the University of California at Berkeley law school, as a law clerk. Tigar's credentials were impeccable: He had headed the law review and graduated first in his class. But he was also one of the most outspoken radicals on America's most radical campus. When the right-wing press got wind of the hire, they tore into Brennan, charging that the left-leaning justice was a closet Communist. Before long, J. Edgar Hoover got involved, compiling a dossier on Tigar's protest activities and secretly passing it on to President Lyndon Johnson. LBJ instructed his Court stooge, Abe Fortas, to pressure Brennan to fire Tigar; Fortas complied, through Brennan's friend, Chief Justice Earl Warren. Unwilling to invoke the wrath of the White House, Warren asked Brennan to rescind the job offer. Brennan complied, to the eternal consternation of his liberal ally William O. Douglas, who considered him a coward for knuckling under. Tigar went on to become a respected attorney in the office of Washington D.C. power lawyer Edward Bennett Williams, on a recommendation from—who else—William Brennan.

Mini Me

If Brennan was the undisputed intellectual leader of the Court's liberal faction, Thurgood Marshall was his most reliable deputy. During their thirteen years of service together, the two men voted virtually in lockstep. Clerks of both men even started referring to them in the singular, calling them "Justice Brennan-Marshall."

TRADING UP

In 1982, Brennan's wife, Marjorie, died after a long battle with throat cancer. They had been married more than half a century, but the seventy-six-year-old justice wasted no time getting back on the horse. Three months later, Brennan married his secretary, Mary Fowler, who had been working for him for more than twenty-five years. The whirlwind courtship was all the more curious because of the way Brennan announced it to colleagues. "Mary Fowler and I were married yesterday, and we have gone to Bermuda," he informed the other justices via interoffice memo. The news came as a bit of a surprise, since hardly anyone knew the two were even dating. That same day, Mary submitted her resignation and the honeymooning lovebirds flew out of town.

HARDCORE JUSTICE

Brennan may be the only Supreme Court justice with a hardcore following. In 1991, Washington D.C.–based indie band Fugazi recorded the song "Dear Justice Letter." The propulsive tune, which laments Brennan's retirement from the Court, includes the lyrics

> Justice Brennan, take out some insurance on me, baby . . .
>
> You let your gown to the ground,
>
> but I'm not waiting around until the kiss-off.

BYRON
WHITE

June 8, 1917–April 15, 2002

BIRTHPLACE:

Fort Collins, CO

NICKNAME:

"Whizzer"

ASTROLOGICAL SIGN:

Gemini

TERM:

April 16, 1962–June 28, 1993

APPOINTED BY:

John F. Kennedy

WORDS OF WISDOM:

"Where else can one be so isolated and alone, yet turn from hero to heel or from heel to hero in just ten pages or so? Where else does the telephone ring so seldom?" (on life at the Supreme Court)

What happens when you appoint a former football star with no judicial experience to the highest court in the land? America found out the hard way in 1962, when President John F. Kennedy named his old war buddy Byron "Whizzer" White as associate justice. White lingered on the Supreme Court for more than thirty years, carving out a spectacularly undistinguished record and vexing his erstwhile political backers with his consistently conservative voting record. His crabby personality and inexplicable loathing of the press did little to endear him to colleagues, reporters, and historians.

Before turning to law, Byron White was a Rhodes Scholar and even played in the National Football League. In fact, White led the NFL in rushing in 1938.

Byron Raymond White was born in Fort Collins, Colorado, on June 8, 1917, spending his childhood in the beet farming community of nearby Wellington. "By the normal standards of the day, we were all quite poor," he recalled. Nevertheless, he worked his way out of the fields and into a full scholarship at

the University of Colorado, a reward for finishing first in his high school class. The consummate high achiever, in college White was Phi Beta Kappa and student body president. He was also a football hero, earning All-America honors and a spot on the Buffalos 1937 Cotton Bowl team. It was Leonard Cahn, a sportswriter for *The Rocky Mountain News*, who first gave him the nickname "Whizzer," a moniker White soon grew to hate.

Torn between academics and the glory of the gridiron, White pursued both. As a Rhodes Scholar, he schmoozed with the Kennedy family at Oxford, and when football was in season he carried the pigskin first for the Pittsburgh Pirates and later the Detroit Lions. He led the National Football League in rushing in 1938 and earned the princely sum of $15,000. Nevertheless, in the off-season he continued to wait tables and work on his law degree. "It's a good way to earn your food, and you don't make money to go to school," he told reporters wondering why he was still slinging hash on an NFL star's salary.

During World War II, White served in the navy and renewed acquaintances with his old Oxford chum John F. Kennedy. In fact, it was White who wrote the official incident report on the sinking of Kennedy's PT boat, the runetext of the Kennedy legend that later formed the basis for the film PT-109. It was a favor the ambitious JFK would not soon forget. Still, a Supreme Court appointment seemed a long way off in 1947, when White returned to his native Colorado resolved, in his words, "to practice law, raise a family, and keep my name out of the goddamn newspapers."

His plan might have worked if his pal Jack Kennedy had not decided to run for president in 1960. White joined the campaign team and, when JFK was elected, was named deputy attorney general. White was just the kind of man Kennedy wanted for the face of his "New Frontier": vigorous, intelligent, full of manly virtues. He was not, however, particularly liberal. The world would discover that two years into the president's term, when White was named to replace the retiring justice Charles E. Whittaker on the high court. Although White remained loyal to Kennedy personally and to the Democratic Party, his jurisprudence was more conservative than anyone could have imagined. To wit:

In 1966, White dissented in the landmark *Miranda v. Arizona* case, arguing that requiring police officers to advise suspects of their rights would "return a killer, a rapist, or other criminal to the streets and to the environment which produced him, to repeat his crime whenever it pleases him."

In 1973, White issued a scathing dissent in the *Roe v. Wade* abortion case. He called the decision "an exercise in raw judicial power" that was "improvident and extravagant," and he derided the majority for reaching the conclusion "for no reason at all, and without asserting or claiming any threat to life or health, [that] any woman is entitled to an abortion at her request."

In the 1986 case of *Bowers v. Hardwick*, White voted—this time in the majority—to uphold a Georgia state law that criminalized anal and oral sex between consenting adults. In his opinion, he railed that "to claim that a right to engage in such conduct is 'deeply rooted in this nation's history and tradition' or 'implicit in the concept of ordered liberty' is, at best, facetious."

A justice who was pro-life, apprehensive about civil liberties, and deeply hostile to gay people may not have been what progressives thought they were in store for when White joined the Court, but that's what they got—and kept on getting for more than thirty-one years. About the only good thing to come out of White's tenure, from a progressive's point of view, was his determination not to leave the Court until a Democrat was in the White House, a final gesture of gratitude to his patron, JFK. Soon after Bill Clinton took office, White made good on his word and paved the way for the nomination of Ruth Bader Ginsburg. He died of pneumonia nine years later.

★ ★

CALL ME BYRON

Woe unto those who called White by his football nickname. It was a well-known fact that he hated being referred to as "Whizzer." White believed that it demeaned his accomplishments as a judge, and he refused to allow even his old gridiron teammates to use the name. Nevertheless, many people did. (Adding insult to injury, U.S. representatives often erroneously referred to White as "Buzzer.") Justice Harry Blackmun once remarked: "There are two things not to do with Byron White. One is to call him Whizzer. And the other is to say that he wants to be commissioner of baseball."

TAKE A LOOK AT THESE HANDS

At six feet two inches tall and 190 pounds, White was one of the most impressive physical specimens ever to sit on the high court. He also had one especially distinguishing characteristic that undoubtedly helped him on the football field: enormous paws. "What hands!" crowed the *Brooklyn Eagle* during his days as a collegiate star. "They look like the business end of a brace of steam shovels."

YOUNG MAN IN A HURRY

White was nothing if not ambitious, and he didn't mind letting you know about it. He once asked an official from a Washington D.C. law firm that considered hiring him if he could become a partner within two years. "Certainly not," came the answer. "Then I'm not interested," White replied. End of interview.

RUBBER STAMP OF APPROVAL

Senators must have had spring fever when they considered White's Court appointment in 1962. His confirmation was a decidedly quick and nondeliberative affair. Nominated on March 31, White was confirmed by the Senate on a voice vote twelve days later and took his seat on the Court five days after that. His confirmation hearing before the Senate Judiciary Committee lasted all of fifteen minutes and consisted of only eight questions.

Welcome Back, Whizzer

White was the first former Supreme Court law clerk to return to the Court as a justice.

TOUGH CUSTOMER

Lawyers charged with making oral arguments before the Court during White's tenure found him maddeningly hard to persuade. Said the eminent constitutional attorney Floyd Abrams: "I cannot think of a single answer that I made in the years that I argued before the Court while Justice White sat on it that seemed to satisfy him. While I won a number of cases that I argued before him, and he voted for my side in most of them, I never had the sense that anything I said pleased him."

NOBODY BEATS THE WHIZ

White made a name for himself as an athlete, and he never lost his competitive edge. He was known to be one of the dirtiest pick-up basketball players in the annals of the Supreme Court. Playing against law clerks thirty years his junior in the top-floor gymnasium known as "the highest court in the land," White developed a reputation for setting hard picks, pushing off on his jump shot, and traveling with the ball whenever he touched it. A notorious crybaby, he called fouls against his defenders on virtually every play and complained loudly if one was called against him. During one Friday afternoon game, White threw a vicious hip check on an opponent in an attempt to beat him out for a rebound. The clerk got the better of the justice, however, and White landed awkwardly, injuring his ankle. He showed up to work on Monday balanced on crutches, swearing everyone to secrecy about the cause of his injury.

What Goes Around . . .

One of White's many controversial dissents came in 1976 in the case of *Runyon v. McCrary*, in which he railed that the Court should have ruled against an African American couple trying to enroll their son in a whites-only private school. Oddly enough, the child at the center of that racial-discrimination case was Michael McCrary, who grew up to become a professional football player. In 2001, McCrary won the National Football League Players Association's Byron "Whizzer" White award, given each year to the player who serves his team, community, and country through public service.

ZEN AND THE ART OF CONSTITUTIONAL LAW

White had an unusual method for dealing with the most difficult decisions: he ignored them. Whenever he was presented with a particularly vexing case, he simply set it aside for weeks—sometimes months—and then returned to it at the last possible minute to render his opinion. "You may think you are not thinking about it," he once observed, "but maybe you are."

PRESS THIS

White was famously scornful of the press. The antipathy dated back to his days as an All-American football star at the University of Colorado, when reporters shadowed his every move. Some of his opinions in First Amendment cases seemed to reflect this hostility, including one in which he referred to newspaper journalists as "snoops." He joined in numerous decisions denying constitutional protections to journalists. At his retirement party in 1993, revelers serenaded White with a ditty that went: "He knows the First Amendment / He learned it up at Yale / But when he writes opinions / Reporters go to jail."

ABE
FORTAS

June 19, 1910–April 5, 1982

BIRTHPLACE:

Memphis, TN

NICKNAME:

"Fiddlin' Abe"

ASTROLOGICAL SIGN:

Gemini

TERM:

October 4, 1965–May 14, 1969

APPOINTED BY:

Lyndon Johnson

WORDS OF WISDOM:

"Judging is a lonely job in which a man is, as near as may be, an island entire."

I f being a presidential crony were the mark of a great Supreme Court justice, then Abe Fortas would merit enshrinement in the American judicial pantheon. A tiresome hack who worked his political connections more assiduously than any other lawyer in Washington, Fortas milked his close friendship with Lyndon Johnson for all it was worth over the course of thirty years, including a seat on the Court and, very nearly, the chief justiceship itself. Ironically, it was Fortas's willingness to do political favors for others that eventually brought about his downfall.

Abraham Fortas was born into a poor Orthodox Jewish family in Memphis, Tennessee, in 1910. His father was a cabinetmaker, originally from England, who instilled in his son a lifelong love for music. Fortas's childhood nickname, "Fiddlin' Abe," was inspired by his skill on the violin, which he honed in a traveling jazz combo, the Blue Melody Boys Band, while still in high school. A straight-A student, Fortas won a scholarship to Southwestern College in Memphis and graduated first in his class. He continued his stellar academic career at Yale Law School, where he edited the law journal and graduated second in his class in 1933.

After law school, Fortas really began to exploit his Rolodex. He beseeched his old law professor (and future Supreme Court colleague) William O. Douglas for a job in President Franklin D. Roosevelt's administration. After

résumé-burnishing stints at the Securities and Exchange Commission and the Department of the Interior, Fortas moved on to private practice in Washington D.C. He represented an accused Soviet spy before the Senate Internal Security Committee and successfully argued the case of Clarence Earl Gideon, an indigent defendant seeking court-appointed legal counsel, before the Supreme Court.

During this period, Fortas also nurtured a relationship with the man who would become his own personal Don Corleone, Lyndon B. Johnson of Texas. The two had met in 1939, when Johnson was an up-and-coming congressman. Fortas soon became Johnson's "fixer," intervening with friends at the Supreme Court on the Texan's behalf when allegations of vote-rigging threatened to invalidate Johnson's election to the Senate in 1948. LBJ never forgot a favor, and upon ascending to the presidency in 1963, he made a mental note to get his buddy Fortas a seat on the Court as soon as possible.

That moment came in the summer of 1965, when Johnson persuaded Fortas to set aside his lucrative private practice and replace the departing Arthur Goldberg. Even after taking a seat on the high court, Fortas continued

> How much does it cost to bribe a Supreme Court justice? If you're dealing with Abe Fortas, the answer is "$20,000 a year for life."

to do LBJ's bidding. He referred to Johnson as "the boss," often left Court conferences to attend meetings with the president, and had a private telephone line to the White House installed in his office. No one was permitted to interrupt him when he was talking to the president. As a general proposition, Fortas voted the way Johnson wished on key issues: liberally in cases involving civil rights and criminal procedure, and more conservatively as it related to the regulation of business.

Meanwhile, Fortas continued to "do business" the same way he always had since coming to Washington. In 1968, that practice finally started to catch up to him. That summer, Johnson nominated him to replace the retiring Earl Warren as chief justice, but confirmation stalled when it was revealed that

Fortas had accepted $15,000 to teach a legal seminar at nearby American University. A contentious set of hearings resulted in a Senate filibuster, prompting Fortas to withdraw from consideration.

The following spring, the news worsened. *Life* magazine published an exposé linking Fortas to a shady financier named Louis Wolfson, who had been convicted of securities fraud several years before and was hoping to get his conviction overturned. He agreed to pay Justice Fortas $20,000 a year for life in exchange for Fortas's "consultation" on his case. Given Fortas's close relationship with Johnson, the implication of a "cash for pardons" deal was clear. With Richard Nixon now occupying the White House, Fortas, for the first time in his life, had no powerful friends to call on for help. Faced with the possibility of impeachment, he resigned his Court seat on May 14, 1969. He lived another thirteen years, returning to private practice and arguing one last time before the bench he had disgraced, just two weeks before he died.

THE JEW CARD

Though hardly devout, Fortas was sensitive about his Jewish heritage. Appalled by the atrocities committed during World War II, he bore a longstanding grudge against Germans. He even refused to have anything to do with his law firm's German clients. With younger Jewish lawyers, he could be a stern taskmaster, apparently convinced it was his job to toughen them up for a Gentile-dominated world. Sometimes his criticisms bordered on the obsessive, as when he ordered one Jewish attorney to start wearing longer socks. But Fortas could be playful about his cultural identity as well. When writing to someone he knew was an observant Jew, he signed the letter "Yours in Christ."

I Am the Egg Man

For a proud Jew, Fortas sure loved Christian holidays. He was so enamored with Christmas that he spent hours elaborately wrapping small, inexpensive presents for friends. He gave one lucky recipient a pair of pliers. Easter was an even greater cause for celebration. Fortas and his wife threw an annual egg-coloring party at which they handed out prizes for "most ridiculous egg," "egg most likely to succeed," and "most political egg."

POWER PLAYER

How close was Fortas to the president? For years, he listed his business address in Who's Who as "c/o White House, 1600 Pennsylvania Avenue, Washington D.C." When John F. Kennedy was assassinated, the first call Lyndon Johnson made after being sworn in as president was to—guess who—Abe Fortas.

Open Marriage

Like his patron Lyndon Johnson (who once bragged that he had "more women by accident than [John F.] Kennedy had on purpose"), Fortas was an unapologetic horndog who indulged himself in many extramarital affairs. He was known to have an impish charm that attracted a wide range of Washington D.C. beauties. Fortas's wife, prominent tax attorney Carolyn E. Agger, seemed perfectly content with this arrangement. The couple slept in separate bedrooms and considered their marriage to be more of a business partnership than a romantic arrangement.

I'M LOVING IT

As a partner in a somewhat unconventional marriage, Fortas was hardly in a position to deny others the right to buddy up with whomever they chose. So it's no surprise that he joined in the unanimous decision in the 1967 case of *Loving v. Virginia*, which struck down state laws prohibiting interracial marriage. In fact, Fortas was so tickled by the case that he even wrote a poem about it. It began:

> For a Negro to marry a White
>> Results in serious Blight
> So argues the State of Virginia
>> But science is all agin' ya. . . .

OK, it wasn't exactly "Ebony and Ivory," but his heart was in the right place.

BLACK AND BLUE

A born glad-hander, Fortas got along well with his Supreme Court colleagues—with one notable exception. Hugo Black came to despise him, in part because Fortas bested him in fashioning a 5–4 majority in a 1966 case involving a sit-in at a Louisiana public library. Fortas had sided with the plaintiff, a black man who was forcibly ejected from the segregated library. When Black took the side of the white librarians, Fortas brought up his racist past. "Look, Hugo was in the Klan and now he's coming to the aid of Southern white womanhood," he railed. Black was so peeved that he refused to invoke the author of the majority opinion in his dissent. "The use of your name would disturb me," Black seethed. In future cases, even when they agreed, Black refused to sign his name to any of Fortas's opinions "just because Justice Fortas is writing," as his clerks explained. He also made a point of marking up Fortas's draft opinions with snarky criticisms of the latter's famously florid writing style. For his part, Fortas took to making jokes about Black's alleged senility and trashing his opinions behind his back, calling one "a disgraceful subversive job of attempted sabotage of this Court." Not surprisingly, when Fortas was embroiled in the legal troubles that forced him off the Court in 1969, it was Black who put the final shiv in and personally implored him to resign.

THE LARRY KING CONNECTION

Fortas's would-be sugar daddy, Louis Wolfson, also had a sordid association with another famous figure: aged TV gabber Larry King. It seems that soon after Fortas's career circled the drain in 1969, Wolfson sought out King—at the time a Miami radio host—for help in having his conviction for securities fraud overturned. King promised to lobby President Nixon's attorney general, John Mitchell, for a pardon, in exchange for $48,500. King never delivered, and Wolfson later filed charges against him for grand larceny. The ultimate result was King's infamous 1971 mug shot, which has been frightening small children ever since it first started circulating on the Internet in the 1990s.

After the Ball

Fortas's decision to resign from the Supreme Court is usually chalked up to the allegations of financial impropriety that began to swirl around him in late 1967. But could there have been another skeleton in his—*ahem*—closet? FBI documents obtained by an investigative journalist in the mid-1990s reveal that the bureau maintained an explosive "morals" file on Fortas that included allegations of homosexual relations with a teenager. According to the documents, a reliable informant told an FBI agent that "he had 'balled' with Abe Fortas on several occasions prior to Mr. Fortas's becoming a justice of the United States Supreme Court." (The document helpfully went on to point out that "to 'ball' is to have a homosexual relationship with another male.") Apparently, the feds thought the allegation was serious enough that they sent an agent to Fortas's home to warn him about it, "strictly for his own personal protection and knowledge." Fortas vehemently denied that he had ever engaged in a gay liaison of any kind. Yet, just months after receiving the heads-up, he resigned from the Court, leading some to speculate that FBI director J. Edgar Hoover may have threatened blackmail to force the staunch Democrat out of town, at the behest of the incoming Republican president, Richard Nixon.

THURGOOD
MARSHALL

July 2, 1908–January 24, 1993

BIRTHPLACE:
Baltimore, MD

NICKNAME:
"Mr. Civil Rights"

ASTROLOGICAL SIGN:
Cancer

TERM:
October 2, 1967–October 1, 1991

APPOINTED BY:
Lyndon B. Johnson

WORDS OF WISDOM:
"I have a lifetime appointment and I intend to serve it. I expect to die at 110, shot by a jealous husband."

The Supreme Court's first African American Justice was also one of the most important figures of the civil rights movement. As a lawyer, Thurgood Marshall successfully argued the *Brown v. Board of Education* case that declared school segregation inherently unequal and unconstitutional. As an associate justice, he eschewed legal formalism and brought the wisdom borne from real-world experience to bear on cases involving free speech, capital punishment, and affirmative action. But there was a

> **Thurgood Marshall often suspended deliberations at 1 P.M. so he could hurry back to his chambers and watch the soap opera Days of Our Lives.**

lighter side of this judicial icon that the public rarely saw. Marshall was also an inveterate prankster, womanizer, and two-fisted drinker known for throwing elaborate parties every time he won a case. *Collier's* magazine once noted that he was "equally at home on a dance floor or before the Supreme Court." Outspoken and combative, he seldom passed up an opportunity to prick the pretensions of his more buttoned-up colleagues. And when he wasn't giving good interviews, he could often be found squirreled away in his office with a

bottle of hooch, watching his favorite soap.

Born in Baltimore in 1908 to William and Norma Marshall, a railroad porter and an elementary school teacher, the future Mr. Justice Marshall was originally called Thoroughgood. He later had the name officially changed on his birth certificate. "It was too damn long, so I cut it," he explained. In school, Marshall was the class clown, notorious for throwing chalk at his teachers. After one such incident, the principal banished him to the school basement with a copy of the U.S. Constitution, ordering him to memorize it before he could leave. By the end of the day, he knew the entire document by heart.

Marshall attended Pennsylvania's Lincoln University, the nation's oldest all-black college. As a young man, he cut a lean and lanky figure and walked with a pronounced strut. The girls called him "Legs." His college friends called him "Turkey." He pledged a fraternity, worked as a bellhop, and ran with a posse of soon-to-be-famous friends that included "hi-de-ho" man Cab Calloway, poet Langston Hughes, and the future president of Ghana, Kwame Nkrumah. He also briefly considered a career in dentistry. Debating proved to be Marshall's real passion, however, and he quickly abandoned the care of teeth for the study of law. Unable to attend the all-white University of Maryland Law School, Marshall opted for Howard University. He graduated first in his class in 1933 and began a long and distinguished career as a lawyer for the NAACP.

His crowning achievement, the 1954 *Brown* decision, proved to be a bitter-sweet victory, for his first wife, Buster, died of cancer a few months later. Marshall remarried in December 1955, though his reputation as a ladies' man preceded him. During the next twelve years, Marshall earned the sobriquet "Mr. Civil Rights" and with it no small measure of celebrity. He indulged his love for whiskey, women, and late-night games of pinochle. None of that deterred Lyndon Johnson from adding him to the Court in 1967, declaring it "the right thing to do, the right time to do it, the right man, and the right place."

Once ensconced on the bench, Marshall proved to be a reliable liberal vote. Over the next quarter century, he voted repeatedly to overturn the death penalty and expand the notions of individual rights and civil liberties. He became such a close ally of the Court's liberal stalwart William Brennan that the clerks took to calling him "Mr. Justice Brennan-Marshall." Regarding his other colleagues, Marshall was most skeptical of Chief Justice Warren Burger, whom he called "an enigma." He had more respect for Burger's successor, William Rehnquist, even though they came from opposite sides of the political divide. "He has no problems, wishy-washy, back and forth," Marshall once observed. "He knows exactly what he wants to do, and that's very important as a chief justice."

Marshall resigned from the Court in June 1991, years after many had predicted (and some had hoped) he would step down. Worn out, bitter, and decrepit, he announced his departure in characteristically pungent fashion, saying, "I'm old and I'm coming apart." He died of heart failure eighteen months later in Washington D.C., at age eighty-four.

★ ★

THURGOOD MASON

Freemasons are thought of as an elite, secret society—not exactly the kind of outfit you'd expect one of America's foremost civil rights champions to join. And yet, Marshall was indeed a Mason, a member of an all-black branch founded in 1784 by an ex-slave named Prince Hall. Marshall was often seen wearing a gold ring bearing the gold numeral "33"—the mark of the highest Masonic degree, and throughout his career he received substantial financial support from American Freemasons. In 1954, Marshall received more than $12,000 from the Prince Hall Grand Lodges of Louisiana and Georgia. He admitted to interviewers that he could not have won his most important Supreme Court cases without Masonic backing. "Whenever and wherever I needed money and did not know of any other place to get it, the Prince Hall Masons never let me down," he said.

MERRY PRANKSTER

As a member of the elite Alpha Phi Alpha fraternity at Lincoln University, Marshall developed a reputation as a master of practical jokes. Some of his best pranks were the most revolting. **Once, a group of frat brothers exacted revenge on a rival from a competing fraternity who had doused them with water. At Marshall's urging, they filled a bucket with urine, saliva, and expectorated tobacco juice and dropped it through a trap door onto the offending party's head. "Bet it broke him of that habit of throwing water," cracked the future civil rights icon. On another occasion, Marshall devised a hazing scheme for freshman pledges that involved forcing them to run around the frat house with pickles wedged in their butt cheeks. Just when they thought the ordeal was over, the pledges would be presented with a punch bowl full of pickles (fresh ones, unbeknownst to them) and ordered to pick one out and eat it. "Everyone would say 'Can't I get my own pickle?'" a gleeful Marshall recalled afterward.**

THOU SHALT NOT SMOKE

A chain-smoker, Marshall was notorious for bumming cigarettes off passersby. On his way to an important NAACP meeting at a Baptist church in Atlanta at the height of the civil rights movement, Marshall seemed concerned less with the agenda and more with the church's no smoking policy. "The planning committee got together with Reverend Borders a while back," Marshall told a journalist traveling with him. "He said, 'I won't mind if you smoke.' We all looked real happy. And then he said, 'But God will mind—and it's his house.' You should've seen our faces fall. We were sad."

Drink to Me

Along with smoking and card-playing, Marshall loved to drink and did so at every opportunity. As a young lawyer, he kept a bottle of bourbon in his desk drawer, from which he would swig during late-night legal skull sessions. He continued to tipple well into his eighties. Once, when a journalist asked if he had a problem with alcohol, Marshall replied: "Hell, yes. Not enough! Not enough to go around!"

I WON'T HAVE WHAT HE'S HAVING

When he wasn't drinking his companions under the table, Marshall liked to disconcert them in restaurants by ordering unusual meals. Two of his favorites: fried beef bones, and raw steak surrounded by onions and capers and topped with a raw egg.

PRESIDENT, SHMESIDENT

Marshall wasn't exactly deferential when it came to dealing with the commander in chief. He liked John F. Kennedy and Lyndon B. Johnson but had little use for the other presidents who served during his Court tenure. Richard Nixon, he claimed, was eager to see him leave the bench. When Marshall was hospitalized with pneumonia in 1970, Nixon put in a request for his medical reports. From his sickbed, Marshall authorized the release, provided that the words "Not yet" be written across the bottom. Jimmy Carter also wanted Marshall to resign so that he could replace him with his solicitor general, Wade McCree, but he wouldn't deliver the message personally. "Carter and I stayed away from each other," Marshall recalled. Instead, the president sent emissaries with the bad news. "Fuck yourself!" was Marshall's reply, and the talk of retirement soon ended. Marshall thought even less of Carter's successor, Ronald Reagan, whom he credited with backsliding on civil rights. When the idea of Marshall succeeding Warren Burger as chief justice was floated, Marshall dismissed it. "I wouldn't do the job of dogcatcher for Ronald Reagan," he sniffed. He later instructed a clerk: "If I die while that man's president, I want you to just prop me up and keep me voting."

SOAP FLAKE

Apparently the cases that came before the Court didn't provide enough drama for Marshall. He was a soap opera junkie. In 1976, *Time* magazine reported that Marshall suspended deliberations every day at 1 p.m. so that he could hurry back to his chambers to watch *Days of Our Lives*.

WARREN
BURGER

September 17, 1907–June 25, 1995

BIRTHPLACE:

Saint Paul, MN

NICKNAME:

"The Admiral"

ASTROLOGICAL SIGN:

Virgo

TERM:

June 23, 1969–September 26, 1986

APPOINTED BY:

Richard Nixon

WORDS OF WISDOM:

"The notion that ordinary people want black-robed judges, well-dressed lawyers, and paneled court-rooms as the setting to resolve their disputes is not correct. People with problems, like people with pain, want relief, and they want it as quickly and as inexpensively as possible."

Warren Burger, wrote one Supreme Court historian, "looked as though he had been cast by Hollywood for the part of chief justice." Tall, broad-shouldered, and with a shock of snow-white hair that resembled one of the old-school judge's wigs he pined to wear, Burger had the perfect look to run the nation's highest court. Unfortunately, he had none of the people skills, judicial acumen, or strength of character. A blustering, imperious phony, Burger exasperated his colleagues and became an object of widespread mockery within the Court's own hallowed halls. The authors of one behind-the-scenes book about the Burger Court derided him as "a product of Richard Nixon's tasteless White House, distinguished in appearance and bearing, but without substance or integrity."

It didn't have to be that way. Warren Earl Burger came from good, solid Minnesota stock. His grandfather, Joseph Burger, was a Medal of Honor recipient

Warren Burger is one of the only justices who supported wearing traditional British judicial attire—including the powdered wig.

who joined the Union army at age fourteen and was wounded during the Civil War. Young Warren was born on Constitution Day, September 17, and showed a talent for drawing and sculpting. When he was fifteen years old, he created a bust of Benjamin Franklin that was later reproduced by the Franklin Mint and sold to benefit the Commission on the Bicentennial of the U.S. Constitution, which ex–Chief Justice Burger was then chairing.

After working his way through law school, Burger entered private practice in his native St. Paul. During the 1930s, he dived into Republican Party politics, helping to elect Harold Stassen as governor and making some powerful friends. In 1952, he played a pivotal role helping Dwight D. Eisenhower secure the GOP nomination. Ike returned the favor by giving Burger a job in his Justice Department. Working out of the Civil Division, Burger became an expert on maritime law, earning the nickname "The Admiral." He was elevated to a seat on the D.C. Court of Appeals in 1955.

In 1969, when the next Republican president, Richard Nixon, was casting about for a law-and-order man to take over as chief justice, Burger seemed the ideal pick. A stolid conservative with impeccable party credentials, he would represent a clean break from his liberal predecessor, Earl Warren. Fortunately, he was respected enough on both sides of the aisle that he won easy confirmation in the Senate.

The respect seemed to end there. Almost immediately, Burger began to alienate his new colleagues with his haughty, high-handed demeanor. Chief among their complaints was the slipshod way he ran their weekly conferences. Burger often showed up inadequately prepared; clerks reported that he seemed to be reading about the cases for the first time as he introduced them. When it came time to vote, he invariably refused to take a stand, revealing only that he was "inclined" to vote a certain way, then changing his mind later to vote with the majority. It was Burger's backhanded way of controlling who got to write which opinions—a practice known among the clerks as "phony voting." Burger once voted five different ways on the same case: twice in favor, twice against, and one "pass." One justice quipped that Burger's tombstone should read: "I think I'll pass for the moment."

In the most notorious example of phony voting, Burger joined the majority in the 1973 abortion decision in *Roe v. Wade* just to keep the opinion away from William O. Douglas, who, as senior justice, would have had priority. Douglas was an unabashed liberal, and Burger feared he would write an overly sweeping opinion. So he retained assignment privileges for himself and instead asked his old Minnesota chum Harry Blackmun to do the honors. Be careful what you wish for. Blackmun ended up writing an opinion every bit as sweeping as the one Douglas could have produced. The liberals had executed a perfect end run, circumventing their hapless chief.

They would continue doing so for the next thirteen years. Even though Burger's appointment was supposed to swing the Court back into a more conservative direction after years of judicial activism under Earl Warren, Burger's inept administration allowed ideological opponents to run rings around him. As a result, there would be no right-wing "counterrevolution"—at least not until William Rehnquist replaced Burger in 1986.

After retiring from the Court, Burger presided over the Constitutional bicentennial and attended to other ceremonial duties, for which he was much better suited. Yet, even in these endeavors he could not escape his own incompetence. No one paid attention to his bicentennial celebration, and his plan to house retired justices in a newly constructed Federal Judicial Center proved equally disastrous. None of the old justices wanted to go. When Burger died of congestive heart failure in 1995, he was remembered more for his overweening pomposity than for anything he had accomplished during his seventeen years on the high bench. Looking the part, it seems, will get you only so far.

★ ★

WIGGED OUT

Burger is one of the only justices in history to go on the record in favor of wearing traditional British judicial attire. He once declared that, as chief justice, he "should be in a wig and gown, and had been cheated out of it by Thomas Jefferson." He was referring to Jefferson's ardent opposition to the ceremonial hairpiece worn by royal jurists, best expressed in his plea to Justice William Cushing: "For heaven's sake, discard the monstrous wig which makes the English judges look like rats peeping through bunches of oakum!"

So why the wig fetish? Burger was an avowed Anglophile with a particular affection for British barristers, whom he considered to be more "civilized" than American lawyers.

CHEF JUSTICE

His name may have been Burger, but the chief justice's tastes were decidedly soignée. A pretentious gourmand, he reveled in life's finer things. He drank only the finest Bordeaux and was never happier than when he stumbled upon cases of a rare Château Lafite in a Washington D.C. wine shop. He developed his own recipe for cheddar cheese and had a small kitchen installed near his Supreme Court office, in which he would regularly whip up epicurean treats for his clerks and other distinguished guests.

HEAR YE, HEAR YE, HERE COMES A POMPOUS ASS!

A stickler for ceremony, Burger loved to point out that his official title was not Chief Justice of the Supreme Court, but Chief Justice of the *United States*. For a time he even instructed his valet to precede him into a room and herald his impending arrival by announcing, "Gentlemen, the Chief Justice of the United States!" ("You've got to be shitting me," blurted one astonished clerk the first time he witnessed this spectacle.)

On another occasion, William Rehnquist and some of his clerks were enjoying an informal picnic lunch in the Court's enclosed courtyard. Before long, Burger's valet arrived and set up a small table with silverware and a white linen tablecloth. Then the chief himself arrived, in a dinner jacket, and began pouring some wine. Rehnquist and the clerks collapsed with laughter and scurried back inside.

Pimp My Court

If he seemed ill at ease in the role of chief justice, perhaps interior decoration was Burger's true calling. He redesigned the Supreme Court cafeteria, even selecting the china and glassware, and had flowers planted in the courtyards and rubber plants placed in the hallways. He was the first chief justice to install computers and photocopiers in the Court building (the justices had previously relied on carbon paper).

Even the benches the justices sat on fell within his micromanaging purview. Dissatisfied with the conventional straight benches, Burger ordered them thrown away, to be replaced with a winged, half-hexagonal style that he preferred. When the Court carpenter informed him that a chair being prepared for incoming justice John Paul Stevens wouldn't be ready in time for his swearing-in, Burger decreed, "I have ruled that it will be done on time"—and so it was. As for his own bench, Burger had a large cushion placed on it so that he would appear taller than his colleagues. Not all of these self-aggrandizing design innovations were well received. In the early 1970s, some justices objected when Burger moved one of his personal desks into the Court conference room.

GAY AGENDA

Burger may have been the most homophobic justice in Supreme Court history. As an appeals court judge, he ruled in favor of the Civil Service in a case involving a Department of Labor employee who lost his job because he frequented a gay cruising spot in Lafayette Park. "Homosexual conduct warrants a disqualification from federal employment," Burger declared. In his opinions and private correspondence, he repeatedly compared gay sex to rape. As chief justice, he would only schedule the Court to consider a case involving homosexuality if he felt sure that the "gay rights" side would lose.

Burger's finest hour of judicial gay bashing may have come in the 1986 case of *Bowers v. Hardwick*, in which the Court upheld a Georgia law criminalizing sodomy. Terrified that the justices might rule narrowly for the gay plaintiff, Burger personally lobbied a wavering Lewis Powell to change his vote to overturn. In a private memo to Powell, he equated gay sex to incest, drug addiction, and exhibitionism and gay men to Jack the Ripper. He called the case the most important one in his thirty years on the bench and implied that Powell should vote his way as a kind of early retirement present.

The arm-twisting worked. Powell switched his vote and ruled in favor of the sodomy ban. A few weeks later, a gleeful Burger whipped up a bitingly hateful concurring opinion—one in a series of "little snappers," as he called them—in which he consigned homosexuals to the guillotine of history. After pointing with approval to the fact that gays were once executed under Roman law, he quoted the eighteenth-century legal scholar William Blackstone to the effect that sodomy was a "crime against nature . . . the very mention of which is a disgrace to human nature." "To hold that the act of homosexual sodomy is somehow protected as a fundamental right," Burger concluded, "would be to cast aside millennia of moral teaching."

Gun Crazy

Burger was nominated for the Court because of his strong law-and-order credentials. But there was one area of criminal law where he departed from right-wing orthodoxy: gun control. "If I were writing the Bill of Rights now, there wouldn't be any such thing as the Second Amendment," Burger told TV news correspondent Charlayne Hunter-Gault in a 1991 interview. The right-to-bear-arms clause, he continued, "has been the subject of one of the greatest pieces of fraud, I repeat the word *fraud*, on the American public by special-interest groups that I have ever seen in my lifetime." To the consternation of firearms enthusiasts everywhere, Burger went on to endorse even stricter weapons restrictions than even the most ardent gun control advocates were then proposing. "Someone asked me recently if I was for or against a bill that was pending in Congress calling for five days' waiting period. And I said, yes, I'm very much against it. It should be a *thirty*-day waiting period, so they find out why this person needs a handgun or a machine gun!"

PRESIDENT BURGER?

In his memoirs, President Richard Nixon revealed that he sounded out Burger about a potential run for president in 1972, if he were forced to eschew reelection due to political fallout from the 1970 invasion of Cambodia. As it turned out, Nixon was able to weather the controversy and didn't need the chief justice to replace him in the White House. About the same time, Nixon also put Burger on his short list of possible replacements for Vice President Spiro Agnew, should he be forced to resign in the face of bribery charges. In the end, he opted to go with Gerald Ford.

Mutiny on the SS Burger

His rare combination of imperiousness and ineptitude made Burger one of the most unpopular chief justices in history. Colleagues could barely contain their disdain. "On ocean liners, they used to have two captains," Justice Potter Stewart observed. "One for show, to take the women to dinner. The other to pilot the ship safely. [Burger] is the show captain. All we need now is a real captain." William O. Douglas refused to refer to Burger by the traditional honorific "The Chief," calling him "this chief" instead. William Rehnquist once said that Burger "gives the impression of a southern Senator conducting a filibuster." Lewis Powell, one of the most mild-mannered men ever to sit on the high bench, called Burger "the Great White Doughnut," according to one of his clerks, "because he had white hair and a bald spot in the middle, and it signified nothing inside." Journalists quickly got wind of the low esteem in which the chief was held and eagerly reported every last bit of sniping. The situation was so bad that the court's press officer kept a file of negative news clippings about Burger locked in a safe in his office.

BROTHER RAT

Burger's bad reputation reached a near-nuclear level with the publication of Bob Woodward and Scott Armstrong's book *The Brethren* in 1979. The tell-all best seller relied on interviews with unnamed law clerks—as well as, reportedly, sitting justice Potter Stewart—to paint a picture of Burger as a dithering, disorganized tyrant. It caused considerable embarrassment to the Court, such that the justices briefly contemplated taking action to suppress its dissemination. In the end, the free market was allowed to run its course. When informed that remaindered copies of the book were selling for ninety-eight cents in a Washington D.C. bookstore, Burger could barely contain his glee.

CUT UP

Burger's overweening pomposity made him the perfect target for an April Fool's Day joke—or so thought his junior colleague, William Rehnquist. In 1985, Rehnquist hired a photographer to pose outside the Supreme Court building with a life-size cutout of Burger and a sign reading "Have your picture taken with the chief justice, $1." He then made sure Burger drove with him to work that morning so he could watch his horrified reaction.

WORDPLAY

In an odd coincidence, transposing Burger's first and middle names—Warren and Earl—gives you the name of his predecessor, Earl Warren.

Harry
BLACKMUN

November 12, 1908–March 4, 1999

BIRTHPLACE:

Nashville, IL

NICKNAME:

"Old Number Three,"
"Hip Pocket Harry"

ASTROLOGICAL SIGN:

Scorpio

TERM:

June 9, 1970–August 3, 1994

APPOINTED BY:

Richard Nixon

WORDS OF WISDOM:

"What is the matter with me? I
seem to have absolutely no
courage, physically or mentally."

If you think women should have the right to a safe and legal abortion, you'll love Harry Blackmun. If you don't, you probably think he's the devil incarnate. The man who authored the landmark *Roe v. Wade* opinion in 1973 didn't want that to be his only legacy. He constantly reminded people that seven of the nine Supreme Court justices had voted with him. Still, Blackmun became the target of pro-life opprobrium. "Think of any name; I've been called it," Blackmun once remarked of the hate mail he received. Epithets included "butcher of Dachau," "Pontius Pilate," and "King Herod," to name a few. "You are the lowest scum on earth," wrote one detractor, who signed his missive "an American Patriot." It was quite an outpouring for the man whom fellow Minnesotan Garrison Keillor called "the shy person's justice."

In person, Blackmun was a diffident worrywart who agonized over his opinions and questioned his fitness to serve on the Court. On the mornings when major decisions were to be issued, he could often be seen on the steps of the Supreme Court building with his head in his hands, mulling it over. A plainspoken eccentric, Blackmun ate the same breakfast every day for decades—one egg, toast, and coffee—and drove the same blue Volkswagen Beetle he had first driven into Washington D.C. in 1970. Yet he could never escape the controversy generated by the sweeping decision that he came to realize he would carry with him to his grave.

Born in Illinois, Blackmun grew up in the Dayton's Bluff section of St. Paul, a blue-collar neighborhood where his father ran a small hardware and grocery store. He attended Harvard University on a scholarship and majored in mathematics, but he gave up the study of medicine to pursue a legal career. After graduating from Harvard Law School, he practiced law in Minnesota while raising a family with his wife, the former Dorothy Clark. His big break came in 1959, when he was named counsel for the Mayo Clinic, based in Rochester, Minnesota.

After a decade there, Blackmun was appointed to the U.S. Court of Appeals by President Dwight D. Eisenhower. He carved out a reliably conservative record, which caught the eye of Richard Nixon in 1970, as he was casting about for a successor to the disgraced Supreme Court justice Abe Fortas. Blackmun was in fact Nixon's third choice. ("Old Number Three," he liked to call himself.) But after Nixon's first two nominees went down in flames, Blackmun's childhood chum (and then chief justice) Warren Burger interceded on his behalf. Not that Blackmun was all that thrilled about his new gig. "The roof, indeed, has caved in upon my family and me," he kvetched after taking his place on the bench. If only he knew how bad it was going to get.

Blackmun took a pronounced left turn after just a couple years on the Court, infuriating his patron, Warren Burger, and setting the stage for the *Roe* apostasy. That decision cemented his public image as one of the Court's leading liberals, a role he played to the hilt in subsequent cases involving affirmative

An unpretentious man, Harry Blackmun delighted in shocking onlookers by arriving at official Washington D.C. functions in his bright blue Volkswagen beetle.

action, privacy rights, and criminal procedure. Blackmun even renounced his previous support of capital punishment, announcing grandly in a 1994 dissent that he would "no longer tinker with the machinery of death." When he stepped down from the bench later that year, he was lionized as an icon in liberal legal

circles, even as right-wingers toasted "Good riddance" to one of their longtime bêtes noires. Blackmun died on March 4, 1999, of complications following hip-replacement surgery. He was ninety years old.

THE TWINS

Blackmun was recommended for his seat on the Court by his close pal and fellow Minnesotan, Chief Justice Warren Burger. The two had grown up six blocks apart in St. Paul, attended grade school and Sunday school together, and competed against each other in softball and tennis. As teenagers, they double-dated and went to their high school proms together (each with his own date, one presumes). In 1933, Blackmun served as best man at Burger's wedding. The Chief repaid his friend's loyalty by endorsing his candidacy to President Richard Nixon in 1970. Assured that Blackmun would be a reliably conservative justice in Burger's image, Nixon went with his newly minted chief justice's recommendation.

It all worked out as planned—at first. During his early days on the Court, Blackmun voted so often with Burger that he earned the derisive nickname "Hip Pocket Harry" (as in "Burger's got Harry in his hip pocket"). Court watchers also referred to the two like-minded jurists as the "Minnesota Twins." But Blackmun broke with Burger on the issue of—surprise, surprise—abortion. Burger hoped to temper the Court's support for abortion rights by assigning Blackmun, rather than liberal firebrand William O. Douglas, to write the *Roe v. Wade* decision. Blackmun responded by holing himself up in the Mayo Clinic library, where he communed with the "emanations" and "penumbras" of privacy rights said to be oozing out of the Constitution. Egged on by the Court's liberals, Blackmun came to see the *Roe* decision as his big chance to separate himself from Burger and establish his own judicial legacy. He succeeded, but at considerable personal cost. He and Burger were never close again. In his diary, Blackmun recorded every detail of their increasingly frosty relationship. "CJ [Chief Justice] keeps yapping," he remarked of one conference during which the long-winded Burger droned on. "CJ picks on me at conference," he wrote on another occasion, indicating that his one-time mentor had now become something of a schoolyard bully. During their final years on the Court together, the two barely spoke. When Burger died in June 1995, Blackmun refused to attend the funeral. Instead he sent a check for $50 in Burger's memory to the Supreme Court Historical Society.

ORGAN GRINDER

Stricken with appendicitis at age fourteen, Blackmun developed a weird fascination with the disease, even writing a five-page essay on his experience. Entitled "My Illness—Appendicitis," it describes in excruciating detail the pains associated with the condition. Eleven years later, when Blackmun's sister came down with her own case, he became obsessed with *her* appendicitis. He went so far as to record in his diary the size, shape, and color of her surgically removed appendix. Every year, for the rest of his life, Blackmun "celebrated" the anniversary of his appendectomy—March 8— babbling on to friends, associates, and even Court colleagues like Sandra Day O'Connor about what he called the "curious experiment" that left him with a six-inch scar.

GRADE A

An inveterate note-taker, Blackmun occupied his mind during the often tedious arguments before the Court by assigning letter and number grades to the lawyers. He also recorded his own pithy comments about the attorneys' appearance and wardrobe. Assessments included "Licks fingers," "balding," and "hard of hearing." In the rare cases for which women argued before the Court, Blackmun invariably documented details about their attire. Of Ruth Bader Ginsburg, the ACLU attorney who would one day join him on the Court, he noted her red dress and ribbon and observed that she was "very precise."

Dear Diary

When he wasn't acting as chief of the fashion police, the anal-retentive Blackmun was recording every last detail of his own life in the running quasi-diary he called his "Chronology of Significant Events." To be accurate, it was anything but. The journal catalogs, in a terse, deadpan style, the daily goings-on during Blackmun's twenty-four years of service on the Court. The deaths of close friends and momentous historic events such as the fall of the Soviet Union receive the same concise treatment as his attendance at legal conferences and charity banquets. Separately, Blackmun kept extensive lists of every movie he saw, concert he attended, and book he read. He even saved receipts from the hotels he stayed at. It was a boon, perhaps, to biographers but also a window into the mind of one of the quirkiest men ever to sit on the Supreme Court.

LIGHTS . . . CAMERA . . . HARRY!

Long a celebrity in liberal judicial circles, Blackmun became a full-fledged movie star in 1997, when he accepted a role in director Steven Spielberg's epic film *Amistad*. The dramatic true story of a nineteenth-century slave ship mutiny and the ensuing legal battle, *Amistad* was nominated for four Academy Awards. Blackmun's role was a small but important one. He played—what else—a Supreme Court justice, Joseph Story, the crusty New England jurist who ruled in favor of the captured Africans. Blackmun's daughter and grandson also appeared in the film, for which the retired justice was paid $540 a day. It is the first and only time a Supreme Court justice has ever played another Supreme Court justice in a major motion picture.

Buggin' Out

A truly unpretentious man, Blackmun delighted in shocking onlookers by arriving at official Washington D.C. functions in his bright blue Volkswagen Beetle. He even ensured that the tradition continued after his death. At his funeral procession in 1994, Blackmun's cremains were carried to Arlington National Cemetery in a container set on the front seat of his Beetle—the only blue bug in a long line of dark limousines.

LEWIS
POWELL

September 19, 1907–
August 25, 1998

D rawn and gaunt, with the courtly manners of the Virginia aristocracy into which he was born, Lewis Powell looked like a kindly country pharmacist from the 1930s—the kind of benevolent coot you'd expect to see dispensing hair tonic and Bromo seltzer in the background of a Frank Capra movie. That's the way he lived and judged as well: with great caution, steady moderation, and impeccable decorum. No wonder the other justices loved him. He was like everybody's idealized grandfather.

Maybe it's in the blood. Powell's was pedigreed Virginia royalty. His father was a descendant of Nathaniel Powell, one of the original settlers of Jamestown and once acting governor of the colony. His mother, Mary Lewis Gwathmey, was raised by an uncle who had served under Gen. Robert E. Lee and been present for the Confederate surrender at Appomattox. The family's fortunes had declined *somewhat* over the years—Powell's dad worked as a manager in a corrugated box factory in Richmond—but there was no denying that young Lewis started life with all the advantages necessary for success.

A prep-school product, he attended Washington and Lee University and graduated first in his class from its law school. He went on to earn a degree from Harvard Law School, where one of his teachers was future Supreme Court justice Felix Frankfurter. In 1936, he married Josephine Pierce Rucker, the daughter of a prominent Richmond obstetrician. They had met several years earlier, but Powell became impressed only after learning that she owned the broad jumping record at Sweet Briar College: an astounding 22 feet.

During World War II, Powell worked as a decoder for the top-secret military intelligence unit known as Special Branch. When he wasn't busy trying to crack encrypted German communications, he presented daily intelligence briefings to Supreme Allied Commander Dwight Eisenhower. Powell also met Alan Turing, the flamboyantly gay cryptographer and mathematician now considered the father of modern computer science. Turing's homosexuality would later become a cause célèbre in his native Britain (and eventually led to his suicide in 1954), calling into question Powell's oft-quoted assertion that he had never met a gay person.

> Lewis Powell once remarked, "I don't believe I've ever met a homosexual," even though his office was reportedly full of gay male law clerks.

After the war, Powell spent more than twenty-five years in private practice, mostly in the arena of corporate mergers and acquisitions. One of his formative experiences involved a nineteen-year-old messenger for his firm who faced possible murder charges after helping his girlfriend arrange an abortion. Always eager to help, Powell got the man off the hook with the police—and would remember the incident years later when he cast one of the critical votes in the Supreme Court abortion decision in Roe v. Wade.

Powell was in his mid-sixties when President Richard Nixon approached him about taking a seat on the Supreme Court. He was making a killing in private practice, served on numerous prestigious boards, and was president of the American Bar Association. He also thought he was too old for the job. But a persistent Nixon prevailed upon his sense of patriotic duty and, on the third try, convinced Powell to accept the nomination. The Senate quickly confirmed him in December 1971.

Powell wasn't exactly thrilled by the appointment. "The truth is that I'd

rather be a lawyer than a judge," he told friends. "I really prefer to be competitive rather than neutral, detached, and disinterested." His wife, Josephine, was even less sanguine. At the swearing-in ceremony, when William Rehnquist's wife, Nan, asked if this was the most exciting day of her life, she replied, "No, it is the worst day of my life. I am about to cry."

Maybe she had gotten a look at her husband's pay stub. During his time on the Court, Powell constantly groused about the low compensation and the heavy workload. The sixty-hour-week schedule was "considerably more than my chargeable hours ever were at the peak of a large and demanding law practice." Nevertheless, Powell went about his judicial duties with characteristic good humor. Though a bit of a dinosaur in terms of social attitudes, he was known to be one of the more polite men ever to serve on the high bench. His jurisprudence, like his personality, was modest and restrained. He toed a moderate conservative line on most issues—most famously in the 1978 case of *Regents of the University of California v. Bakke*, in which he cast the deciding vote to curtail, but not eliminate, the use of racial quotas in university admissions.

The Supreme Court's historical roster is filled with individuals whose bad temper and poor manners are legendary—Felix Frankfurter and James McReynolds jump to mind—but Lewis Powell was that rare justice about whom few people could say a bad word. It was ironic then, that his retirement in 1987 precipitated one of the most acrimonious confirmation battles in American judicial history, as first Robert Bork and then Douglas Ginsburg went down in flames trying to fill Powell's comfortable, sensible shoes.

★ ★

HERE COME THE JUDGE

Journalism icon Edward R. Murrow was one of Powell's closest friends. They first met in 1930, at a student leadership conference in Palo Alto, California. Later that year they shared a stateroom on a cruise ship across the Atlantic to attend a similar confab in Brussels, Belgium. With uncanny prescience, Murrow christened the twenty-two-year-old Powell with what would become his lifelong nickname: "Judge."

Watch Your Language!

Powell's other nickname, "Great Heaven Above," was given to him by his fly-boy chums in the 319th Bombardment Group during World War II. "Great Heaven Above" was apparently the most colorful exclamation the demure Virginian ever issued. In fact, Powell was such a prude, he never uttered *any* profanity. When he needed to include the word "hell" in a letter, he simply wrote the letter "h" followed by a long blank space. Later, when he took his seat on the Supreme Court, Powell faced the daunting prospect of opining on a case involving a radical group called Up Against the Wall, Motherfucker. When writing about the case, he substituted the notation "Motherf———" wherever the offending word appeared.

DID YOU GET THE MEMO?

Today, the name Lewis Powell is synonymous with moderation and judicial restraint. But the cautious jurist may have won his place on the high court in part due to his authorship of an intemperate right-wing screed. In August 1971, Powell penned a memorandum to his friend Eugene Sydnor Jr., an official at the U.S. Chamber of Commerce. In it, he drew the battle lines in what he saw as an ongoing cultural war against the U.S. free enterprise system, issuing a dark, Orwellian vision of a counterattack by corporate America.

"The American economic system is under broad attack," Powell wrote. This assault came not only from the usual suspects—"the Communists, New Leftists, and other revolutionaries"—but also from "perfectly respectable elements of society . . . the college campus, the pulpit, the media, the intellectual and literary journals, the arts and sciences, and from politicians." Using textbooks and TV shows as their weapons, Powell argued, these dangerous radicals sought to undermine the public's faith in the beneficence of big business.

To combat this menace, Powell issued a charge to U.S. businessmen to "fight back" with a sustained public relations offensive. He also called on the U.S. Chamber of Commerce to serve as a watchdog on the media and the educational establishment, looking for signs of anticapitalist bias. "The national television networks should be monitored in the same way that textbooks should be kept under constant surveillance," Powell suggested. He went on to decry what he saw as the repugnant content-cramming the nation's bookshelves. "The newsstands—at airports, drug-stores, and elsewhere—are filled with paperbacks and pamphlets advo-cating everything from revolution to erotic free love," the aged lawyer warned. Unless an effort was made to counter this propaganda onslaught with more wholesome fare, an "opportunity for educating the public will be irretrievably lost."

The so-called Powell Memo proved to be a big hit in the Nixon admin-istration. Two months later, President Nixon—who had run his 1968 cam-paign on similar anti-elitist themes—nominated Powell for a seat on the Supreme Court. The memo also inspired the creation of many right-wing think tanks, including the Heritage Foundation, the Manhattan Institute, and Citizens for a Sound Economy—organizations that would carry on Powell's call to arms over the ensuing decades.

Queer Studies

The epitome of bland, respectable corporate conservatism, Powell did stand out from the other justices in one most unlikely way: his penchant for hiring gay law clerks. In fact, during the 1980s, it was hard to find a clerk in Powell's office who *wasn't* gay. In 1985, one of them was even rumored to be having an affair with a Reagan administration attorney. The next year, when a case involving gay sex came before the Court, Powell decided to use his unusual hiring practices to his advantage. He approached Cabel Chinnis, a gay clerk, for insight into the "homosexual lifestyle." Told that gay men and lesbians might constitute as much as 10 percent of the U.S. population, Powell was flabbergasted. "I don't believe I've ever met a homosexual," he admitted, which surely would have been news to his human resources director. "I was surprised by that remark," Chinnis later remarked. "[It] just struck me as the kind of thing a grandmother would say." Powell then dug an even deeper hole for himself, quizzing the mortified clerk about why gay men don't simply have sex with women. When Chinnis bluntly informed Powell that a gay man likely could not maintain an erection with a female partner, the elderly jurist's circuit board nearly melted. Unable to grasp the concept that a man could be aroused by another man, he was reduced to a stammering husk. Another clerk, eavesdropping from a neighboring office, felt her jaw drop to her desk. "What struck me," she recalled, "is that the concept of homosexuality had no content for him. He had no frame of reference." Little wonder, then, that despite his best efforts to educate himself about the issue, Powell found against the gay plaintiff in the case. Sodomy, he opined in a memo outlining his thinking on the matter, threatens to destroy civilization itself, "as the perpetuation of the human race depends on normal sexual relations, just as is true in the animal world."

BUDWEISER AND SKIPPY

Like most Supreme Court justices, Powell had his quirks. Though he barely spoke above a whisper, he loathed writing and spent hours speaking his memoranda into a Dictaphone. During lunch hours, he would often head into the Supreme Court courtyard for his favorite snack: peanut butter on crackers, washed down with half a bottle of beer, which he swigged out of a paper bag.

Regrets . . . He Had a Few

Powell never hid that he wished he'd never given up his law practice for a seat on the high court. One day while having lunch with Larry Brown, the star running back for the Washington Redskins, Brown asked him which he preferred: being a lawyer or being a judge. For Powell, the answer was obvious. "Would you rather be a player or a referee?" he replied.

MY BAD!

Powell was a notorious flip-flopper who often regretted the votes he cast after he could no longer do anything about them. Of his decision to vote with the 5–4 majority in *Bowers v. Hardwick*, to uphold the criminalization of consensual anal sex, Powell admitted in a 1990 interview that he had originally voted the other way but changed his mind at the last minute. "I think I made a mistake in the Hardwick case," he conceded. The dissenters "had the better of the arguments." D'oh!

The death penalty was another issue about which Powell belatedly changed his mind. "I have come to think that capital punishment should be abolished," he declared in 1991, four years after he left the Court, having cast many deciding votes to uphold the constitutionality of executions. To which the thousands of retarded, indigent, and unjustly executed Americans could only say: "Thanks, pal."

WILLIAM
REHNQUIST

October 1, 1924–
September 3, 2005

BIRTHPLACE:

Milwaukee, WI

NICKNAME:

"The Lone Ranger"

ASTROLOGICAL SIGN:

Libra

TERM:

January 7, 1972–
September 3, 2005

APPOINTED BY:

Richard Nixon

WORDS OF WISDOM:

"In the long run, it is the majority who will determine what the constitutional rights of the minority are."

"Who the hell is that clown?" President Richard M. Nixon asked White House counsel John Dean after meeting William Rehnquist for the first time. It was July 1971—a low point in the history of men's fashion—but assistant attorney general Rehnquist's attire was appalling even by the standards of the day: loud pink shirt, Hush Puppies, and a garish psychedelic tie. "Is he Jewish?" Nixon mused. "He looks it. That's a hell of a costume he's wearing, just like a clown." Six months later, Nixon would nominate "that clown" for a seat on the U.S. Supreme Court. Rehnquist would remain there, his fashion sense scarcely improving, for the next thirty-three years. A right-wing revolutionary in Gilbert and Sullivan–inspired robes, he brought theatrical flair to the cause of strict constructionism.

William Hubbs Rehnquist grew up in the suburbs of Milwaukee, where his father sold paper wholesale and his mother worked as a translator for local export businesses. The product of a rock-ribbed Republican family, the young Rehnquist set his sights on a career in government. When his elementary school teacher asked what he wanted to do when he grew up, he replied, "I'm going to change the world." Before he could do that, though, he had to find his path. He dropped out of college after one quarter because he didn't find it intellectually challenging enough, then spent three years working during World War II as a weather observer for the Army Air Corps in Egypt and Morocco. Apparently the climate suited him. "I wanted to find someplace like North Africa to go to school," he recalled. That place turned out to be Stanford, where he enrolled on the GI Bill. (The absence of marauding panzer divisions might have been part of the draw as well.)

When William Rehnquist checked himself into a hospital for "back pain" in 1981, he was experiencing severe hallucinations brought on by an addiction to sedatives.

After graduating at the top of his class from Stanford Law School in 1952 (and briefly dating Sandra Day O'Connor; see page 213), Rehnquist clerked at the Supreme Court for Justice Robert Jackson. Always seeking sunnier climes, he relocated to Phoenix in 1953, joined a local law firm, and struck up a sideline as a right-wing gadfly. In 1957, he wrote an article for *U.S. News & World Report* decrying the influence of liberal Supreme Court clerks on the Warren Court, with their "extreme solicitude for the claims of Communists" and other undesirables. During the 1964 presidential campaign, he wrote speeches for Republican candidate (and fellow Arizonan) Barry Goldwater. That same year, he spoke out in opposition to the Phoenix city council's proposed public accommodations law, arguing that it would interfere with "the historic right of the owner of a drug store, lunch counter, or theater to choose his own customers"—that is, to refuse to serve black people.

All this agitprop endeared Rehnquist to influential conservatives in the Republican Party. When the GOP returned to power under Richard Nixon in 1969, Rehnquist was rewarded with the plum job of assistant attorney and head of the Office of Legal Counsel. In this job, he was constantly in the president's ear and managed to win Nixon's confidence, despite his muttonchop sideburns and ghastly taste in ties. In 1971, when Nixon was casting about for a Supreme Court appointee to replace the departing John Marshall Harlan, he tapped Rehnquist. It was a surprising, and somewhat controversial, choice.

Democrats groused about his dismal record on civil rights. Nevertheless, after a spirited debate in the Senate, Rehnquist was confirmed by a vote of 68–26.

Arriving at the Court, Rehnquist admitted feeling "like I'd entered a monastery." It took him a year or two to get his sea legs, and even then he often found himself swimming against the ideological tide. *Newsweek* dubbed him "The Court's Mr. Right"; the *New York Times* called him "the Court's most predictable conservative member." But those designations meant little if he was unable to persuade the Court's liberal majority to vote with him. During his early years, he dissented so many times, and so often by himself, that his clerks gave him a Lone Ranger doll as a gift.

By the end of the decade, however, the tide had turned. Ronald Reagan's election in 1980 ushered in a golden age of American conservatism, and Rehnquist was ideally situated to lead its judicial auxiliary. In 1986, Reagan nominated him as chief justice, to replace the retiring Warren Burger. Once again, the confirmation hearings were bruising, with Democratic senators raising the issues of Rehnquist's erstwhile opposition to school desegregation and allegations that he had harassed black voters while working as a Republican Party official in Phoenix. Rehnquist's nomination prevailed by a less than overwhelming 65–33 vote.

As chief justice, Rehnquist managed to earn the respect of his colleagues, no matter what their political persuasion. He toed a strict conservative line in his votes, but he allowed every justice to have a say, and he ran the Court's conferences smoothly and efficiently. Substantively and stylistically, he was seen as a breath of fresh air when compared with is dour, pompous predecessor. Having long since toned down his hideous '70s wardrobe, Rehnquist allowed his natural eccentricities to come to the fore. He displayed an impish sense of humor and a fondness for trivia, often starting his morning meeting by asking clerks to name the five largest U.S. states in order of surface area. While sitting on the bench, he and Justice Harry Blackmun would pass Trivial Pursuit questions back and forth on notepaper. A devotee of musical theater, Rehnquist loved to lead the Court in sing-a-longs, using a conductor's baton given to him by one of his clerks. Occasionally, his flair for frivolity got him in trouble. He famously warbled a few choruses of "Dixie," the Confederate marching song, at a federal judicial conference, angering the African American judges in the audience. And his hostility to homosexuality was deep rooted. He repeatedly compared gays to measles patients and suggested they should be quarantined.

For all his eccentricities, Rehnquist is widely regarded as an effective chief justice. Even if he failed in remaking the Court along conservative lines, as he'd intended, at least he returned some of the popular cachet that had been lacking in the grim Burger years. What would the impeachment trial of Bill Clinton have been like, for instance, without the sight of Rehnquist morbidly presiding over the festivities in a bespoke robe inspired by a Gilbert and Sullivan operetta? When Rehnquist died in September 2005, after a long battle with thyroid cancer, eight of his former law clerks—including his eventual successor, John Roberts—served as pallbearers, a testament to the high regard in which he was held by the extended Court family.

GET ME BILL RENSLER!

President Nixon eventually came to understand that Rehnquist was not Jewish, as he'd originally suspected, but he never quite mastered his assistant attorney general's name. Nearly a month after being introduced, Nixon was still calling Rehnquist "Renchburg." Several months later—and less than three weeks before nominating him for the Supreme Court—he referred to him as "Bill Rensler" several times during a telephone conversation with Senator Barry Goldwater. (To his credit, Nixon did mention that "Rensler" was "an excellent man.")

Reindeer Games

Perhaps someone in the White House could have provided President Nixon with a mnemonic. Rehnquist is the grandson of Swedish immigrants. In Swedish, his surname translates as "reindeer twig."

A DIP IN THE POOL

Not since Felix Frankfurter had such a world-class gambler sat on the Supreme Court. Rehnquist had a special fondness for betting pools. Every year without fail he ran the Court pools on NFL football, the NCAA basketball tournament, and the Kentucky Derby, and every four years he arranged a pool on the U.S. presidential election. During President Bill Clinton's impeachment trial in 1998, he even ducked away from the proceedings periodically to take part in an impromptu poker game with his law clerks in the Senate cloakroom.

Pill Popper

On the list of qualities one might want to see in a Supreme Court justice, "addicted to sedatives" and "prone to hallucinations" would probably fall somewhere near the bottom. Yet, for the better part of a decade, Rehnquist gulped down enormous quantities of a powerful drug that reportedly made him see and hear things that weren't there. Only the intervention of some conscientious doctors saved America from having its highest court presided over by a stark raving loon.

The trouble started in 1971, when Rehnquist went to see Congressional physician Dr. Freeman H. Cary about his chronic back pain. Cary prescribed Placidyl, a potent sedative-hypnotic developed to help people suffering from insomnia. The drug worked—all too well. By 1977, according to a 1986 medical report, Rehnquist was addicted to the stuff, and he remained so for the next four years. He was known to consume three month's worth of Placidyl in one month's time, then return to Cary to refill his prescription. He was also, by his own admission, popping four Valiums a day. By the end of 1981, the then associate justice was showing some serious side effects. He slurred his way through speeches, stumbled over hard-to-pronounce words, and routinely lost his train of thought. That December, he checked himself into George Washington University Hospital, ostensibly for back pain but ultimately for a little forced detoxification. According to the hospital's official records, Rehnquist was pretty much bouncing off the walls the whole time. A nurse noted that Rehnquist told her he could hear "voices outside the room . . .

saying they're going to kill the president." At one point, a doctor told investigators, the justice went "to the lobby in his pajamas in order to try to escape." On another occasion he bolted from his room in horror, screaming, "There is gas coming out of the radiator!" Hospital security nabbed him before he could get on the elevator and escorted him back to his bed. In the end, doctors determined that Rehnquist's withdrawal symptoms were so severe that they started giving him the drug again. They then slowly weaned him until he stopped taking it entirely by early February 1982.

LET THERE BE LITE

Once Rehnquist conquered his Placidyl habit, he returned to less mind-altering vices—and practiced them in moderation. He smoked precisely two cigarettes a day—one in the morning while opening his mail and one in the afternoon with his lunch. A man of fixed routines, he invariably ordered the same thing every day: a cheeseburger and a light beer, which he referred to (incorrectly) as a "Miller's Lite."

AT LEAST HE DIDN'T DRESS LIKE BUTTERCUP

As if President Bill Clinton's 1998 impeachment trial weren't surreal enough, Rehnquist had to add his own antic touch. Inspired by a costume he saw worn by the Lord Chancellor in a local Washington D.C. performance of Gilbert and Sullivan's *Iolanthe*, he decided to outfit himself for his role as presiding judge by donning a black robe with four gold stripes on each sleeve. "We thought it was a joke," said Justice Sandra Day O'Connor after Rehnquist first showed up wearing the comic opera get-up. But Rehnquist was all too serious. A huge Gilbert and Sullivan fan, he drew inspiration from the whimsical composers throughout the impeachment experience. Three years later, in an interview for PBS, he even quoted from *Iolanthe* when assessing his own part in the spectacle: "I did nothing in particular, and I did it very well."

THROW THE BOOK AT HIM!

Rehnquist was the perfect person to preside over Bill Clinton's impeachment trial—and not just because he knew how to dress for the occasion. As the author of the 1992 tome *Grand Inquests: The Historic Impeachments of Justice Samuel Chase and President Andrew Johnson*, he was one of the world's foremost experts on the subject.

No Friend of Bill

Rehnquist's problems with Bill Clinton began long before the impeachment trial. At Clinton's second inaugural, the chief justice stunned the reelected president by concluding the swearing-in ceremony with the cryptic warning, "Good luck. You're gonna need it." When rumors circulated that Clinton was thinking of naming his wife Hillary to be attorney general, Rehnquist could barely contain his glee. "They say Caligula appointed his horse consul of Rome," he joked.

PULLING RANK

Like his predecessor Warren Burger, Rehnquist was a bit of a stickler for ceremony. He often snapped at lawyers who addressed him as "Justice Rehnquist." "That's *Chief* Justice!" he bellowed.

HE GOT GAME

Warren Burger may have liked to treat his clerks to gourmet lunches and glasses of fine Bordeaux, but Rehnquist had decidedly more plebeian tastes. Basketball was his game, and he was known for challenging his clerks to fiercely contested pick-up games in the Supreme Court building's top-floor gymnasium, known informally as "the highest court in the land." He was also responsible for the acquisition of an official Court ping-pong table. However, some of Rehnquist's other proposed democratic innovations, like opening the justice's dining area to clerks, were overruled by his colleagues.

TOO MUCH INFORMATION

Rehnquist once admitted to a clerk that he had been "pretty lousy about flossing my teeth," having made his dentist a wealthy man as a consequence.

Party On!

An unrepentant party animal, Rehnquist savored every opportunity to get together with fellow justices for a little tippling and light entertainment. The Court's annual Christmas party was an especially raucous affair, during which Rehnquist invariably indulged his love of musical comedy. In 1975, he and one of his clerks composed an entire light opera from parody Christmas carols. The standout number, sung to the tune of "Angels from the Realms of Glory," mocked the Court's liberal majority for its continued support of the rights of criminal suspects as set forth in *Miranda v. Arizona*: "Liberals from the realm of theory should adorn our highest bench / Though to crooks they're always chary / at police misdeeds they blench." The chorus then dropped to its knees and sang "Save *Miranda*, save *Miranda*, save it from the Nixon Four"—the four justices, including Rehnquist, appointed by former president Richard Nixon. Some years later, at another Rehnquist-hosted affair, the chief justice mesmerized guests by acting out the film *All Quiet on the Western Front* during a spirited game of charades. His histrionics included crawling under the coffee table, pantomiming rifle fire with his fingers, and mouthing the sound of gunshots.

Strange Justice: Eight of the Most Unusual Supreme Court Cases

RADICH V. NEW YORK (1971)

American flag shaped like a phallus, anyone? The justices consider the case of Stephen Radich, a New York City art-gallery owner convicted of "casting contempt on the American flag" for sponsoring an art exhibit in which Old Glory was depicted in several provocative ways, including being shaped into a penis and affixed to a seven-foot cross topped by a bishop's miter. The Court's 4–4 vote (Justice William O. Douglas abstained) fails to clarify the matter, and Radich's conviction is later overturned by a federal judge.

COHEN V. CALIFORNIA (1971)

The year 1971 proves to be a banner one for weird cases, as the Court takes on the appeal of Paul Robert Cohen, a California teenager arrested and convicted of disturbing the peace after striding through a municipal court building in Los Angeles wearing a jacket that bore the legend "Fuck the Draft," in a protest against the Vietnam War. "There were women and children present in the corridor," noted the lower court that originally rejected Cohen's appeal. By a vote of 5–4, the Supreme Court overturns Cohen's conviction, reaffirming the principle that offensive speech isn't in and of itself a criminal offense. In a blistering dissent, Justice Harry Blackmun calls Cohen's protest an "absurd and immature antic," which could be construed as an incitement to violence.

SIERRA CLUB V. MORTON (1972)

In perhaps the loopiest opinion since the Court ruled that African Americans are not people in *Dred Scott v. Sanford*, Justice William O. Douglas uses his dissent in an environmental protection case to advance his contention that inanimate objects ought to be able to file suit in federal courts. Specifically, Douglas asserts the right of "valleys, alpine meadows, rivers, lakes, estuaries, beaches, ridges, groves of trees, swampland, or even air" to take developers to court to block their impending destruction. "The voice of the inanimate object . . . should not be stilled," Douglas bellows from the bench. No other justices join in his opinion.

HUSTLER MAGAZINE V. FALWELL (1988)

In a case depicted in the 1996 film *The People Vs. Larry Flynt*, the rotund, wheel-chair-bound pornographer rolls into the highest court in the land to challenge his libel conviction for a *Hustler* magazine ad parody in which the Reverend Jerry Falwell "talks about" an incestuous sexual encounter with his mother inside an outhouse. Lower courts had found in favor of Falwell, but the Supreme Court rules unanimously that *Hustler*'s parody is protected under the First Amendment.

BARNES V. GLEN THEATRE (1991)

Lap dancing is not an activity you would expect to have grand Constitutional implications, but the Court has taken up the issue *twice*. In the 1991 decision in *Barnes v. Glen Theatre*, the justices ruled that state governments have the authority to regulate nude dancing. The case involved a South Bend, Indiana, strip club called The Kitty Kat Lounge that wished to allow its female "entertainers" to perform without the encumbrance of g-strings and pasties, as mandated by state law. "Nudity itself is not inherently expressive conduct," Justice David Souter wrote for the majority. Nine years later, the justices gathered 'round the stripper pole once again for the case of *City of Erie v. Pap's A.M.* This time, the proprietors of an Erie, Pennsylvania, adult establishment named Kandyland cleverly argued that their nude dancers were being unfairly discriminated against while the actors in a nearby production of the play *Equus*, which featured full-frontal male nudity, were allowed to disrobe without interference. Once again, the Court sided with municipal authorities and upheld the constitutionality of Erie's pasty requirement.

MOSELEY V. V SECRET CATALOGUE, INC. (2003)

Lest people think the Supremes only take cases involving hard core photography, they hear the plea of lingerie retailer Victoria's Secret, which sues for trademark infringement against the "adult specialty store" Victor's Little Secret. In a unanimous decision, the justices rule that Victoria's Secret must provide proof that Victor's Little Secret's purveyance of sex toys actually damaged the company's reputation before it can recoup any damages.

MARSHALL V. MARSHALL (2006)

In a case that brought tabloid trash culture into the hallowed halls of the Supreme Court, Vickie Lynn Marshall (aka Anna Nicole Smith) brings her claim against the estate of her late oil tycoon husband, J. Howard Marshall, before the justices. Although the Court chooses not to rule on the merits of her claim, they do rule in her favor, unanimously, that she can continue her fight in a lower court. Sadly, her death by overdose the next year rules out a return appearance before the robed eminences in Washington D.C.

MORSE V. FREDERICK (2007)

In the so-called BONG HiTS 4 JESUS case, an Alaska high school student brings a civil rights lawsuit against his school board after he is suspended for unfolding a banner bearing that message at a school-sponsored outing to watch the Olympic torch pass by. The school board argues that encouraging people to do bong hits in the name of the redeemer violates the school's antidrug policy—and the Supreme Court buys it. A five-vote majority rules that the student's free speech rights were not unfairly abridged.

JOHN PAUL
STEVENS

April 20, 1920–

BIRTHPLACE:

Chicago, IL

NICKNAME:

"The FedEx Justice,"
"Wild Card"

ASTROLOGICAL SIGN:

Taurus

TERM:

December 19, 1975–

APPOINTED BY:

Gerald Ford

WORDS OF WISDOM:

"Few of us would march our
sons and daughters off to war
to preserve the citizen's right
to see 'Specified Sexual
Activities' exhibited in the
theaters of our choice."

Not since King Lear has an elderly man's health been as intensely scrutinized as that of John Paul Stevens. In 2008, he became the second-oldest person ever to sit on the Supreme Court. Because his departure would tilt the Court's ideological balance, partisans on both sides of the political spectrum feverishly anticipated his every move. As a Republican justice whose voting record trended leftward from the day he arrived on the bench, the unassuming, bow-tied Midwesterner became a favorite target of conservatives. "We need somebody to put rat poison in Justice Stevens's crème brûlée," declared the right-wing firebrand Ann Coulter in 2006. After conservative Samuel Alito replaced moderate Sandra Day O'Connor in 2005, the liberal radio network Air America started playing the parody "Hang on Stevens"—to the tune of the of the 1960s pop hit "Hang on Sloopy"—in a desperate attempt to keep the octogenarian justice from kicking the bucket.

A long time ago—a *very* long time ago—John Paul Stevens was a young man. He was born into a wealthy Chicago family on April 20, 1920. His grandfather, J. W. Stevens, had made the family fortune as founder of the Illinois Life Insurance Company. His father, a hotelier, built the Stevens Hotel, now the

Hilton Chicago, one of the city's largest and swankiest. The palatial building took up an entire block and featured three thousand guest rooms, a rooftop golf course, a barbershop, a movie theater, and an in-house ice cream factory. As children, Stevens and his brothers posed as models for the bronze sculptures that greeted guests in the hotel's grand hall. Visitors constituted a veritable who's who of Jazz Age society; Babe Ruth stayed there, as did Amelia Earhart. Charles Lindbergh dropped by after returning from his transatlantic flight to Paris and presented seven-year-old John Paul Stevens with a pet dove named Lindy.

> While his colleagues freeze in Washington D.C., John Paul Stevens prefers to dictate his opinions from a condo in sunny Florida.

The good times ended abruptly with the Great Depression. In 1934, the Stevens Hotel went bust, and Stevens's father was found guilty of embezzling $1.3 million to pay off his mounting debts. ("A totally unjust conviction," John Paul maintains to this day.) With no family sinecure to fall back on, Stevens considered a career in teaching. Then, caught up in the patriotic fervor that accompanied the outbreak of war in Europe, he enlisted in the Navy on December 6, 1941—just hours before the Japanese attack on Pearl Harbor. He saw no action but worked as an intelligence officer in Washington D.C., helping break the code that led to the shoot-down of a plane carrying Japanese admiral Isoroku Yamamoto, the mastermind of the Pearl Harbor attack. For his efforts, Stevens was awarded the Bronze Star.

After the war, Stevens attended Northwestern University Law School, graduating in 1947 with the highest grades in school history. He clerked for Supreme Court justice Wiley Rutledge, then returned to Chicago to enter private practice. His successful prosecution of a public corruption case in 1969 attracted the attention of the new U.S. president, Richard Nixon, who appointed Stevens to the U.S. Court of Appeals in 1970. In one of the more noteworthy rulings during his tenure on the federal bench, Stevens wrote the

majority opinion in the infamous "Seven Dirty Words" case involving comedian George Carlin. His ruling upheld the right of the FCC to punish radio stations for airing so-called indecent speech over public airwaves.

When in 1975 President Gerald Ford was searching for an inoffensive moderate to replace the departing William O. Douglas on the Supreme Court, he could not have found a better nominee than Stevens. Unquestionably qualified, he was universally respected on both sides of the aisle and cruised to Senate confirmation, 98–0. Once ensconced on the high bench, Stevens proved to be an independent-minded pragmatist. He voted to reinstate capital punishment and against affirmative action in college admissions, but sided with his liberal colleagues on issues such as abortion rights, gay rights, and federalism. By the turn of the millennium, the political ground had shifted far enough to the right so that Stevens was now widely considered one of the Court's most liberal justices—hence the heated proxy war over the exact nature and timing of his departure.

★ ★

I WILL SQUASH YOU

Before settling on a legal career, Stevens was one of the nation's top squash players.

TIE ONE ON

Stevens has a thing for bow ties—silk bow ties, to be precise. He wears them underneath his robes at all times and is so obsessed he often mentions them in his opinions. Once, during his days in private practice, an opposing attorney suggested to the court that lawyers in clip-on bow ties could not be trusted. Stevens quietly rose from his seat and untied his tie for all to see, then retied it and sat back down.

POISON PEN

Although Stevens is known to be charming and warm hearted in person, a caustic and occasionally nasty streak courses through his Supreme Court opinion writing. In the 1970s, he gained a reputation for writing dissents ridiculing other justices' reasoning. He sometimes derided the majority for advocating criminal procedures more appropriate to the Soviet Union or Nazi Germany than the United States. Stevens also developed an irritating habit of quoting himself in his opinions. Often he would reprint passages from his own previous opinions (sometimes even from a lower court), to prove to his colleagues that he had been right all along.

I'll Fly Away

He's left his mark on American jurisprudence, but Stevens also packs quite a carbon footprint, if his travel records are any indication. A licensed pilot and longtime aviation enthusiast, Stevens spends much of his downtime flying around the country in his private jet. He often flies himself from Washington to his home in Florida—even while the Supreme Court is in session. Asked once about his passion for planes, Stevens admitted that his dream was to take the president for a ride. "Any plane that contains the president becomes Air Force One," he gushed. "I would be able to call the tower and say, 'This is Air Force One!'"

GET ME MY SUNSCREEN—AND A COPY OF BOWERS V. HARDWICK!

Stevens is the only member of the Court who refuses to stay in Washington while the Court is in session, an aversion he attributes to the capital's inclement winter weather. While his colleagues freeze, he prefers to dictate his opinions while poolside at his Florida condo. (Early in his Supreme Court career, Stevens earned the nickname "the FedEx justice" because of his predilection for overnighting opinions back and forth to Washington for transcription and editing. "That was cumbersome," he admitted, and ceased the practice.) He spends so much time reading briefs on the beach that he once had to shake out the sand upon his return to Washington. When not tanning, Stevens adheres to a strict fitness regimen: a daily swim in the ocean, two or three rounds of golf, and three games of tennis a week.

PICK A CARD

Justice Potter Stewart gave Stevens his other nickname, "Wild Card," in recognition of the latter's tendency to change his vote on a moment's notice. Justice Byron White, who detested Stevens, invented a less charitable variation. He called Stevens "the one-eyed jack" behind his back.

POETIC JUSTICE

Stevens is an amateur Shakespeare scholar who has publicly speculated that the Bard's plays may have been written by Edward De Vere, the 17th Earl of Oxford. In 1988, he teamed up with Justices Harry Blackmun and William Brennan, fellow literary buffs, to hear oral arguments in a mock Supreme Court hearing about the authorship of Shakespeare's plays. After the "lawyers" finished their debate, Stevens and his colleagues came down on the side of the Bard, although Stevens conceded, "I don't think the contrary view is wholly frivolous."

Take Me Out to the Ballgame

On September 14, 2005, the eighty-five-year-old justice fulfilled a lifelong dream by throwing out the first pitch at a game between the Chicago Cubs and the Cincinnati Reds at Wrigley Field in Chicago. "It was a thrill for him, an absolute thrill," said his daughter Susan Mullen, who warmed him up for the big event. "It was more the little boy in him than the Supreme Court justice." A lifelong Cubs fan, Stevens was in the stands for Game 3 of the 1932 World Series between the Cubs and the Yankees, at which Babe Ruth hit his famous "called shot" home run. Stevens keeps a scorecard from that game, hung on the wall of his chambers.

WELCOME TO THE CLUB

Baseball wasn't the only game occupying Stevens's mind in 2005. According to newspaper reports, he became hooked on Sudoku number puzzles that year.

DEAR DAVE

Like a lot of older men, Stevens aggressively searches for ways to curb his flatulence. His fart inhibitor of choice is Beano, a dietary supplement designed to reduce gas in the digestive tract. Stevens is such a fan that he once extolled the product's virtues in a letter to newspaper columnist Dave Barry. The missive, sent, according to Barry, "on his official John Paul Stevens stationery," inspired a September 1991 Barry column entitled "The Winds of Change," wherein the humorist tested out Beano's efficacy on a visit to a Mexican restaurant.

MEDICAL MARVEL

It's no wonder that Stevens has lived longer than almost any other justice in history. Apart from his penchant for breaking wind, the man has an iron constitution. He has survived heart bypass surgery, had a polyp removed from his colon, and was briefly treated for prostate cancer in the early 1990s. Determined to defy critics and live as long as possible, he now adheres to a strict low-fat diet, eating only grapefruit for lunch.

SANDRA DAY
O'CONNOR

March 26, 1930–

BIRTHPLACE:

El Paso, TX

ASTROLOGICAL SIGN:

Aries

TERM:

September 25, 1981–
January 31, 2006

APPOINTED BY:

Ronald Reagan

WORDS OF WISDOM:

"Slaying the dragon of delay is
no sport for the short-winded."

Sandra Day O'Connor graduated third in her class from
Stanford Law School. Yet, amazingly
enough, her only job offer was as a legal
secretary. Such were the limitations in
the 1950s for even the most accomplished career women. Oddly, one of
the partners at the firm that offered
her that job was William French Smith,
who went on to become U.S. attorney
general. Nearly thirty years later, he
rectified his firm's mistake by recommending O'Connor for a far more important job—that of associate justice of the U.S. Supreme Court. She was the first
woman to hold that position.

In one of her first actions as justice, Sandra Day O'Connor
hired a YMCA instructor to teach Jazzercise to female
employees in the Supreme Court gym.

She's also the only gun-totin', truck-drivin', horse-ridin' cowhand to sit
on the high Court—at least until Hank Williams Jr. takes his rightful place on
the bench. Sandra Day grew up on a working cattle ranch, the Lazy B, which
stretched over nearly two hundred thousand acres in southeastern Arizona.
Animals were a major element of her upbringing, with the ranch boasting
more than two thousand head of cattle as well as scores of horses. Her personal childhood menagerie included several javelina hogs and a large bobcat.

("When he purred, you could hear him all over the house," she later recalled.)

Day spent the school years in El Paso with her maternal grandmother and her free time back in Arizona, hanging around the cowboys, learning to shoot her .22, and tooling around the ranch in a battered pickup truck. From her mother she gained an awareness of current events; they spent hours reading newspapers and magazines together. From her father she inherited a political ideology. He was a rock-ribbed Republican who loathed Franklin Roosevelt and his New Deal economic programs.

After graduating from high school at age sixteen, Day enrolled at Stanford University and earned a degree in economics. She continued her studies at Stanford Law, where William Rehnquist edged her out of the top spot in a class of 102. Six months after graduation, she married a fellow Stanford law alum, John Jay O'Connor III. Unable to secure a job as a lawyer in private practice, she took various positions in the public sector, including deputy county attorney in San Mateo County and assistant attorney general of Arizona. In 1969, the governor of Arizona appointed her to fill a vacant seat in the state senate. She served there for five years, rising to the rank of majority leader. She later served as a judge on the Maricopa County Superior Court and the Arizona Court of Appeals. It was there that President Ronald Reagan found her when he was looking to make good on a campaign pledge to nominate a woman to sit on the U.S. Supreme Court.

O'Connor's appointment was not without controversy. Abortion opponents, in particular, were dismayed at what they deemed her insufficiently dogmatic position on *Roe v. Wade*. At her confirmation hearings, O'Connor largely fudged on the issue and rode a wave of public goodwill generated by her pioneer status. She was confirmed by a vote of 99–0 and took her seat in September 1981. The nine-person body known for decades as "the Brethren" at last had a sister in its ranks.

By all accounts, O'Connor didn't face much resistance from her colleagues on the basis of gender. They dithered briefly over whether to drop the appellation "Mr. Justice" when addressing one another—with Harry Blackmun insistent that it be retained—but eventually decided to do so. O'Connor quickly established herself as a mainstream conservative justice who, in her early years on the Court, voted with fellow Arizonan William Rehnquist more than 90 percent of the time. Later, she grew more moderate, establishing a reputation as the ultimate "swing vote" in critical cases involving abortion, capital punishment, and affirmative action.

O'Connor's "case by case" approach to the law infuriated some Court watchers, particularly those with a partisan or ideological bias. Especially enraging to those on the left was her vote with the 5–4 majority in the case of *Bush v. Gore*, which curtailed the recounting of votes in the 2000 presidential election and delivered the contest to then governor George W. Bush. O'Connor was mulling retirement at the time, and was reportedly disinclined to vacate her seat if a Democrat in the White House would be able to nominate her successor. "This is *terrible*," she had exclaimed at an election night party when early returns indicated a victory for Vice President Al Gore. Her husband later admitted to other guests that Gore's election would put the kibosh on their retirement dream—a fact that must have been on her mind a month later when she voted with her conservative colleagues to pull the plug on his presidential prospects once and for all.

Although controversial in liberal circles, O'Connor's role in the *Bush v. Gore* decision did little to damage her reputation with the public. She remained a revered figure and a role model for young women until her retirement from the Court in 2006.

MARRY ME, BILL

Talk about a power couple. If Cupid had been on his mark, O'Connor and Chief Justice William Rehnquist might have been the Supreme Court's first husband-and-wife judicial team. The two briefly dated while students at Stanford Law School. ("We went to a few movies" is how O'Connor remembers it.) Asked by a Fox News reporter whether Rehnquist had shown the appropriate level of "judicial restraint" in the darkened theater, O'Connor opted for evasion. "He was a brilliant, entertaining young man," was all she would say.

HAVE A BALL

The man Sandra Day *did* end up marrying, John O'Connor, first had to pass an unusual trial by fire, courtesy of Sandra's cantankerous father, Harry Day. When she brought O'Connor back to the ranch to meet the family, Day made a point of castrating a bull, putting its testicles on a skewer, and cooking them over a branding fire as a gesture of good fellowship. "Here, John, try these," he said, offering up the grilled nuts as an hors d'oeuvre. Eager to impress his future father-in-law, O'Connor scarfed them down in one swallow, *Fear Factor* style, with compliments to the chef. Having passed muster with both father and daughter, he was soon welcomed into the family.

TAKE IT TO THE BRIDGE

The O'Connors sure knew how to party—and did so at the slightest opportunity. They once threw a shindig to celebrate the construction of a footbridge over their backyard pool. The elaborate "dedication ceremony" featured bleating bagpipers, helium balloons, and a buffet of boiled beef, potatoes, and English muffins. Male guests came dressed in top hats, tails, white shorts, and tennis shoes; their female counterparts sported formal gowns and pith helmets. The *Arizona Republic* even sent a society reporter to cover the bizarre soirée.

Let's Get Physical

Legal scholars may argue over O'Connor's judicial legacy, but there's one area where everyone can agree she revolutionized the Supreme Court: Jazzercise. One of her first actions was to hire a YWCA aerobics instructor to teach a daily Jazzercise class for female employees, which was held in the Court gym. Setting aside her judicial robes and donning a leotard, O'Connor personally attended the early-morning sessions, which incorporated "stretches, extensions, twists, head rolls, and leg lifts," according to an account published in the *Saturday Evening Post*. "I think physical fitness is enormously important to your capacity to do mental fitness work," O'Connor once remarked. She even had T-shirts printed for her workout buds, bearing such slogans as "Exercise Defends

Your Constitution" and "Supreme Sport and the Highest Court." In her later years on the Court, she supplemented her cardio work by attending Pilates and yoga classes with fellow justice Ruth Bader Ginsburg.

OUT OF HER GOURD

Like Linus awaiting the Great Pumpkin, O'Connor had a tendency to take Halloween way too seriously. Every year she made her law clerks decorate a jack-o'-lantern, with a theme keyed to news events. In 2001, shortly after the September 11 attacks, the scary squash was dubbed "Osama Bin Pumpkin." In 2002, it was painted to look like Martha Stewart, complete with prison garb.

RIDE 'EM COWGIRL

Who knew there was a National Cowgirl Hall of Fame? Who knew O'Connor was in it? In 2002, O'Connor joined Annie Oakley, Patsy Cline, and Laura Ingalls Wilder—among more than one hundred others—in the pantheon of legends honored by the institution, based in Fort Worth, Texas, for "exemplifying the pioneer spirit of the American West."

SHE GOT GAME

A staunch advocate for Title IX and the cause of women's athletics, O'Connor once invited the American women's Olympic basketball team to shoot some hoops with her on the Supreme Court's top-floor basketball court, known as "the highest court in the land." Her own roundball skills were decidedly less than Olympian: She tossed an airball on her first shot.

Vanity, Thy Name Is Sandra

Few justices have reveled in their status on the high court quite as much as O'Connor. She had vanity license plates for her car that bore the legend "USSC102," to commemorate her place as the 102nd Supreme Court justice in American history.

UNSPORTSMANLIKE CONDUCT

Bad things happen when you put a drunken NFL star and a Supreme Court pioneer at the same table. Witness the kerfuffle that ensued at the Washington Press Club's black-tie Salute to Congress dinner in 1985. Inexplicably, Justice O'Connor was seated next to John Riggins, the hulking running back for the Washington Redskins. "Riggo," or "The Diesel," as he was popularly known, imbibed a bit too much that night and was soon sidling up to O'Connor with decidedly seamy intentions. "Come on, Sandy Baby, loosen up. You're too tight," he told her, before passing out on the floor. According to newspaper reports, he lay there for several minutes while the waitstaff served dessert to the mortified VIP diners.

To his credit, Riggins realized the error of his ways and sent roses to O'Connor the next morning, by way of an apology. For her part, O'Connor was more amused than annoyed by the wasted pigskinner's boorish come-on. She was soon outfitting her Jazzercise classmates in T-shirts reading "Loosen up at the Supreme Court." Several years later, after Riggins had retired from football and was trying to make a go of it as an actor on the D.C. theater circuit, O'Connor even attended opening night of one of his plays and gave *him* a dozen roses for his curtain call.

THE PLAY'S THE THING

Perhaps O'Connor empathized with Riggins because she secretly harbored theatrical aspirations her own. If so, she realized them in 1996, when she made a surprise appearance as Queen Isabel of France in the Washington D.C. Shakespeare Theatre's production of *Henry V*. Appropriately enough, her dialogue included the famous line "Haply a woman's voice may do some good."

BUSH, GORE, FORE!

O'Connor may have anguished over the prospect of a Constitutional crisis precipitated by the disputed 2000 presidential election, but she quickly got over it. Just six days after casting the deciding vote in *Bush v. Gore*, she hit the links with her husband and a group of friends for a round of golf at the Paradise Valley

Country Club in Arizona. As fate would have it, that wasn't just George W. Bush's lucky week—it was O'Connor's as well. She recorded her first hole-in-one on the 150-yard ninth hole.

It was the culmination of more than thirty years of duffing for the golf-crazy justice, who didn't take up the game in earnest until age forty. "My father thought it was a game for effete Easterners," O'Connor once said, "and that no self-respecting ranch girl would play golf." Prodded by her husband, she eventually became quite a good player, and even used the game to illuminate her deliberations on the Court. When disabled golfer Casey Martin sued the Professional Golfers Association for the right to use a golf cart during PGA events, O'Connor joined the Supreme Court's 7–2 majority ruling in his favor. "I imagine I could envision the situation better because of my golf experience," she said afterward. Elsewhere O'Connor explained the allure of the game this way: "Golf, like skiing, is something you have to do all by yourself. You can't blame it on anybody. It's your problem to make a good swing."

Coming Up Roses

On January 1, 2006, O'Connor became only the second Supreme Court justice—and the first since Chief Justice Earl Warren in 1955—to serve as the Grand Marshal of the Tournament of Roses Parade in Pasadena, California. (Oddly enough, it rained on both occasions.) Her duties included presiding over the ceremonial coin toss before the ninety-second annual Rose Bowl game between USC and the University of Texas.

FOR THE KIDDIES

Until someone discovers an unpublished manuscript of William Howard Taft's locked away somewhere, O'Connor will probably remain the only Supreme Court justice to write a children's book. *Chico*, published in 1995, tells the story of O'Connor's childhood on her family's Arizona ranch and her love for the eponymous horse.

ANTONIN

SCALIA

March 11, 1936–

BIRTHPLACE:

Trenton, NJ

NICKNAME:

"Nino"

ASTROLOGICAL SIGN:

Pisces

TERM:

September 26, 1986–

APPOINTED BY:

Ronald Reagan

WORDS OF WISDOM:

"I'm a conservative, I'm a textualist, I'm an originalist, but I'm not a nut."

There have been other ornery justices on the Supreme Court, but few who could match the intellectual heft and partisan pugnacity of Antonin Scalia. A cantankerous conservative with a zest for verbal combat (his critics would say verbal bullying), Scalia loves nothing more than a good scrap. If he isn't blowing off journalists with one of his obscene Sicilian salutes, he's changing the outcome of a U.S. presidential election and then telling anyone who doesn't like it to "Get over it!" Gotta love that Nino!

An avid hunter, Antonin Scalia has killed more animals than any other Supreme Court justice—and he kept the heads to prove it.

Scalia was born on March 11, 1936, in Trenton, New Jersey. His family moved to the Elmhurst section of Queens after his father, a professor of Romance languages, got a teaching job at Brooklyn College. "Nino," as he was known from early childhood, picked up a passion for learning from his old man and graduated first in his class from an elite Jesuit military prep school. "I was something of a greasy grind," Scalia has said of his school days—and if that's Scaliaspeak for "Big Man on Campus," then few were greasier. Scalia was

a Boy Scout, was elected president of the Dramatic Society, and played the lead role in the school's production of *Macbeth*. He was also a musician and a crack shot. Classmates remember seeing him riding on the subway with one of two objects: his French horn or his .22 carbine, which he used on the junior varsity rifle team. Luckily, he never confused the two, or there'd have been a mess of dead bodies at band practice.

Scalia followed up prep school with another first-in-his-class performance at Georgetown, followed by a stint at Harvard Law School. He married his college sweetheart, Maureen McCarthy, in 1960 and embarked on a legal career—first as an attorney and later as a law professor. In 1971, he left academia for a position in the Nixon administration. After Nixon had drowned in the mire of Watergate, President Gerald Ford tapped Scalia to determine who had legal ownership of the surreptitious recordings Nixon had made while in the White House. Not surprisingly, Scalia—a staunch conservative and loyal Republican—sided with his ex-boss. The decision would later be overturned by the Supreme Court.

With the end of Republican rule in 1977, Scalia returned to the teaching of law. In 1982, the next GOP chief executive, Ronald Reagan, plucked him out of the academy once more and placed him on the D.C. court of appeals. That appointment was but a prelude to his 1986 nomination to the Supreme Court, which came as no surprise to those who knew of Scalia's growing reputation as one of the most intellectually gifted—and ideologically right-wing—judges in America. Despite his politics, Scalia breezed through the confirmation process. Senators seemed interested more in his Italian heritage than in his opinions on abortion, civil rights, or gun control. ("I would be remiss if I did not mention the fact that my great-great-grandfather married a widow who was married first to an Italian American," Senator Howell Heflin of Alabama observed, to which Scalia replied, "Senator, I have been to Alabama several times, too.") Scalia sailed through on a 98–0 vote.

Scalia emerged as the leader of the Court's "originalist" faction, which holds that the Constitution is a "dead document" whose meaning is limited to the literal words inscribed by its framers. "Once we depart from the text of the Constitution," he once asked, "just where short of that do we stop?" He has voted repeatedly to uphold restrictions on abortions, limit the ability of the government to curtail expressions of religious worship in the public square, and empower the executive in the area of detaining and interrogation of terror suspects. In the case of *Bush v. Gore*, which helped decide the 2000 presidential election, Scalia blamed Al Gore for bringing the dispute before the Court in the first place, then admonished critics who charged him with partisan meddling to "get a life and get over it."

That line was hardly out of character. To the consternation of liberals, Scalia has earned a reputation as a scrappy intellectual pugilist whose erudite, tartly worded opinions have been described as "verbal hand grenades." One lawyer who argued before the Court compared Scalia's style of questioning to "a big cat batting around a ball of yarn." The belligerent justice once taunted a litigator who had to search for his brief inside a folder full of papers: "When you find it, say 'bingo.'" He has dismissed those who disagree with his originalist interpretation of the Constitution as "idiots" and labeled his colleagues' dissenting opinions "perverse" and "irrational." In one of his more whimsical moods, he called a decision by Justice Stephen Breyer "sheer applesauce." During a discussion of affirmative action with Justice Sandra Day O'Connor, he derided it as the evil fruit of a bad seed. "But Nino," O'Connor replied, "if it weren't for affirmative action, I wouldn't be here."

Like him or hate him, no one can fail to be entertained by Scalia's "no apologies" approach to jurisprudential combat. He falls within the grand tradition of justices like William O. Douglas who infuriate their ideological opponents and endear themselves to their partisan brethren.

★ ★

PAPANAZI

Deeply suspicious of the press, Scalia imposes a strict "no cameras" policy on those unfortunate enough to cover him. Until recently, he has demanded that no video or audio recordings be made of his personal appearances, claiming he has a "First Amendment right not to speak on the radio or television when I do not wish to do so."

In April 2004, Scalia's press policy ignited a minor firestorm when a U.S. marshal confiscated a journalist's tape recording of a Scalia speech in Hattiesburg, Mississippi. Scalia later apologized for the incident. He has since changed his press policy, partly on the recommendation of his children, who believe he will be less easy to "demonize" if he presents a more cuddly public face.

FIVE FINGER EXERCISE

In April 2006, while attending a special Mass for lawyers and politicians at Cathedral of the Holy Cross in Boston, Scalia issued his own special benediction for a *Boston Herald* reporter who asked what he would say to critics questioning his ability to rule impartially on matters about the separation of church and state. "You know what I say to those people?" Scalia replied, while flicking his fingers out from underneath his chin in a well-known obscene Italian gesture. "*Vaffanculo!* That's Sicilian." (In fact, it is a contraction of a common Italian curse that translates as "Go take it in the ass.") After the newspaper reported on the incident, Scalia refused to apologize, claiming he had merely "responded jocularly" to the writer's request for comment, using a gesture that meant simply "I could not care less." He then went on to chide the reporter for "watching too many episodes of *The Sopranos* and for referring to him as an "Italian jurist." "I am, by the way, an American jurist," Scalia scolded.

WILD GAME

An avid sportsman, Scalia once found himself in hot water for going duck hunting with Vice President Dick Cheney. No, he didn't wind up on the wrong side of Cheney's shotgun. Some viewed their weekend in the wild as a conflict of interest: Scalia and the other justices were in the process of hearing a lawsuit against Cheney over his role as chairman of a White House energy task force.

The walls of Scalia's chambers are filled with the mounted and stuffed heads of animals he has killed, including an enormous elk. When Scalia took the meat of a deer he had bagged and served it up to his colleague Ruth Bader

Ginsburg for New Year's dinner, she quipped that he "has been more successful at deer hunting than he has at duck hunting."

"Vatican Roulette"

Scalia and his wife, Maureen, have nine children and twenty-eight grandchildren—a prodigious output the justice attributes to his strict adherence to Catholic doctrine outlawing the use of contraception. "We didn't set out to have nine children," he told *60 Minutes* in 2008. "We're just old-fashioned Catholics, you know? Playing what used to be known as 'Vatican roulette.'" During Scalia's Supreme Court nomination hearings in 1986, one of the Senators remarked that as a father, he had a lot of experience working with groups of nine.

BAWD OF AVON

Scalia is known for his quick wit, which he often displays during oral arguments. In 2001, while lawyers were debating a case involving child pornography, Justice John Paul Stevens pointed out that images of minors engaged in sexual acts might have some redeeming social value—and cited Shakespeare's *Romeo and Juliet* as a case in point. "I must have seen a different version!" Scalia interjected, causing the entire Court to erupt in laughter.

SIR LAUGHSALOT

In 2005, a Boston University law professor conducted a study that determined Scalia was by far the funniest Supreme Court justice—if instances of laughter recorded in Court transcripts are used as the criteria. During the nine months of the 2004–5 term, there were seventy-seven "laughing episodes" denoted at Scalia's expense, indicating that he was responsible, on average, for just over one laugh per argument. Coming in second place was that other king of comedy, Justice Stephen Breyer, with forty-five laughs. The ever-silent Clarence Thomas inspired no laughs at all.

LEMON LAW

Of all the colorful, bombastic opinions for which Scalia is famous, his master-work may be his majority opinion in the case of *Lamb's Chapel v. Center Moriches Union Free School District*, in which he excoriates the so-called Lemon Test, the Supreme Court doctrine that lays out the requirements for laws that impact organized religious worship. It is so vividly written that it is worth quoting at length:

> Like some ghoul in a late-night horror movie that repeatedly sits up in its grave and shuffles abroad after being repeatedly killed and buried, Lemon stalks our Establishment Clause jurisprudence once again, frightening the little children and school attorneys of Center Moriches Union Free School District. Its most recent burial, only last term, was, to be sure, not fully six feet under. . . . Over the years, however, no fewer than five of the currently sitting Justices have, in their own opinions, personally driven pencils through the creature's heart (the author of today's opinion repeatedly), and a sixth has joined an opinion doing so. . . .
>
> The secret of the Lemon test's survival, I think, is that it is so easy to kill. It is there to scare us (and our audience) when we wish it to do so, but we can command it to return to the tomb at will. When we wish to strike down a prac-tice it forbids, we invoke it; when we wish to uphold a practice it forbids, we ignore it entirely. Sometimes, we take a middle course, calling its three prongs "no more than helpful signposts." Such a docile and useful monster is worth keeping around, at least in a somnolent state; one never knows when one might need him.

If I May Quote Myself

On the wall in Scalia's office hangs a plaque that reads "'Nothing is easy.'—Antonin Scalia, 1985." The self-attributed maxim is meant as a rebuke to clerks who complained that crafting opinions according to a rigorous judicial philosophy was hard work.

LA JUSTICE È MOBILE

In keeping with his Italian American heritage, Scalia is an opera buff who often attends productions in and around Washington D.C. In January 1994, he took his buffery one step further when he and fellow aria aficionado Justice Ruth Bader Ginsburg appeared as extras in the Washington Opera's production of Richard Strauss's *Ariadne auf Naxos*. Scalia remained onstage for about an hour and a half, wearing a white wig and knee breeches first worn by Plácido Domingo during the world premiere of *Goya* in 1986.

CARNAL KNOWLEDGE

Scalia must have grown up in a different country than the rest of us. In June 2003, when the Court issued a decision in the case of *Lawrence v. Texas*, striking down several state anti-sodomy laws, Scalia dissented, saying that if sodomy bans were unconstitutional, then so were "laws against bigamy, same-sex marriage, adult incest, prostitution, masturbation, adultery, fornication, bestiality, and obscenity." Somebody needed to inform him that masturbation and fornication are perfectly legal.

PIZZA PAN

As inflexible as he is in his judicial philosophy, Scalia is even more rigid when it comes to fast food. According to his friend and fellow judge Alex Kozinski, Scalia will eat pizza delivered from only one Washington D.C. pizzeria: AV Ristorante Italiano on Capitol Hill. "I realize it's not the best restaurant in town," Scalia has said, "but I've been going there for nearly fifty years, so I have a special connection to the place." In fact, on one occasion when Kozinski ordered up a pie from a competing pizzeria he considered far superior to AV Ristorante, Scalia refused to nosh. "It's not from AV Ristorante," he declared, shooting daggers at Kozinski with his eyes. "I *won't* eat it."

Leonard Bernstein He Aint

Reportedly, President Ronald Reagan was so jazzed by his selection of Scalia to serve on the Supreme Court, he wrote a song about it. Sung to the tune of

"Maria" from *West Side Story*, the presidential paean went something like this:

Scalia, I just picked a judge named Scalia
And now the Court Supreme
Won't cause Ed Meese to scream, at me;

Scalia, I just picked a judge named Scalia
His writing is so fine
He'll pull in five votes every time

Scalia
Say it loud
'cause for life he's staying
Say it soft
And you'll hear liberals praying;

Scalia, I'll never stop saying Scalia
Scalia . . .

COURT OF PUBLIC OPINION

Scalia is known to play a mean game of tennis and carries the Court's internal math with him wherever he slings a racquet. One day in 1998, he was exchanging volleys with a friend in Washington D.C. When the score reached 4–4, Scalia picked up his play and won the next game: "5–4!" he exulted, claiming the set.

ANTHONY
KENNEDY

July 23, 1936–

BIRTHPLACE:

Sacramento, CA

ASTROLOGICAL SIGN:

Leo

TERM:

February 18, 1988–

APPOINTED BY:

Ronald Reagan

WORDS OF WISDOM:

"Sometimes you don't know if
you're Caesar about to cross
the Rubicon or Captain Queeg
cutting your own tow line."
(on the vicissitudes of being a
Supreme Court justice)

How squeaky clean is Anthony Kennedy? As a teenager, he avoided movies if he suspected they might show a woman's cleavage or contain the word *virgin*. About the worst thing he ever did as a child, according to his classmates, was to drop a piece of chewing gum off the Washington Monument while on a high school trip. His father once offered him $100 if he would do something—*any-thing*—to get himself arrested. The old man never collected. Nevertheless, the beaming, law-abiding homebody from northern California—whom the *New York Times* once called "energetic, self-effacing, and immensely polite"—has won some powerful enemies. In 2003, James Dobson, the right-wing evangelical leader and founder of Focus on the Family, called Kennedy "the most dangerous man in America."

Anthony McLeod Kennedy was born in Sacramento, California, on July 23, 1936. His father, Anthony J. "Bud" Kennedy, was his polar opposite: a hard-drinking, cigar-chomping, poker-playing lawyer who lobbied for various shady local concerns: a liquor distiller, a record company, the oil industry, and even a factory that wrapped sausages in animal intestines. His mother, Gladys "Sis" Kennedy, was a teacher and volunteer. Little Anthony was a self-described "skinny kid" and super straight arrow. "I think we all tried to coax Tony as often as possible into breaking any of his rules," said one of his childhood chums. "I can't remember that we ever did." Whenever his friends tried to entice him into mischief, Kennedy would beg off, saying he had to do something at home. Friends recall an archetypal nerd who didn't date, go to parties, or play sports. "He was your ninety-pound weakling," recalled a former classmate. "He didn't stand out in a crowd, but he was always very, very bright."

On weekends, Kennedy served as an altar boy at Holy Spirit Catholic Church, and during the week he worked as a page in the California State Senate. It was there that he first encountered Earl Warren, the California governor who later became chief justice of the Supreme Court. The young Kennedy befriended Warren's children and played in the governor's mansion. One of his prized possessions is a letter he received from Warren as a nine-year-old boy, informing him, "You're going to go very far in government."

> An ardent fan of Shakespeare, Anthony Kennedy once staged a mock trial to determine Hamlet's sanity at the time of Polonius's murder.

Still, there were those who thought the fresh-faced youngster needed some toughening up—chief among them his rough-hewn father. During his college years, Kennedy traveled around Europe one summer in a red Volkswagen. His dad presented him with a bottle of one-hundred-proof Yellowstone whiskey to take with him on the trip, but presumably not for the medicinal purposes to which it was put. Instead of drinking it, Kennedy gargled it to soothe a sore throat.

After graduating from Stanford and then Harvard Law School, Kennedy embarked on a legal career in San Francisco. When his father died suddenly in 1963, he returned to Sacramento to take over the family practice. He also married and began raising a family. The well-connected Kennedy made several powerful friends, including California governor Ronald Reagan, for whom Kennedy helped draft a tax-cut ballot proposition in 1973. Though the initiative failed, the Gipper was impressed with Kennedy's constitutional acumen and two years later recommended him to President Gerald Ford for judicial appointment.

Kennedy spent twelve years on the court of appeals, earning a reputation as a moderate conservative and a conciliator. That was exactly the type of judge that Reagan, then president, sought to fill a seat on the Supreme Court, after the flame-out of right-wing fire-breather Robert Bork in 1987. Kennedy's bland demeanor and the relative absence of controversial rulings on his résumé enabled him to pass unscathed through the Senate, which voted unanimously in his favor. The consummate straight-A student was now a Supreme Court justice.

On the bench, Kennedy quickly found a niche in the political center, alongside fellow Reagan appointee Sandra Day O'Connor. He took more of an incrementalist approach than the more strident conservative justices, such as Antonin Scalia and Clarence Thomas—a philosophy that drew the ire of right-wing interest groups like Focus on the Family. Also grinding their gears was Kennedy's fascination for consulting foreign courts and citing international precedents in his opinions. For years, Kennedy has spent much of his "me time" in Salzburg, Austria, drinking in the classical music he loves so much and hosting intercontinental bull sessions for legal scholars. Conservatives charge that he has "gone native" on issues like gay rights and capital punishment. Liberals, on the other hand, increasingly came to view him as the Court's key swing vote, especially in the aftermath of O'Connor's retirement.

★ ★

MR. GOOD EXAMPLE

Kennedy takes his reverence for the law to the extreme. To this day, friends report, he refuses to jaywalk.

EXCLUSIONARY RULE

Jaywalking may be abhorrent to Kennedy, but apparently discrimination was just fine, at least until 1987. At Harvard, he recalled, "we regularly excluded all women from our study group and thought nothing of it. We just weren't aware of the problem." Later, he eagerly accepted membership in several all-white private clubs and defended their right to exclude people of color, doing so almost to the day he was nominated for the Supreme Court. At that point, Kennedy did an about-face. He resigned from both the Del Paso Country Club of Sacramento and the Olympic Club of San Francisco, admitting that their bylaws limited membership to white men. In his statement, he conceded that "real harm can result from membership exclusion regardless of its purported justification."

To Tony, with Love

Teaching may have been Kennedy's true calling. He still spends part of his time instructing about international law before rapt audiences. Eschewing notes, he delivers three-hour lectures extemporaneously and takes a theatrical approach to pedagogy. He occasionally teaches classes in costume, dressed as James Madison. So energetically does Kennedy convey his passion for the law that a colleague once called him "a human hydroelectric project." Students also seem to appreciate his performances. They've been known to give him standing ovations.

TO BE OR NOT TO BE

Kennedy is obsessed with *Hamlet*, often referring to Shakespeare's great tragedy in his opinions. When the Court, at the instigation of Bard buff John Paul Stevens (see "Poetic Justice," page 208), held a mock trial to determine the true author of Shakespeare's plays, Kennedy was the only justice to find against. In his dissent, he posited the notion that Shakespeare might not have existed at all.

In March 2007, Kennedy (who apparently has a lot of time on his hands for literary flights of fancy), presided over yet another mock trial, this one conducted to ascertain whether Hamlet was legally insane at the time of Polonius's murder. The courtroom spectacle unfolded over several hours at Washington D.C.'s John F. Kennedy Center for the Performing Arts, as part of the capital's six-month Shakespeare festival. Vowing to "put this issue to rest for all time," Kennedy served as judge, with two prominent local trial lawyers presenting the prosecution case and Court TV anchorwoman Catherine Crier arguing for the defense. In the end, the jury deadlocked six to six. Thankfully, Kennedy reconsidered his original plan to rewrite some of Shakespeare's dialogue for the occasion, admitting that it would be "marginally presumptuous." *Marginally?*

RED FACED

Beware Supreme Court justices bearing gifts. On a trip to the People's Republic of China to meet with that country's vice premier, Kennedy brought along a little gift he had picked up in the Supreme Court gift shop: a leather-bound page-a-day calendar filled with dates of important cases in Supreme Court history. Hoping to impress his host even more, Kennedy proceeded to ask him what his birthday was. The vice premier told him, and Kennedy dutifully looked up the date in the calendar. As soon as the interpreter began reading, Kennedy knew he was in trouble. The case in question was *United States v. Dennis*, in which the Court affirmed the prison term of American Communist Party leader Eugene Dennis in 1951.

STAR CHAMBER

According to Jeffrey Toobin, author of the best seller *The Nine*, Kennedy has quite the pimped-out office. Chief among the accoutrements is a plush, deep red carpet "festooned with gold stars" that makes his chambers look like a cross between the Oval Office and a French courtesan's boudoir. Toobin also reports that Kennedy hasn't been shy about "borrowing" masterpieces from the National Gallery to hang on his office walls. Finally, the self-important jurist has made it a point to situate his desk in the far corner, so that all who enter must cross the entire grand expanse to pay their respects. And don't even think about disturbing his view. Reportedly, Kennedy once torpedoed plans by Congress to build an aboveground visitors center between the Supreme Court building and the Capitol because he was afraid it might obscure his spectacular vista.

DAVID
SOUTER

September 17, 1939–

BIRTHPLACE:

Melrose, MA

ASTROLOGICAL SIGN:

Virgo

TERM:

October 9, 1990–

APPOINTED BY:

George H.W. Bush

WORDS OF WISDOM:

"The day you see a camera
come into our courtroom, it's
going to roll over my dead
body."

David Souter is the Henry David Thoreau of the contemporary Supreme Court. An eccentric New England bachelor who eschews modern conveniences and cultivates a profound love of nature, he could have stepped into our century straight out of a cabin on Walden Pond. Souter even keeps a vintage 1850s print of the Merrimack River hanging on the wall in his living room. His ramshackle home in Weare, New Hampshire, is crammed to the rafters with dusty volumes of Dickens, Oliver Wendell Holmes, and other nineteenth-century writers. ("It looks like someone was moving a bookstore and stopped," Souter once quipped.) But you won't find a fax machine or a workable TV anywhere in the place. As for computers, well, forget it—this justice prefers to record his opinions with a fountain pen, just like his forefathers did. And yet here he is sitting on a court that regularly rules on cases involving digital downloading, software piracy, and other sophisticated technical matters. Like *Saturday Night Live*'s Unfrozen Caveman Lawyer, David Souter is frightened and confused by our complicated modern world, but he does the best he can to understand it.

Souter's journey to our planet began on September 17, 1939, when he was born the only child of an assistant bank manager and a gift shop clerk in Melrose, Massachusetts. When he was eleven years old, his family moved into the farmhouse in Weare, New Hampshire, where he still resides. In high

school, Souter was voted "most likely to succeed" and "most sophisticated"— early evidence that his throwback style was regarded as charming, at least in some quarters.

Souter went on to Harvard, where he majored in philosophy and joined the prestigious Hasty Pudding Society. Already his career path was set. At graduation, a group of his friends put together a scrapbook of fake newspaper stories touting his future achievements as a lawyer. One of the headlines read: "David Souter nominated to the Supreme Court." Moving on to Harvard Law, he began putting the finishing touches on his weirdo persona. He became known for donning three-piece suits for campus parties and telling long-winded stories in a thick New England accent. Oddly enough, in the rarefied milieu of 1960s Cambridge, this actually made him *more* popular.

After earning his law degree in 1966, Souter returned home to Weare. He joined the staff of the New Hampshire attorney general's office and steadily rose through its ranks, becoming deputy attorney general in 1971. When Attorney General Warren Rudman, Souter's political mentor, moved on to the U.S. Senate in 1976, he recommended his younger colleague for the top job. Souter accepted, although in typically frugal fashion he declined to take the larger office that accompanied his new position.

> **How much does David Souter love his job? Even a vicious beating by two thugs didn't deter the faithful justice from going to work.**

After two years as attorney general, Souter moved on to the New Hampshire superior court and later to the state supreme court, where he likely could have been happy for the rest of his life, reading briefs, deciding cases, and serving in his spare time as the vice president of the state historical society. During this time, his typical weekend involved helping an elderly neighbor cross the street to the general store to buy her Sunday *New York Times* and visiting his aged mother at her retirement home a few miles from his house. But in 1990, fate came calling, again in the person of Warren Rudman, who prevailed upon

President George H. W. Bush to nominate Souter for the latest vacancy on the U.S. Supreme Court.

Souter was well prepared for the job, but not for the media scrutiny that came with his confirmation process. Dubbed a "stealth candidate" for his lack of a clear and consistent judicial record, he had to fend off insinuations that he was gay and that he might be a closet pro-choicer. (From 1971 to 1985, Souter had served on the board of a Concord hospital that performed abortions.) But his calm and reasonable demeanor during the confirmation hearings won over all but the most stalwart detractors, and Souter was confirmed by a vote of 90–9. On the Court, he validated the worst fears of his conservative critics, voting with the liberal bloc on several important cases. He provided the critical swing vote in the 1992 case of *Planned Parenthood v. Casey*, which reaffirmed *Roe v. Wade*, and voted with the minority to reject the arguments of the Republican candidate (and the son of the man who had nominated him) in *Bush v. Gore*.

Not surprisingly, Souter became something of a folk hero in liberal circles, cherished as much for his crunchy granola affectations as his generally progressive jurisprudence. Likening the experience of serving on the Supreme Court to "walking through a tidal wave," Souter regularly retreats to his New Hampshire homestead for a little low-tech R&R in the company of nature. "I need some period of the year when I can make a close approach to solitude," he says, using terminology that could have come straight out of a Thoreau notebook. Others have noted a similarity in spirit between Souter and some of the judicial icons of yore, such as Oliver Wendell Holmes and Learned Hand. Or, as one of Souter's friends once said of him, when in his presence, "you really feel as if you are with one of our Founding Fathers."

★ ★

LET'S GET ON WITH IT!

The consummate flinty New Englander, Souter doesn't suffer fools—or foolish procedures—gladly. He's on record as disapproving of a time-honored tradition in which attorneys about to offer oral arguments are ceremonially sworn in as members of the Supreme Court bar. During the ten-minute ceremony, Souter invariably glowers silently over what he considers to be a colossal waste of time.

COOL CUSTOMER

Apparently the bitter New England winters have left no impression on Souter. No matter what the weather, he refuses to don an overcoat and wears only a scarf as protection against the elements—a predilection that dates back to his college days at Oxford.

A JUDICIOUS DIET

Souter eats the same exact thing for lunch each day: one whole apple— core, seeds, and all—and a cup of plain yogurt, both served on the finest Supreme Court china. When a friend once suggested that apple seeds might be poisonous, Souter did some independent research to determine they were only harmful if consumed in large quantities.

Tightwad

Souter is a notorious skinflint, or, as one of his closest friends put it, the man who "put the 'c' in 'cheap.'" He rarely picks up a restaurant check and regularly lists $0 on his end-of-year expense report. Colleagues have also remarked about how he drives around in the same dilapidated car until it runs into the ground. While he was serving as New Hampshire's deputy attorney general in the 1970s, his vehicle of choice was a broken-down fifteen-year-old Chevrolet with personalized state-government license plates. Motorists would routinely honk and ridicule him for defiling the highway with such a clunker, to the point where Attorney General Warren Rudman had to implore him to upgrade his ride. Souter then invested in a used Volkswagen Rabbit, followed by an equally sensible Volkswagen Golf, which he continued to drive well into his tenure on the Supreme Court.

SUPREME IGNORANCE

Souter isn't exactly the most plugged-in justice, especially when it comes to popular culture. Upon arriving on the Court in 1990, he had never heard of Diet Coke, even though it had been on the market for nearly a decade. At a friend's wedding in 2003, Souter was clueless when one of the guests joked about getting the Supremes to play at the reception. He had never heard of Diana Ross and the most famous "girl group" of the 1960s.

PARTY ANIMAL

He may not win much at Trivial Pursuit, but Souter can let his hair down when the occasion requires. "No one I've ever met is more fun at a party," said college friend Dr. Melvin Levine. "He has that British satirical sense of humor, does wonderful impressions." Souter is in fact an accomplished mimic, although his repertoire of impersonations is somewhat limited. He is especially proud of his uncanny imitation of former New Hampshire governor Meldrim Thomson Jr., the archconservative who appointed him state attorney general in 1976.

CATCHING SOME RAYS

During daylight hours, Souter eschews the use of electric lights, preferring to read by the light of the sun. If necessary, he moves his chair around the room to catch the necessary illumination.

Ink-Stained Wretch

No fan of computers, Souter still does all his writing with a fountain pen.

TECHNOPHOBE

When Souter is back home in Weare, New Hampshire, the telephone is just about his only concession to the age of electronic communications. But he keeps a landline only and has no answering machine, fax, or e-mail capability. His friend and patron Senator Warren Rudman once gave him a television set as a gift, but Souter never has bothered to plug it in.

PICK YOU UP AT SEVEN?

A lifelong bachelor, Souter isn't exactly a ball of fire when it comes to romancing the ladies. One of his old flames has said that going out with him was like "knowing someone from another century"—not exactly a ringing endorsement. During their time on the Court together, Justice Sandra Day O'Connor routinely tried to hook Souter up with eligible bachelorettes. So did former first lady Barbara Bush. But the dog wouldn't hunt. At the end of one promising evening, Souter informed his date that he'd had a good time and bid her goodnight with the words, "Let's do this again next year."

MAKING BANK

Souter may be eccentric, but he's crazy like a fox when it comes to personal finance. In 2003, it was revealed that he was worth as much as $25 million—not bad for a guy who had worked in state government most of his life. His secret? Buying bank stocks and watching their values soar through mergers and acquisitions.

Into the Breyer Patch

For some reason, Souter is often mistaken for fellow justice Stephen Breyer. One time a couple approached him in a restaurant and struck up a conversation. When they asked "Breyer" what his favorite part of being a justice was, Souter replied, "Well, I'd have to say it's the privilege of serving with David Souter."

LUCKY MUG

When the Court deals with criminal justice cases, Souter brings personal experience to the table. In April 2004, the unassuming jurist was viciously beaten by two men while jogging near his home in Washington D.C. The bizarre, apparently motiveless assault occurred about nine o'clock at night. True to form, Souter was back at work the next morning—a Saturday.

EMPTY CLOSET

As America's first unmarried justice since Frank Murphy in the 1940s, Souter has been dogged for years by rumors that he is gay. A 1990 *Time* magazine cover story on his nomination raised the issue directly, citing the names of two women who had gone on dates with Souter over the years—as if that proved anything about his sexual preference. *Newsweek* dug even deeper, quoting a gay New Hampshire lawyer as saying there was "not a particle of evidence" to prove that Souter was homosexual. "The law [is] his mistress," raged Souter's political godfather, Warren Rudman, suggesting that the bachelor judge's abstemious lifestyle merely reflected his professional devotion. During the confirmation process, Souter's supporters even brought in President Ronald Reagan's former chief of staff, Kenneth Duberstein, specifically to beat back charges that the nominee might be batting for the other team. Not surprisingly, all the unsubstantiated innuendo took a toll on the soft-spoken Yankee. "Warren, if I had known how vicious this process is, I wouldn't have let you propose my nomination," he told Rudman.

CLARENCE
THOMAS

June 23, 1948–

BIRTHPLACE:

Pin Point, GA

NICKNAME:

"The Silent Justice"

ASTROLOGICAL SIGN:

Cancer

TERM:

October 23, 1991–

APPOINTED BY:

George H. W. Bush

WORDS OF WISDOM:

"Who has put pubic hair on my Coke?" (attributed)

Say what you want about Clarence Thomas, but he's overcome a lot to get where he is. From squalid origins, he's risen to a seat on America's highest court—though with bizarre detours into self-admitted alcohol abuse and allegations of sexual harassment and hardcore porn addiction. Nobody ever said that becoming the nation's second African American justice would be easy.

Thomas was born on June 23, 1948, in the tiny town of Pin Point, Georgia. A dirt-poor community given over to freed slaves after the Civil War, Pin Point was hardly the birthplace of America's judicial titans. It had no sewers, running water, or paved roads. Basically, if you could survive into adulthood and get a job shucking oysters, you considered yourself lucky. For most people, having your father abandon the family and your house burn down wouldn't be considered a stroke of good fortune, but for young Clarence it was. It meant that he could go to live with his grandfather in nearby Savannah.

A devout Catholic who made his living selling heating oil from the back of a pick-up truck, Thomas's gramps instilled in him a strong work ethic and a sense of personal discipline. He also nudged him toward the priesthood as a career choice. Thomas attended a series of Catholic boarding schools and seminaries but kept running up against the era's pervasive bigotry. As the only African American in his class, he was often the subject of racist taunting.

"Smile, Clarence, so we can see you," a white classmate joked when the lights were turned off. A "friend" wrote in his yearbook: "Keep on trying, Clarence. One day you will be as good as us." When he discovered a fellow seminarian cheering on the news that Martin Luther King had been assassinated, Thomas had had enough. "I knew I couldn't stay in this so-called Christian environment," he later remarked.

> Until injuring his knee, Clarence Thomas was one of the most avid users of the Court building's top-floor basketball facility, the so-called highest court in the land. Once he even played Charles Barkley in a game of H.O.R.S.E.

Quitting the seminary enraged Thomas's grandfather, who promptly threw him out of the house, screaming, "I'm finished helping you. You'll probably end up like your no-good daddy or those other no-good Pin Point negroes." Determined to prove the old man wrong, Thomas worked his way into Holy Cross, a Jesuit college in Massachusetts. There he joined the Black Student Union, a militant group on campus, and briefly adopted radical politics. He also developed a severe drinking problem that would last more than a decade. College friends remember Thomas as the beer-guzzling black radical with the foul mouth and a fondness for dirty jokes. It was at Holy Cross, Thomas's roommate later revealed, that the future Supreme Court justice first peered inside a can of soda and declared, "Somebody put a pubic hair in my Coca-Cola." The ribald gag would come up again more than a decade later, at his confirmation hearings before the U.S. Senate.

After graduating from Yale Law School in 1974, Thomas found himself deeply in debt and in desperate need of cash. He tried selling his own blood for money, but was turned away because his pulse was too slow. "I trudged home," Thomas recalled, "thinking to myself that a man who couldn't even sell his own blood to buy a decent meal had sunk pretty low. The only good thing about not having any money to spare was that it helped to keep my consumption of alcohol under control." Help came in the form of a job offer from

Missouri attorney general John Danforth, who would become Thomas's chief political patron. He joined Danforth's staff and later moved with him to Washington when Danforth became a U.S. senator. By this time, Thomas's own politics had taken a hard right turn. He started reading the collected works of libertarian writer/philosopher Ayn Rand and driving a BMW in short order. In 1981, incoming Republican president Ronald Reagan rewarded him for his conservative activism by appointing him assistant secretary for civil rights at the Department of Education. After only ten months, he was bumped up to director of the Equal Employment Opportunity Commission (EEOC).

With a plum job in a popular administration, Thomas seemed to be on easy street at last. But he was still drinking like a fish. ("I spent too many nights in the early eighties, drinking alone in a dreary efficiency apartment," he confessed in his memoirs.) His marriage had collapsed, and there were still more money problems. After nearly being kicked out of one apartment for failing to pay the rent on time, he found another that was infested with cockroaches. "I couldn't afford anything better," he recalled. About this time, Thomas met a younger EEOC attorney named Anita Hill. More on her later.

By 1986, Thomas had controlled his drinking and gotten his life in order. He met and married his second wife, Virginia Lamp, a GOP Congressional aide who shared his love for Ayn Rand. In 1990, President George H. W. Bush capped his rapid rise through the ranks of official Washington by appointing him to sit on the D.C. court of appeals. Thomas had no judicial experience at the time. He sat on the court for only eighteen months, until Bush came calling again, this time with an offer of a Supreme Court nomination. Thurgood Marshall, the Court's lone African American justice, had resigned, and Bush was eager to appoint the high-profile black conservative to replace him.

Thomas's confirmation before the Senate was already going to be dicey. Even the Bush administration official who coached him for his appearance before the Senate judiciary committee called his performance "terrible." Thomas later admitted that he misled the White House when they asked whether he had ever used illegal drugs. "I don't remember," Thomas replied—an answer he insisted was accurate because he may have been too drunk to recall smoking marijuana. Still, Thomas gave a reasonable enough account of himself before the committee and seemed likely to be confirmed before the full Senate. That's when Anita Hill reentered his life. In a big way.

In an incendiary letter that was leaked to the press, Hill charged that, in the 1980s, Thomas had repeatedly pressured her for dates and subjected her to graphic descriptions of his genitalia while supervising her at the EEOC. Worse still, she alleged, Thomas had an insatiable love of porn involving animals, freaks, and sexual marvels such as the grotesquely endowed cowboy stud Long Dong Silver. (A Washington D.C. video store proprietor later confirmed that Thomas was something of a connoisseur of adult films; one of his favorite titles, *Bad Mama Jamma*, depicted the erotic exploits of a 450-pound woman.)

Special hearings were immediately convened to address the veracity of Hill's allegations. Although several corroborating witnesses came forward, little hard evidence emerged to prove that Thomas had broken the law—or even acted outside the bounds of office propriety. Thomas himself called the televised hearings "a national disgrace" and "a high-tech lynching" engineered by his political opponents to keep an outspoken black conservative off the nation's highest bench. After a surreal week of questioning, Thomas's nomination was sent to the full Senate, which confirmed him by a vote of 52–48.

"Whoop-dee damn-doo!" Thomas exclaimed from the bathtub when his wife informed him of the outcome. "Mere confirmation, even to the Supreme Court, seemed pitifully small compensation for what had been done to me," he later wrote. A bitter and angry Thomas took his seat on the Court in October 1991, determined to flummox and frustrate all those who had opposed him by being even more conservative than they could have possibly imagined. A proponent of the "Constitution-in-exile" philosophy that seeks to restore federal law to its state before the New Deal and the civil rights revolution, Thomas has been a stalwart member of the Court's right-wing bloc, led by Justice Antonin Scalia. Although widely reported to have a warm personal relationship with Court staff and fellow justices—he and liberal Stephen Breyer often pass teasing notes during oral arguments—Thomas delights in taking every opportunity to twist the knife in the backs of those he sees as having tried to destroy his reputation. In 2007, that list grew to include Anita Hill, whom Thomas derided in a best-selling memoir as a grasping, shrewish whack job driven by her own romantic frustration.

THE QUIET MAN

If you visit the Supreme Court while it's in session, expect to see the justices engage in vigorous constitutional question-and-answer sessions with the lawyers appearing before them—all except Clarence Thomas. Since he arrived on the Court, he's more than earned his nickname, "The Silent Justice," by refusing to utter a word during oral arguments. At one point, Thomas went more than two years without asking a single question—surely a record for a bench whose seats have been filled by some of American history's most notorious blowhards. One prominent legal blog even started a "When-Will-Justice-Thomas-Ask-a-Question Watch" to try to predict the occurrence of his next query.

So why the silent treatment? Thomas has offered various explanations. He once blamed his reluctance to speak on shyness caused by his inability to master the English language as a teenager. (Thomas grew up speaking Geechee, an African American regional dialect used in his native Georgia.) He later claimed that he would open his yap when he was good and ready—and not a moment before.

"If I think a question will help me decide a case, then I'll ask that question," he told Brian Lamb of C-SPAN. "Otherwise, it's not worth asking, because it detracts from my job." At other times, Thomas has derided the practice of anyone asking questions in oral arguments. "My colleagues should shut up!" he told an audience at Michigan's Hillsdale College in 2007. "Suppose you're undergoing something very serious like surgery, and the doctors started a practice of conducting seminars while in the operating room, debating each other about certain procedures and whether or not this procedure is this way or that way. You really didn't go in there to have a debate about gallbladder surgery. You actually went in to have a procedure done. We are judges. This is the last court in a long line in our system. We are there to decide cases, not to engage in seminar discussions." Besides, Thomas contends, once the cases get to the Supreme Court, most justices' minds are already made up, and there's very little chance anything will happen to change that. "This is not Perry Mason," he contends.

COKE FIEND

"Who has put a pubic hair in my Coke?" became one of the most bizarre catchphrases in judicial history after Anita Hill accused Thomas of asking her the question during their time together at the Equal Employment Opportunity Commission. Thomas's fondness for the smutty interrogative allegedly dated to his college days, although its origin and meaning remain obscure. One of the more colorful theories was offered by Senator Orrin Hatch of Utah, Thomas's staunchest backer on the Judiciary Committee. In a "stop the presses" moment at Thomas's confirmation hearings, Hatch appeared waving a tattered copy of William Peter Blatty's 1971 horror novel *The Exorcist*, from which, he alleged, Anita Hill had plagiarized the entire anecdote. There was just one problem. Blatty's version doesn't mention a Coke, and it isn't phrased in the form of a question. In the passage Hatch cited, one character simply talks about what appears to be "an alien pubic hair floating around in my gin."

FINE WHINE

Thomas is no fan of the NAACP. When an interviewer asked him to name one area where the venerable civil rights organization has done good work, he replied, "I can't think of any." He complained that all civil rights leaders do is "bitch, bitch, bitch, moan and moan, whine and whine."

Bum Rap

Thomas may have no use for the civil rights establishment, but for many in the black community the feeling is mutual. In their 1992 song "Build and

Destroy," hip-hop group Boogie Down Productions informs listeners that "the white man ain't the devil, I promise / You want to see the devil, take a look at Clarence Thomas."

RAND FAN

Thomas is a huge fan of the libertarian writer/philosopher Ayn Rand, particularly her 1943 novel, *The Fountainhead*. For years, he has required his staff to watch the film version of the book during their lunch hour. One former aide called it "a sort of training film" for working for Thomas.

I WILL BURY ALL OF YOU!

In the wake of his bruising confirmation battle, Thomas is determined to get back at his critics—and living a long time is his idea of the best revenge. "I was only going to stay on the Supreme Court for ten years," he once told a staffer, "but since they pissed me off, I think I'll stay on for life." Early in his tenure, Thomas even masterminded the renovation of the Supreme Court gym, specifically for the purposes of getting into top shape so that he could outlast all his enemies. A workout freak, the thickly built justice once ran the Marine Corps Marathon and enjoys lifting weights.

POISON IVY

High on Thomas's long enemies list are members of the mainstream media, or "smart-aleck commentators and self-professed know-it-alls," as he calls them. He once told a friend that the day he cancelled his *Washington Post* subscription was the happiest day of his life. Ivy Leaguers also grind his gears. For years, Thomas kept a "Yale Sucks" bumper sticker on the mantelpiece in his chambers. On his bookshelf is a sign that reads "Save America. Bomb Yale Law School." Why all the hatred toward his alma mater? Thomas believes that Yale faculty and alums took sides against him in the Anita Hill controversy. He even threatened to send his law degree back to New Haven in protest. When asked to speak at law schools, Thomas adheres to a strict policy encapsulated in the phrase "I don't do Ivies."

A Diss Best Served Cold

One campus Thomas won't be speaking at anytime soon is **Bennett College** in **North Carolina**, where economist **Julianne Malveaux** reigns as president. In 1994, Malveaux pronounced Thomas "an absolutely reprehensible person" and declared, "I hope his wife feeds him lots of eggs and butter and he dies early like many black men do, of heart disease." The diss must have stuck in Thomas's craw, because five years later he was still looking for payback. In December 1999, at a banquet for the right-wing **Media Research Center** in Washington, Thomas accepted an "**I'm a Compassionate Liberal but I Wish You Were All Dead Award for Media Hatred of Conservatives**" on Malveaux's behalf.

HOOP DREAMS

Until he injured his knee, Thomas was one of the most avid users of the Court building's top-floor basketball facility, known informally as "the highest court in the land." He once invited NBA star Charles Barkley for a game of H.O.R.S.E. and some light conversation. The meeting also had a political purpose: Thomas was trying to convince Sir Charles to run for Congress in Alabama as a Republican.

RACE MAN

Basketball isn't Thomas's only game. He also loves **NASCAR** and once served as the grand marshal of the **Daytona 500**.

KING OF SWAG

Membership on the Supreme Court has its privileges, and Thomas has not been shy about exercising them. According to his financial disclosure forms, he accepts more gifts than any sitting justice. Among the freebies collected over the years: $100 worth of cigars from radio host Rush Limbaugh; a $500 cowboy hat from a Houston men's club; an $800 Daytona 500 commemorative jacket; $1,200 worth of tires from a businessman in Omaha, Nebraska; and $1,375 worth of western attire, including a rawhide coat and a silver belt buckle.

On the Road Again

Every justice has an extracurricular passion. Thomas's is driving. On weekends, he likes to tool around town in his black Corvette ZR-1. The vanity plate reads "REZ IPSA," after the Latin legal phrase *res ipsa loquitur*, or "the thing speaks for itself." During the summer, Thomas leaves the 'vette at home and piles the family into the forty-foot custom-built RV he calls his "condo on wheels." Together they tour Wal-Mart parking lots and out-of-the-way trailer parks, where Thomas can escape the Beltway elites he so despises and interact with "ordinary" Americans. "Being an RVer helps me do my job better," the peripatetic justice has said. "The best people in the country can be found in RV campgrounds." In 2004, the Recreation Vehicle Industry Association acknowledged Thomas's contribution to the world of RVing when it presented him its Spirit of America award.

THE BALLAD OF LONG DONG SILVER

One of the more unusual bit players to emerge from the Thomas-Hill hearings was Long Dong Silver, the Bermuda-born porno actor whose work (Hill contended) Thomas greatly admired. A fixture of the 1980s adult film scene, Silver (real name: Daniel Arthur Mead) claimed to have an eighteen-inch-long penis, which he could tie into a half hitch knot, with room to spare. It was later revealed that he used a prosthetic sheath to enhance his endowment. The cowboy-hat-wearing sex performer gave up on porn in 1987 and reportedly now lives in seclusion in the south of England.

RUTH BADER
GINSBURG

March 15, 1933–

BIRTHPLACE:
Brooklyn, NY

NICKNAME:
"Kiki"

ASTROLOGICAL SIGN:
Pisces

TERM:
August 10, 1993–

APPOINTED BY:
Bill Clinton

WORDS OF WISDOM:
"I would not like to be the only woman on the court."

Short, frail, socially awkward, and sporting comically oversized eyeglasses, Ruth Bader Ginsburg could easily be dismissed as the latest in a long line of Supreme Court grotesques—a physical oddity more suited for a Victorian-era specimen box than a postmodern judicial body. But that's probably just what she wants you to think. Inside that mantis-like figure beats the heart of a tough-as-nails survivor from the streets of Brooklyn. She overcame family hardship and institutional sexism to get where she is—and it'll take more than a mighty stiff wind to dislodge her. (Well, okay a mighty stiff wind would probably dislodge her; she's only five feet tall, after all.)

Ruth Joan Bader was born on March 15, 1933, in the Flatbush section of Brooklyn. The second child of furrier Nathan Bader and his wife, Celia, Ruth learned how to deal from an early age. Her older sister Marilyn died of meningitis at age eight, and from then on she was raised, essentially, as an only child. She picked up her love of learning from her mother. A voracious reader, Celia Bader would often take Ruth on trips to the nearest public library, one flight above a Chinese restaurant. (Ginsburg has associated books with the smell of Chinese food ever since.) Her interest in law was kindled in grade school, where she wrote an editorial for the school paper on the meaning of Magna Carta and the Bill of Rights.

In high school, Bader broadened her horizons to include extracurricular activities. She twirled the baton, played the cello in the orchestra, and joined the honor society. As a member of the school pep squad, known as the "Go-Getters," she wore a black satin jacket with gold letters and sold tickets for football games. She also lost a race for student government, but was happy to be defeated by her best friend. For fifteen summers, Bader spent her downtime at Camp Che-Na-Wah in the Adirondack Mountains. There she picked up a nickname, "Kiki," whose origins remain obscure.

In the fall of 1950, Bader left Brooklyn for Cornell University in upstate New York. *Lolita* author Vladimir Nabokov was one of her professors, though young lust doesn't seem to have figured prominently in her college years. While popular, Bader earned a reputation for being "scary smart," in the words of one classmate, and seemed destined for a life of high achievement. She married Martin Ginsburg, a fellow Cornell alum, in 1954, and together they moved on to Harvard Law School. There, Marty contracted testicular cancer, prompting Ruth to take on his classwork as well as her own. She still made law review and graduated tied for first in her class, after transferring to Coumbia Law School, in 1959.

> A devotee of Verdi and Puccini, Ruth Bader Ginsburg has appeared as an extra in two productions of the Washington Opera.

Had she been a man, Ginsburg would have been an attractive hire for dozens of top law firms. Instead she found herself shut out of the job market. "The traditional law firms were just beginning to turn around on hiring Jews," she said later. "But to be a woman, a Jew, and a mother to boot—that combination was a bit too much." After a series of rejections, she managed to wrangle a clerkship and eventually joined the law faculty of Rutgers University. From this perch she began a sideline litigating sex discrimination cases, eventually appearing before the Supreme Court. "I didn't eat lunch for fear I might throw up," she said of her first oral argument. After a few minutes her anxiety evaporated, and "I realized that here before me were the nine leading jurists of America, a captive audience. I felt a surge of power that carried me through." Initially dismissive, over time the justices came to respect her, and between 1972 and 1978 Ginsburg won five of the six cases she argued before the hallowed nine.

In 1980, President Jimmy Carter recognized Ginsburg's growing stature by elevating her to the U.S. court of appeals. She was now one step away from a Supreme Court appointment, but would have to wait thirteen years, until the election of the next Democratic president, before she moved up the ladder. When Bill Clinton announced her nomination, little controversy ensued. Ginsburg sailed through the Senate on a 97–3 vote, becoming the second female justice in history. As one of the liberal stalwarts on a court dominated by conservatives, she's made her mark most often in dissent, although her cautious approach to adjudication and moderate positions on issues of criminal justice have made her surprisingly palatable to conservatives. She's even struck up an unlikely friendship with her ideological opposite, Antonin Scalia; the archliberal and the überconservative are best pals away from the bench. (Not that that's kept Scalia from blasting away at her in his opinions.) Every year their families celebrate New Year's together with a black-tie dinner at the Ginsburgs' swanky apartment in the Watergate complex (the former home of U.S. senator Abraham Ribicoff). While the justices regale each other with work stories, spouses Martin Ginsburg and Maureen Scalia do most of the cooking.

I CAN'T HEAR YOU!

On Ginsburg's wedding day, her soon-to-be mother-in-law presented an unusual gift: a set of earplugs. "In every good marriage, sometimes it pays to be a little deaf," Old Mother Ginsburg confided. Ruth Bader Ginsburg has come to appreciate the wisdom of learning to tune out the negative, and the advice is certainly handy when some of her more overbearing Court colleagues (*cough*— Scalia—*cough*) take it upon themselves to criticize her. "I sometimes find myself alone in chambers momentarily distressed or annoyed," Ginsburg has admitted, "thinking, I'd like to strangle Justice So-and-So."

BIG MOMMA

It was a plot twist worthy of an *I Love Lucy* episode. In 1965, when Ginsburg was pregnant with her second child, she began wearing her mother-in-law's capacious dresses to conceal her condition from her boss, who she suspected would fire her upon learning the truth.

GREAT MOMENTS IN SEXISM I

In 1956, while at Harvard Law, Ginsburg and the eight other female law students attended a dinner hosted by Dean Erwin Griswold. After a pleasant meal, Griswold ruined the evening by asking each of the women how it felt to be taking up places that should have gone to more-deserving males. "When my turn came, I wish I could have pushed a button and vanished through a trapdoor," Ginsburg recalled. She managed to stammer out an answer about how studying law would help her to understand her husband's work better, and could possibly lead to part-time employment.

Great Moments in Sexism II

Felix Frankfurter and Learned Hand were two of the many judges who refused to hire Ginsburg as a clerk because of her gender. Frankfurter didn't even try to hide his sexism. "Does she wear skirts?" he asked when informed she had applied for a clerkship. "I can't stand girls in pants!" Despite being assured that she dressed in the proper, ladylike fashion, he never granted her an interview.

Hand was subtler. He had a policy of never hiring women as clerks, he said, because he swore like a sailor and didn't want to offend their delicate sensibilities. One day Ginsburg was riding in the backseat of a car while Hand and her boss, federal district court judge Edmund L. Palmieri, sat up front. Hand was cursing a blue streak, as always, so Ginsburg worked up the courage to ask what the difference was. "Young lady," Hand replied, "here I am not looking you in the face."

CHUMP CHANGE

How pervasive was the sexism that Ginsburg faced as a young female lawyer arguing before the Supreme Court? During oral arguments, Justice William Rehnquist once asked her why women were still complaining about inequality when Susan B. Anthony's face was on a dollar coin. Wasn't that enough, the future chief justice wanted to know? Ginsburg had to bite her tongue to keep from blurting out what immediately leaped to mind: "No, Your Honor, tokens won't do."

NOW I KNOW HOW FLORENCE BALLARD FELT

During her early days as an associate justice, Ginsburg fretted about being regarded as "the other woman" on the Court, next to the trailblazing Sandra Day O'Connor. In 1993, the National Association of Women Judges even presented her with a T-shirt that read "The Supremes" on the front and "I'm Ruth, Not Sandra" on the back.

DIMINUTIVE DIVA

Like her good friend Antonin Scalia, Ginsburg is an opera buff and can often be observed weeping during performances at the Washington Opera. The wee jurist has also appeared as an extra in two of the company's productions, once in a powdered wig and full costume and once as herself. She counts Mozart, Verdi, and Puccini among her favorite composers.

Mystery Woman

When she's not humming along with *Pagliacci*, Ginsburg likes reading mystery novels, whose intricate plot twists no doubt appeal to her rigorously logical mind. Her favorite authors include Amanda Cross and Dorothy L. Sayers. In her off-hours, she also enjoys watching classic movies, water skiing, and horseback riding.

IT'S IN THE HOLE!

If you're booking tee times for your next Supreme Court golf outing, consider adding Ginsburg to your foursome. The unassuming justice is quite the accomplished duffer. Despite being left-handed, she learned to play with right-handed clubs, prompting a friend to remark that Ginsburg plays golf the same way she decides cases: aim left, swing right, and hit it down the middle.

AIN'T SHE SWEDE

Ginsburg speaks fluent Swedish, having spent two summers in Sweden researching a book about that country's civil procedure. To this day, she boasts, she can follow the films of Ingmar Bergman without subtitles.

PICTURE IMPERFECT

Unlike Clarence Thomas, Ginsburg will gladly speak at her Ivy League alma mater. Just don't ask her to gaze upon her own likeness while she's there. In 1984, Columbia University's law school commissioned a portrait of Ginsburg— the first ever of a woman at the school—as a tribute to the native New Yorker. There was just one problem: the painting was dreadful. In fact, it made her look like a dour, disapproving schoolmarm. Ginsburg hated it. Now, instead of hanging alongside portraits of other fabled Empire State jurists like Charles Evans Hughes, it sits in storage.

Laugh Track

Ginsburg's reputation as a prim, humorless crone may be unfounded. (According to her son James, she can get positively giddy after just one glass of wine.) But her own husband may have something to do with it. For years, Martin Ginsburg made a point of telling his law partners every time he made his wife laugh. In a booklet entitled "Mommy Laughs," Ginsburg's daughter Jane even kept a log of the rare instances when a smile cracked her mother's lips. It's no surprise that in 2005, when a Boston University law professor conducted a study to determine the funniest Supreme Court justice, Ginsburg came in second to last. Only the eternally saturnine Clarence Thomas ranked lower.

STEPHEN
BREYER

August 15, 1938–

BIRTHPLACE:
San Francisco, CA

NICKNAME:
"Blister King"

ASTROLOGICAL SIGN:
Leo

TERM:
August 3, 1994–

APPOINTED BY:
Bill Clinton

WORDS OF WISDOM:
"When you put on the robe, at that point the politics is over."

How badly did Stephen Breyer want to get on the Supreme Court? Even though he was hit by a car while riding his bicycle shortly before his interview with President Bill Clinton in 1993, suffering a punctured lung, he insisted on leaving the hospital and traveling by train from Massachusetts to Washington D.C. He was determined to make a good face-to-face impression. He didn't (not that time, anyway). Clinton passed over the wheezing, obviously uncomfortable appeals court judge in favor of Ruth Bader Ginsburg. But the next year, when another Court opening popped up, Breyer was back in the game. This time he aced the interview—and managed to avoid getting run over in the process.

Stephen Breyer's first try at the Supreme Court was interrupted by a nasty bike accident (and some broken ribs).

Stephen Gerald Breyer was born on August 15, 1938, in San Francisco. His father was a lawyer and a passionate advocate of good government. When Stephen was a child, Irving Breyer would take the boy into the voting booth on Election Day. "We're exercising our prerogative," Papa Breyer would say as little Stephen pulled the lever on his behalf. Breyer's mother, Anne, was active

in Democratic Party politics and a member of the League of Women Voters. She encouraged the studious Stephen to put aside his textbooks every now and then and take up sports, even though he had no aptitude for it. In fact, Breyer had so much trouble staying on the playing field that his summer-camp compatriots nicknamed him "Blister King," for his constantly barking feet. Breyer eventually found a suitable outlet for mind and body in the Boy Scouts, where he made Eagle Scout as at age twelve and earned a reputation as the "troop brain."

In high school, Breyer was a member of the debate team, once squaring off against future California governor and U.S. presidential candidate Jerry Brown. His debate coach remembered him as being lawyer material, a scrupulous researcher who would squirrel himself away at the library to bone up on a debate topic while fellow students were out "stealing hubcaps." Not surprisingly, Breyer excelled academically, earning only one B and being voted Most Likely to Succeed. During summers, he worked a series of odd jobs, including delivery boy, ditch digger for the Pacific Gas and Electric company, and salad mixer at a summer camp in the Sierras.

After high school, Breyer wanted to attend Harvard, but his mother talked him out of it, fearing he would wind up too much of an egghead. He enrolled at Stanford instead, where the atmosphere was maybe a little too relaxed. He was arrested once for underage drinking, though he still managed to graduate Phi Beta Kappa. After a sojourn at Oxford as a Marshall scholar, Breyer moved on to Harvard Law, where he served as editor of the *Harvard Law Review* and graduated—you guessed it—magna cum laude.

A clerkship with Supreme Court justice Arthur Goldberg gave the young Breyer his first taste of Washington D.C. It was there, at a Georgetown house party, that he first met the woman who would become his wife. Joanna Freda Hale was a British national, of aristocratic stock. Her father, Lord John Blankenham, was the former vice chairman of the British Conservative Party. The couple was married in 1967 at a village church in Suffolk, England. Over the next thirteen years, Breyer split his time between Cambridge, Massachusetts, and the nation's capital, teaching law, writing and lecturing on regulatory issues, and serving as counsel to various Senate committees. In 1980, President Jimmy Carter capped his ascent to the top ranks of American jurisprudence by making him a U.S. Court of Appeals judge.

Breyer had to wait another thirteen years for a chance to move up to the Supreme Court—and when he blew his first interview with Bill Clinton, all hope seemed lost. "I don't see enough humanity," Clinton complained after meeting the reserved judge for the first time. "I want a judge with a soul." But with the 1994 retirement of Harry Blackmun, the bald, beaming jurist got another bite at the apple. This time the president was won over, and Breyer's name was sent to the Senate for confirmation. Ralph Nader led the opposition to his nomination. The po-faced consumer advocate bashed Breyer as a tool of big business whose opinions "just happen to please 'corporatists' who do not welcome health and safety regulation." But with the Democrats still clinging to control of Congress, little could be done to derail Breyer's jump to the high court. He was confirmed on a vote of 87–9.

On the Court, Breyer is known for his moderate politics, affable personality, and abstruse writing style. (A friend once told him, "Steve, you think like an eagle but write like a turkey.") Like his colleague Justice David Souter—for whom he is often confused—Breyer also has a bit of eccentricity. Opining on a case involving wireless Internet licenses, Breyer observed that a sign reading "'No Animals in the Park' doesn't apply to a pet oyster"—surely one of the strangest utterances ever to exit the mouth of a Supreme Court justice. To this day, no one is quite sure what he meant by the remark, although that's just fine with the genial Breyer, whose Cheshire cat smile seems to signal that another such gnomic witticism might spill forth from his pen at any moment.

★ ★

STEVE'S HOUSE

An amateur architect, Breyer helped design Boston's new federal courthouse in the 1990s. Determined to create a public space that jurors and other citizens would actually want to spend time in, Breyer met with community groups, visited courts around the country, and engaged the planners responsible for the Holocaust

Memorial Museum in Washington and the John F. Kennedy Library to help him realize his grand vision. Erected under the federal government's $8 billion courthouse construction and renovation program, the resulting ten-story L-shaped palace of justice cost $220 million to build and was derided as "a Taj Mahal" by Senator John McCain.

STUMP THE JUSTICE

In March 2007, at the urging of his sister-in-law, Breyer appeared on the popular National Public Radio trivia program "Wait Wait . . . Don't Tell Me." After chatting about life at the Court with host Peter Sagal and panelists Luke Burbank, Paula Poundstone, and Mo Rocca, Breyer tried his hand at the "Not My Job" segment, in which guests attempt to answer trivia questions outside their area of expertise. Unfortunately, Breyer's topic—the antics of famous rock stars—was completely alien to him, and he fared poorly. The pointy-headed jurist seemed baffled by questions about David Bowie having an exorcism performed on his swimming pool, Iggy Pop eating nothing but German sausages for a year, and Ozzy Osbourne heading straight for the bar upon checking into the Betty Ford Clinic. Breyer failed to answer any of the three questions correctly, prompting an enraged Rocca to dispatch him "back to the appeals court" for more seasoning.

THE ROBE WARRIOR

During his 2007 appearance on "Wait Wait . . . Don't Tell Me," Breyer revealed that he has been wearing the same judicial robe since the early 1980s—principally because of its amazing lint-resistant properties. "It's a synthetic," he explained, pointing out that he had purchased the robe some twenty-five years earlier at a shop in downtown Boston, where he was serving as a federal appeals court judge. Egged on by the show's panel, Breyer also confessed that he was jealous of the snazzy robes worn by his Court colleagues Sandra Day O'Connor and Ruth Bader Ginsburg. "They have very nice collars," the covetous jurist admitted.

Ill Humor

You can mark Breyer down as unfazed by the 2005 study conducted by Boston University law professor Jay D. Wexler, which pegged him as the second funniest justice, behind Antonin Scalia. Being the funniest Supreme Court justice, Breyer quipped, "is like being one of the shortest tall people."

HI YO, STEPHEN!

An avowed epicure, Breyer loves to cook and, when he lived in Cambridge, Massachusetts, used to shop at the same gourmet stores favored by master chef Julia Child. His other hobbies include bird watching and bicycle riding. He's also a fan of old-time radio programs, particularly "The Lone Ranger," which he used to listen to as a child growing up in California.

LEO'S STASH

Breyer is a voracious reader who has amassed an impressive rare book collection. Many of the volumes were bequeathed to him by his nutty Uncle Leo, an avid antiquarian who used to roust him from bed at the crack of dawn so they could be first in the door at Cambridge's used-book sales.

A GIANT AMONG JUNIORS

Breyer was "junior justice"—Court parlance for the justice with the least amount of service time on the high bench—for twelve years, longer than any other justice in history save for Joseph Story. With that title came some unusual responsibilities. The junior justice traditionally goes last in funeral processions and when entering the House chamber for the president's State of the Union address. As low man on the pole, it was also Breyer's job to open the door to the justice's conference room if anybody knocked on it. In interviews, Breyer has often recounted a story about the time he answered the door to find that he was being asked to deliver a cup of coffee to Justice Antonin Scalia. Even after Justice Samuel Alito replaced him in the position of junior justice, Breyer found the old habits hard to break. "When there is a knock at the door I suddenly react and start to get up," he has said. "I had been used to it like a Pavlovian dog."

As it turned out, Breyer fell just twenty-nine days short of being the longest-serving junior justice in history. Story held the position for 4,228 days in the early nineteenth century. "I missed by twenty-nine days becoming immortal as the answer to a trivia question!" a dejected Breyer said upon learning the news.

Nuts to Notes

Alone among current justices, Breyer eschews footnotes in his opinions, in the belief that excessive citations get in the way of the text and impede comprehension by the lay reader.

JOHN
ROBERTS

January 27, 1955–

BIRTHPLACE:
Buffalo, NY

NICKNAME:
"Jackie"

ASTROLOGICAL SIGN:
Aquarius

TERM:
September 29, 2005–

APPOINTED BY:
George W. Bush

WORDS OF WISDOM:
"If the Constitution says that the little guy should win, the little guy's going to win in court before me. But if the Constitution says that the big guy should win, well, then the big guy's going to win."

"I've always wanted to stay ahead of the crowd," wrote thirteen-year-old John Roberts in his application letter to the elite Catholic boarding school La Lumiere. "I won't be content to get a good job by getting a good education; I want to get the best job by getting the best education." The consummate overachiever, Roberts walked a scarily straight-and-narrow path from Midwestern steel town to stewardship of the highest court in the land. If nice guys finish last, someone forgot to tell Roberts, whose nonthreatening manner evokes a bygone era when being brainy, diligent, and white was all you needed to climb the ladder of success.

John Glover Roberts was born on January 27, 1955, in Buffalo, New York. When he was eight, his father, an executive for Bethlehem Steel, moved the family to Long Beach, Indiana. Maybe he was seeking a less "avant-garde" milieu in which to raise his children, but it's likelier that the attraction was more and bigger steel mills. Until age eleven, John Junior was known exclusively as "Jackie." He realized that the only Jackie he'd ever heard of was Jacqueline Kennedy and asked everybody to start calling him by his given name.

A devout Catholic, Roberts attended parochial grade school and an all-male Catholic boarding school. Classmates remember him as an almost eerily overprepared student whose academic performance put them all to shame. One time Roberts boned up for a presentation on Greek philosophy by plowing through seven books on the subject and showing up for class wearing a home-made toga. His lecture droned on for three whole days. On another occasion, his calculus teacher informed the class that more than half the students had failed a test, a few others had earned Ds, and one freak had screwed up the curve by getting every answer correct. Everyone knew who that freak was. Languages were also in the future chief justice's sweet spot. He excelled at Latin and, it was said, could translate the *Aeneid* on par with his teacher.

When not making his fellow students look like slack-jawed yokels in the classroom, Roberts was out-hustling them on the extracurricular circuit. He wrestled, ran track, co-captained the football team, co-edited the student newspaper, served on the student council and yearbook staff, sang in the choir, worked as a dorm proctor, and played Peppermint Patty in the school's production of "You're a Good Man, Charlie Brown." At the school science fair, Roberts overwhelmed the competition with his automatic table fork project, beating out another student's water purification exhibit by acclamation. Even at that early age, his conservative politics were beginning to take shape. He wrote an opinion piece for the school paper, opposing the idea of opening enrollment to girls.

> As associate counsel to Ronald Reagan, John Roberts faced unforeseen challenges. One of the biggest was keeping pop singer Michael Jackson at bay.

Moving on to Harvard, where he shared a class with cellist Yo-Yo Ma, Roberts maintained the same frenzied academic pace. He graduated in only three years, summa cum laude, of course. In 1976, his 175-page undergraduate thesis, "British Domestic Politics: 1900–1914," won the Bowdoin Essay Prize for "the best dissertation submitted in the English language." Refusing to pass "Go," Roberts went straight on to Harvard Law (after briefly considering Stanford and ruling it out because his interviewer wore sandals). He graduated

magna cum laude at age twenty-four and embarked on a series of high-profile clerkships, including one for Supreme Court justice William Rehnquist. (Oddly, just a few years earlier, Roberts had declined to join Harvard Law's "Rehnquist Club," honoring the pioneering conservative jurist.) He served as a legal eagle in the Reagan White House, as deputy solicitor general under George H. W. Bush, and in private practice with the Washington D.C. law firm of Hogan & Hartson.

In 2003, Roberts became a judge on the U.S. Court of Appeals for the D.C. circuit—a traditional stepping stone on the way to the Supreme Court. A suitable vacancy opened up in 2005, with the retirement of Sandra Day O'Connor. Roberts was first nominated for her associate justice's chair, then bumped up to chief less than two months later, after Rehnquist's death. Partisan opposition limited Roberts's confirmation margin to 56 votes in the Senate, though his candidacy was never seriously in doubt. He did little in his first few years on the Court to assuage the fears of liberals, joining a conservative bloc led by Justices Scalia, Thomas, and Samuel Alito (O'Connor's eventual replacement). Still, his genial smile, strong work ethic, and collegial management style was enough to defang most in the mainstream media, who prize bonhomie chief among earthly virtues.

★ ★

YOU WANNA BE STARTING SOMETHING?

Long before he became the Supreme Court's resident P.Y.T., Roberts was telling Michael Jackson to "beat it" in a series of scathing memos written during his time as associate counsel to the president in the Reagan White House. The publicist for the self-appointed "King of Pop" had written to Reagan requesting an official presidential letter recognizing the singer's efforts to combat drunk driving. Charged with handling such correspondence, a beleaguered Roberts hit the ceiling. "The office of presidential correspondence is not yet an adjunct of Michael Jackson's PR firm," he raged in a memo to his boss. "Enough is enough." A few months later, Jackson's camp tried again. This time they asked for a letter thanking Jackson for a concert he had performed in the nation's capital. Again, Roberts exploded. "I hate to sound like one of Mr. Jackson's records, constantly repeating the same refrain," he blasted, "but I recommend that we not approve this letter." He went on to decry the "fawning" treatment Jackson was being afforded by certain members of the White House staff, calling it "more than a little embarrassing." Jackson's concert appearance, Roberts argued, "was a calculated commercial decision that does not warrant gratitude from our nation's chief executive." Finally, in a sign that he was keenly attuned to the mid-80s music scene, Roberts noted that "some youngsters [are] turning away from Mr. Jackson in favor of a newcomer who goes by the name 'Prince,' and is apparently planning a Washington concert. Will he receive a presidential letter?"

BOSS MAN

Roberts may not like the King of Pop, but another 1980s icon is aces in his book. The chief justice is a big Bruce Springsteen fan. In fact, when he was denying M.J.'s request for a presidential thank you, he made a point of mentioning that the Boss didn't receive a letter from Reagan after *his* tour.

SOUSAPHILE

When not pumping his fist to "Born in the USA," Roberts can be found marching along to the strains of John Phillip Sousa. During his days as deputy solicitor general in the George H. W. Bush administration, he played Sousa marches to rev himself up before a big case at the Supreme Court. It must have worked. Roberts won twenty-five of the thirty-nine cases he argued before the Court.

Fry Crook

Talk about "tough love." Roberts dished some out fast food style in one of his most celebrated cases as an appeals court judge. In the 2004 case of *Hedgepeth v. Washington Transit Authority*, Roberts ruled that the D.C. transit police had not violated the constitutional rights of a twelve-year-old girl whom they arrested for eating a single French fry in a Washington Metro station. In Roberts's own recounting of the incident, the ravenous tyke was searched, had her shoelaces removed, and "was transported in the windowless rear compartment of a police vehicle to a juvenile processing center, where she was booked, fingerprinted, and detained until released to her mother some three hours later." But none of that was enough to sway the three-judge panel. "No one is very happy about the events that led to this litigation," Roberts wrote in his majority opinion. "The question before us, however, is not whether these policies were a bad idea but whether they violated the Fourth and Fifth amendments to the Constitution. Like the district court, we conclude that they did not, and accordingly we affirm."

YOU'RE MAKING ME DISNEY!

On most Saturdays, Chef Roberts whips up a special breakfast for his wife and kids: crisp bacon accompanied by Mickey Mouse–shaped waffles.

MR. JUSTICE GOTROCKS

He may strike an unassuming figure, but Roberts is one of the wealthiest men ever to sit on the Supreme Court. At the time of his nomination in 2005, he had a net worth of more than $5 million, according to financial disclosure forms submitted to the Senate Judiciary Committee. Roberts's holdings included about $1.7 million in mutual funds and $1.6 million in individual stocks. (For those wishing to replicate his portfolio, major investments included Dell, Microsoft, Texas Instruments, XM Satellite Radio, and Time Warner.) But the chief can be excused for socking a little away. He took a serious pay cut to join the federal judiciary in 2003. His salary went from $1 million a year in private practice to a comparatively measly $212,100 by 2008.

CHOCOLATE REIGN

A confirmed chocoholic, Roberts always keeps a candy dish piled high with Hershey's Kisses in his chambers. As a law school student, he ate chocolate chip ice cream every day at the same Cambridge ice cream shop. His sister also whipped up a batch of chocolate chip cookies to mark the start of his Supreme Court confirmation hearings.

Green, Green Grass of Home

He may be a multimillionaire, but Roberts doesn't live like one. Neighbors report the unpretentious chief justice still mows his own lawn.

SEIZE THE DAY

Is Roberts an epileptic? That's the conclusion some doctors have reached, citing the two seizures the chief justice has suffered since 1993. The first occurred on a golf course, according to *Newsweek*, and prevented Roberts from driving to work for several months. The second seizure took place in July 2007 at the chief justice's summer home in Maine. He fell backward on a floating boat ramp, suffered minor scrapes, and was rushed to the hospital for treatment. Doctors generally consider a patient epileptic when he or she has had two or more seizures with no known cause.

HELLO, DOLLY!

In one of history's weird little close encounters, Roberts crossed paths with Broadway legend Carol Channing in February 2006. The newly installed chief justice was visiting George Washington University to preside over a law school moot court competition when he bumped into the toothy diva, who was performing on campus as part of the university's 185th birthday celebration. Channing presented Roberts with her autographed photo and posed with him for another. "She was ecstatic to meet him," remarked a university spokeswoman, "and he seemed equally pleased to be meeting her."

MY LITTLE MENAGERIE

Roberts keeps several unusual pets, including two snails and a ladybug named Dora.

SAMUEL
ALITO

April 1, 1950–

BIRTHPLACE:
Trenton, NJ

NICKNAME:
"Scalito," "Strip Search Sammy"

ASTROLOGICAL SIGN:
Aries

TERM:
January 31, 2006–

APPOINTED BY:
George W. Bush

WORDS OF WISDOM:
"I'm not any kind of a bigot. I'm not."

The words *studious* and *diligent* are most often used to describe Justice Samuel Alito, a mild-mannered man who keeps his passions confined to the baseball diamond. When he isn't cavorting with the Phillie Phanatic or fielding grounders for skipper Larry Bowa at a major league fantasy camp, the New Jersey native has been known to pull all-nighters alongside his clerks, with nothing but delivery pizza for fuel. A staunchly conservative Italian American jurist, he is known to the general public as a younger, thinner, less abrasive version of Antonin Scalia—an identity his ideological opponents have tried to perpetuate by hanging the demeaning nickname "Scalito" around his neck.

A lifelong Phillies fan, Samuel Alito was embraced by the Philly Phanatic at his Supreme Court welcoming dinner.

Samuel Anthony Alito Jr. was born on April Fool's Day in 1950 in Trenton. His mother was an elementary schoolteacher; his father worked as the research director of the Office of Legislative Services, a nonpartisan agency that advised the New Jersey legislature. Sam Sr. was known for his persnickety views on correct English grammar, a trait that young Sam inherited, to the

eternal consternation of his future law clerks. Proudly patriotic, Alito grew up in a brick Cape Cod–style home, with a screened porch and an American flag on the front lawn. At Steinert High School, he was a straight-A student, active in more than ten clubs including the debate team, track and field, and honor society. He served as president of the student council and graduated as class valedictorian. He also played the trumpet, but not very well, according to his band director. Tooting his horn was about the only thing Alito didn't excel at. When it came time to take his SATs, he smashed all records. At that time, there were four separate tests, each with an optimal score of 800. Alito notched two 800s, one 796, and one 780. He was admitted to Princeton without difficulty.

In college, Alito stuck to his formula of working hard and keeping his nose clean. One classmate described him as a "teetotalling, early-to-bed and early-to-rise legal scholar." Traditional undergraduate horseplay was largely outside his comfort zone, although he could retaliate when provoked. After a roommate pulled a prank on him, Alito responded by dosing the dorm ice cube tray with salt. "The other guy drank scotch-on-the-rocks every night," reported a fellow Princetonian. "[He] went through a full bottle of terrible-tasting scotch before realizing that his ice cubes had been sabotaged." When it came to politics, Alito kept a similarly low profile. At the time, the university was just starting to admit women, and although Alito didn't agitate against the change, he did join a right-wing alumni group that opposed it. The overall impression is of a genuinely conservative young man playing his cards close to the vest in hopes of securing future employment. The 1972 Princeton yearbook seemed to acknowledge Alito's ambitions when it noted that he "intends to go to law school and eventually to warm a seat on the Supreme Court."

The law school in question was Yale, and after graduating from there in 1975, Alito took a rather eerily conventional route up the legal ladder: clerk for a Trenton law firm and then for an appellate judge; four years as an assistant U.S. attorney; and then a seven-year stint in Ronald Reagan's Justice Department, where he argued several cases before the Supreme Court. It was during this period that Alito wrote on a job application form that he was "particularly proud" of his work on cases arguing that "racial and ethnic quotas should not be allowed and that the Constitution does not protect a right to an abortion"—positions that would be used as ammunition against him in his Supreme Court confirmation hearings twenty years later. It was also during this period that he met and married law librarian Martha-Ann Bomgardner, who played a pivotal role in those same confirmation hearings.

In 1990, President George H. W. Bush appointed Alito to the third circuit court of appeals, where he spent fifteen years building a reliably conservative record, particularly on criminal justice issues. When President George W. Bush's original nominee to replace the retiring Sandra Day O'Connor went down in flames in October 2005, Bush turned to Alito. The ensuing confirmation hearings were marked by vague accusations by Democrats that Alito was a "closet bigot" and a right-wing zealot. He won favor with the public when his wife broke down in tears behind him on national television. Some derided the waterworks as insincere, but clearly there was insufficient public sentiment opposing his nomination. Alito was confirmed in the Senate by a vote of 58 to 42.

POWER STRIP

Alito is known by two distinctive nicknames: "Scalito," for his purported ideological kinship with fellow justice Antonin Scalia; and the more colorful "Strip Search Sammy." He picked up the latter during his days as an appeals court judge. In the 2004 case of *Doe v. Groody*, Alito opined for the minority that a group of Schuylkill County, Pennsylvania, police officers did not violate the constitutional rights of a ten-year-old girl whom they strip searched while executing a search warrant in a narcotics investigation.

APPEAL THIS!

"Hard-ass" doesn't begin to describe Alito's approach to criminal justice. Upon joining the U.S. Court of Appeals in 1990, his colleagues in the U.S. Attorney's Office gave him a rather unique going-away present: a custom-made ink-pad stamp marked "AFFIRMED," so that Alito could literally rubber-stamp all the criminal appeals he was *not* going to overturn. Some months later, an unmarked envelope arrived in the U.S. Attorney's Office. Inside was a copy of the first criminal appeal Judge Alito had heard at his new job. The word "AFFIRMED" was stamped all over the front page.

PHILLIE FANATIC

Alito is a lifelong, hardcore baseball fan who often employs sports metaphors in his speeches and opinions. As a child growing up in Trenton, New Jersey, he rooted for the Philadelphia Phillies and dreamed of one day becoming commissioner of baseball. As a grown man, he largely confined his interest to coaching his son's Essex County Little League team and, on one notable occasion in 1994, attending a major league fantasy camp—a birthday present from his wife. At the camp, Alito manned second base alongside his favorite Phillies. ("Good field, no hit" was the assessment of one of his friends.)

Since being nominated for the high court, however, Alito has taken his Phillie Phandom to an even higher—and, some would say, creepier—level. In November 2005, he urinated next to Senator (and former Phillies' pitcher) Jim Bunning in a Capitol Hill men's room. Alito used the opportunity to give Bunning an earful about the Phillies' epic collapse in the 1964 pennant race. The next spring, Alito capped off his magical mystery tour by throwing out the first pitch at a Devil Rays–Phillies game in Philadelphia. Alito's Court colleagues have also picked up on his passion for the national pastime. At a dinner welcoming the newly installed justice in 2006, Justice Stephen Breyer arranged to have the Phillies' antic, green-furred mascot, the Phillie Phanatic, burst into the dining area and give Alito a congratulatory hug.

Judge Java

Most justices can only hope to have a courthouse named after them someday. But before he even first slipped into his Supreme Court robe, Alito already had a designer coffee christened in his honor. The joe-loving judge's clerks convinced TM Ward, a coffee shop near the Newark federal courthouse where Alito used to work, to whip up a special blend that embodied his muscular approach to jurisprudence. "Judge Alito's Bold Justice Blend"—so named for the boldness of both the judge and the beverage—combines Colombia, Java, and New Guinea coffee beans with just a hint of espresso. The shop's owner described the brew's flavor to the *New York Times* as "strong in the cup, with some sweetness and a winey aftertaste." Customers ask for it by name, saying simply "Give me an Alito." Alito himself stops by to get some whenever he's in town—often buying it by the pound.

BADA-BING!

You can call Sam Alito many things. Just don't call him a fan of *The Sopranos*. He has been an outspoken critic of the wildly popular HBO mob drama, believing that it perpetuates harmful stereotypes about Italian Americans. "You have a trifecta—gangsters, Italian Americans, New Jersey," Alito told an audience at Rutgers University in 2008. For many years, Alito lived in the same New Jersey community inhabited by fictional mob boss Tony Soprano—and he paid the price for it. A friend once sent him a map of locations used in the series. "He wanted me to put down where my house was on the map," Alito related.

A VIGOROUS DISSENT

Never let it be said that Sam Alito lacks a sense of humor . . . or taste. While working as an appeals court judge, Alito passed summary judgment on the decorating choices of a district court colleague whose office was just down the hall. The judge in question had enormous stonework lions installed on either side of the entrance to her chambers. Appalled at this pretentious display, Alito responded by ordering two garish, plastic pink flamingos to guard the doorway of his own chambers. The offending judge quickly took the hint and had her lions removed.

SELECTED BIBLIOGRAPHY

Alexander, Michael. *Jazz Age Jews*. Princeton, N.J.: Princeton University Press, 2001.

Anderson, Judith Icke. *William Howard Taft: An Intimate History*. New York: W.W. Norton, 1981.

Baker, Leonard. *Brandeis and Frankfurter: A Dual Biography*. New York: Harper & Row, 1984.

Baker, Liva. *Felix Frankfurter: A Biography*. New York: Coward-McCann, 1969.

Baker, Liva. *The Justice from Beacon Hill: The Life and Times of Oliver Wendell Holmes*. New York: HarperCollins, 1991.

Biskupic, Joan. *Sandra Day O'Connor: How the First Woman on the Supreme Court Became Its Most Influential Justice*. New York: HarperCollins, 2005.

Cray, Ed. *Chief Justice: A Biography of Earl Warren*. New York: Simon & Schuster, 1997.

Cushman, Clare, ed. *The Supreme Court Justices: Illustrated Biographies, 1789–1995*. Washington, D.C.: Congressional Quarterly, 1995.

Danelski, David J., and Joseph S. Tulchin, eds. *The Autobiographical Notes of Charles Evans Hughes*. Cambridge: Harvard University Press, 1973.

Dean, John W. *The Rehnquist Choice: The Untold Story of the Nixon Appointment That Redefined the Supreme Court*. New York: Simon & Schuster, 2001.

Eisler, Kim Isaac. *A Justice for All: William J. Brennan Jr. and the Decisions That Transformed America*. New York: Simon & Schuster, 1993.

Elliott, Stephen P., ed. *Reference Guide to the United States Supreme Court*. New York: Facts on File, 1986.

Gerhart, Eugene C. *America's Advocate: Robert H. Jackson*. Indianapolis: Bobbs-Merrill, 1958.

Greenhouse, Linda. *Becoming Justice Blackmun*. New York: Henry Holt, 2005.

Hall, Timothy L. *Supreme Court Justices: A Biographical Dictionary*. New York: Facts on File, 2001.

Howard, J. Woodward. *Mr. Justice Murphy: A Political Biography*. Princeton, N.J.: Princeton University Press, 1968.

Hutchinson, Dennis J. *The Man Who Once Was Whizzer White: A Portrait of Justice Byron R. White*. New York: Simon & Schuster, 1998.

Hutchinson, Dennis J. and David J. Garrow, eds. *The Forgotten Memoir of John Knox: A Year in the Life of a Supreme Court Clerk in FDR's Washington.* Chicago: University of Chicago Press, 1997.

Irons, Peter. *A People's History of the Supreme Court.* Rev. ed. New York: Penguin, 2006.

Jeffries, John C. *Justice Lewis F. Powell Jr.* New York: Charles Scribner's Sons, 1994.

Jost, Kenneth. *The Supreme Court A to Z.* Washington, D.C.: Congressional Quarterly, 2007.

Kalman, Laura. *Abe Fortas: A Biography.* New Haven: Yale University Press, 1990.

Kaufman, Andrew L. *Cardozo.* Cambridge: Harvard University Press, 1998.

Lamb, Charles M., and Stephen C. Halpern, eds. *The Burger Court: Political and Judicial Profiles.* Urabana: University of Illinois Press.

Lash, Joseph P. *From the Diaries of Felix Frankfurter.* New York: W.W. Norton, 1975.

Lazarus, Edward. *Closed Chambers: The Rise, Fall, and Future of the Modern Supreme Court.* New York: Penguin, 1998.

Manaster, Kenneth A. *Illinois Justice: The Scandal of 1969 and the Rise of John Paul Stevens.* Chicago: University of Chicago Press, 2001.

Mason, Alpheus Thomas. *William Howard Taft: Chief Justice.* New York: Simon & Schuster, 1964.

Mayer, Jane, and Jill Abramson. *Strange Justice: The Selling of Clarence Thomas.* New York: Houghton Mifflin, 1994.

McElroy, Lisa Tucker. *John G. Roberts Jr.: Chief Justice.* Minneapolis, Minn.: Lerner Publications, 2007.

Murdock, Joyce, and Deb Price. *Courting Justice: Gay Men and Lesbians v. the Supreme Court.* New York: Basic Books, 2001.

Murphy, Bruce Allen. *The Brandeis/Frankfurter Connection.* New York: Oxford University Press, 1982.

Murphy, Bruce Allen. *Wild Bill: The Legend and Life of William O. Douglas.* New York: Random House, 2003.

Newman, Roger K. *Hugo Black: A Biography.* New York: Random House, 1994.

Newmyer, R. Kent. *John Marshall and the Heroic Age of the Supreme Court.* Baton Rouge: Louisiana State University Press, 2001.

Niven, John. *Salmon P. Chase: A Biography*. New York: Oxford University Press, 1995.

O'Connor, Sandra Day, and H. Alan Day. *Lazy B: Growing Up on a Cattle Ranch in the American Southwest*. New York: Random House, 2002.

Pringle, Henry F. *The Life and Times of William Howard Taft*. Hartford, Conn.: Archon Books, 1964.

Pusey, Merlo J. *Charles Evans Hughes*. New York: Macmillan, 1951.

Rosen, Jeffey. *The Supreme Court: The Personalities and Rivalries That Defined America*. New York: Henry Holt, 2006.

Schwartz, Bernard. *The Book of Legal Lists*. New York: Oxford University Press, 1997.

Schwartz, Bernard. *A History of the Supreme Court*. New York: Oxford University Press, 1993.

Sekulow, Jay Alan. *Witnessing Their Faith: Religious Influence on Supreme Court Justices and Their Opinions*. New York: Rowamn and Littlefield, 2006.

Simon, James F. *Lincoln and Chief Justice Taney*. New York: Simon & Schuster, 2006.

Stahr, Walter. *John Jay: Founding Father*. New York and London: Humbledon and London, 2005.

Teubner, Gary. *Learned Hand: The Man*. Brookfield, Conn.: The Millbrook Press, 1963.

Thomas, Marlo. *The Right Words at the Right Time*. New York: Atria Books, 2002.

Toobin, Jeffrey. *The Nine: Inside the Secret World of the Supreme Court*. New York: Doubleday, 2007.

Urofsky, Melvin I., ed. *The Supreme Court Justices: A Biographical Dictionary*. New York & London: Garland Publishing, 1994.

Williams, Juan. *Thurgood Marshall: American Revolutionary*. New York: Random House, 1998.

Witt, Elder, ed. *The Supreme Court A to Z*. Washington, D.C.: Congressional Quarterly, 1994.

Woodward, Bob, and Scott Armstrong. *The Brethren: Inside the Supreme Court*. New York: Avon Books, 1979.

Yarbrough, Tinsley E. *David Hackett Souter: Traditional Republican on the Rehnquist Court*. New York: Oxford University Press, 2005.

INDEX